Landscapes
of the **Mind**
The Music of John McCabe

Landscapes
of the Mind
The Music of John McCabe

Compiled and edited by George Odam

Co-published in 2007 by:
The Guildhall School of Music & Drama
Barbican
Silk Street
London
EC2Y 8DT
Tel: 0044 (0) 207628 2571
Fax: 0044 (0) 20 7382 7212

www.gsmd.ac.uk

and

Ashgate Publishing Limited
Gower House
Croft Road
Aldershot
Hants GU11 3HR
Tel. 0044 (0) 1252 331551
Fax: 0044 for (0) 1252 344405

www.ashgate.com

Ashgate Publishing Company
Suite 420
101 Cherry Street
Burlington, VT 05401-4405 USA

British Library Cataloguing in Publication Data

Landscapes of the mind : the music of John McCabe. –

   (Guildhall research studies)

   1. McCabe, John, 1939– 2. Composers – England
– Biography

   I. Odam, George

   780.9'2

Library of Congress Cataloging-in-Publication Data

Landscapes of the mind : the music of John McCabe / edited by George Odam.

      p. cm. — (Guildhall research studies)

   Includes discography (p.   ) and index.

   ISBN 978-0-7546-5816-0 (alk. paper)

   1. McCabe, John, 1939– 2. Composers—England—Biography. I. Odam, George.

   ML410.M449L36 2008

   780.92—dc22

                                    2008003803

Printed and bound in Great Britain by TJ International Ltd, Padstow, Cornwall

For Damian, Ronan, Peter, Helena, Robin and Deborah without whose contributions this book could not have been produced.

Contents

Foreword

Dr Vernon Handley CBE

It is often said that for every one musical influence an eighteenth-century composer experienced a modern composer is open to ten. Some narrow this down to musical influences, others expand the category to include all influences: cultural, financial, political, as well as emotional, and the response to other artists' works. From this position they argue that music down the centuries has fluctuated between periods of the intellectual and emotional, or cerebral and emotional, or cold and boiling over. The superficiality of this view of a complicated art has had great support, for music is a mysterious influence in our lives and demands a rigorous discipline of study if it is to yield up over a few of its secrets.

In this process of study the performer in us has a valuable contribution to make. Giving physical voice to music exposes its *raison d'être*, and spurs us on to experience more of its magic. This fusion of intellectual and actual voices is something which the composer must possess in some degree if his music is to be available and valuable to all; otherwise it is dead on the page.

John McCabe is both composer and performer, creator and recreator. To hear him play Haydn, or talk about Haydn's music, is to gain possession of the emotional depth of Haydn's vision, not its intellectual content alone; to hear him play Bax or talk about that composer is to understand exactly the same duality of gifts in him, the powerful emotional content at the service of a great mind. Perhaps then, it is not surprising that one should find both elements in John's music. He is aware of both the demands in his mind, but in his composition and performing they are fused.

As a conductor, I cheerfully admit that I am susceptible to the gifts of my players as well as to the inspiration of the score. This fusion of elements that I speak of above is absorbed by orchestral players and soloists

Vernon Handley.

alike in that they rarely, if ever, mention derivations when dealing with his music – in other words, the fusion has worked; we are dealing with an individual voice, a voice like no other. Yet John achieves this without recourse to shocks. He can tear up the earth when the development of an idea demands, but never with easily obtained fireworks. In this he shows the influence of two of his loves, mentioned before, Haydn and Bax: seemingly diverse sensibilities, yet when examined in depth miraculously close in that their compositional procedures have utter integrity.

His solo works, song settings and large ensembles have the same integrity, the original material informing all that comes after, so that *Chagall Windows*, *Irish Songbook* and *Notturni ed Alba* are discernibly by the same man yet wonderfully fresh as to their original inspiration. His inspirations come from endless sources – literary, philosophical, theatrical, natural – and he exposes himself when writing, almost as well, dare I say it, as he does when he composes.

That integrity, supported by a rich but never uncontrolled expression, is presenting us with an unending source of delightful and stimulating music. John McCabe enhances life. Long may he continue to do so.

Vernon Handley

Illustrations

Preface

Over the nearly seventy years of John McCabe's lifetime the classical music business in Britain has changed radically. It has moved from operating within a traditionalist culture in which classical music took its place among the arts without question and was generally admired, performed by many and respected by even those who did not listen to it much, to a diverse and more egalitarian society driven by commercialism and increasingly anti-establishment, where the majority of musical performance is electronically generated and focussed on the lowest common denominator. In Britain, music of all the arts had perhaps been the one least strongly patronised by royalty and the monied classes, and it has suffered the pressures of change even more directly as a result. The old, traditional and patronising Reithian model for broadcasting gave way to a more generally popular one based on success in audience ratings. The brave new world, so stunningly and accurately predicted by Constant Lambert in his 1931 book of essays *Music Ho!* has materialised just as he predicted it would, with the reality of what he termed 'the appalling popularity of music'.

The advent and establishment of television over this period helped accelerate the change towards a commercially driven model for the broadcasting media, where classical music had to find its level. Despite this, as a country, we still manage to maintain our many London and regional orchestras partly through subsidy and patronage alongside active repertory and touring opera and ballet, but a significant change in the Performing Rights Society's rules towards the end of the 1990s severely affected the lives and work of many composers, McCabe among them. Whereas up until the end of the twentieth century it was still possible for an active and successful composer to make a reasonable living on commissions and royalties on sales and performances, with the change to a performance payment per head of audience, this ceased to be the case, and the publishing of notated music has become a minority business. Throughout this time McCabe himself has been very active politically in support of classical composers (for want of a better word) and still promotes their work as a performer and recording artist when he has the opportunity. Without work in television and film background music, where the practice of contemporary classical music still finds a natural home in some areas, and a small amount in the classical theatre, composers now rarely have much incentive or inclination to write large pieces for traditional forces, especially those in the symphonic tradition, excepting big commissions such as the BBC Proms.

This is one of the many reasons we have to celebrate this amazingly active composer, still in regular receipt of commissions, with six symphonies in his catalogue and currently planning at least another one or more, and still producing concertos and other symphonically based works at an amazing rate, apparently undeterred by the adverse political, cultural and financial climate. Throughout his composing life his musical style has remained remarkably stable, enduring and ignoring many changes of fashion. Rock music has taken such a hold here in Britain that it is now increasingly rare to find substantial musical criticism of classical music in the press, and the government-funded Arts Council shows little interest in the work of such superb home-grown composers as Elgar, whose 150th anniversary saw the removal of his image from the £20 note to be replaced by an economist and moral philosopher.

We celebrate then, in this volume, not only a remarkable composer of superbly beautiful and intellectually rewarding music, but also a survivor and holder of the line whose work is resonant of many centuries of fine music-making and who continues to charm the ear of his audiences and to win the hearts and minds of musicians with whom he comes into contact. His sympathy with his fellow musicians is paramount, since he is an active one himself, still engaged in playing and recording music of the classical canon as well as by British composers and contemporaries alongside his own music. This volume hopes to show how diverse and fascinating John McCabe's music has always been and remains. Through the writings of critics, musicians, music administrators and academics we hope that we can give a detailed account of McCabe's composing life, providing along the way an insight into his musical personality and a glimpse behind the scenes into the work of this extraordinary artist. *Landscapes of the Mind* was a title suggested by McCabe himself. Much of his music carries titles athat refer to and evoke landscapes of different kinds, but these landscapes exist only as mental images and the music is not directly descriptive.

We have purposely avoided too much technical detail so as to assist general readers, and the reproduced pages of score have an illustrative rather than analytical function. We hope to attract the interest of young performers who have not yet experienced the pleasure and satisfaction of playing such well-crafted music and to provide a perspective and background detail to those listeners who already know some of his music from live and broadcast concerts and through his many recordings. Most of all we hope to awaken the interest of listeners who have not yet had the pleasure and enjoyment that can be gained through direct experience of the music of John McCabe.

McCabe is meticulous in his preparation for first performances and it has been his custom always to write concise but helpfully informative programme notes. Most of these can be obtained through Chester/Novello (Music Sales) on request, or obtained on the Internet at www.johnmccabe.com/publications/chesternovello. Most of the authors in this volume have drawn freely from these notes, and where there are unacknowledged quotations these will be either from such notes or, of course, directly and verbatim from John McCabe himself, who has been so supportive in the production of this book. In addition, Verity Butler made McCabe the focus of her dissertation for her Master's degree at the Royal College of Music and collected much of her information through interviews and correspondence with the composer.

Acknowledgements

It is amazing to me that this should be the first comprehensive book to be written and published on the English composer and pianist John McCabe, who at the time of writing is nearing his 70th year. I have been privileged to follow McCabe's career from its beginning but I would have been entirely unable to have produced such a detailed and comprehensive study without the assistance, generosity, insight and professional skill of all the contributors. They have each given their time most willingly in order to help to promote interest and raise awareness in the music of one of our country's most prolific composers, and both John and I will remain deeply in their debt. Without their hard work, so freely given, this book could never have been produced. They are:

Verity Butler
Paul Conway
Paul Hindmarsh
Tamami Honma

Guy Rickards
John Vorrasi

to whom I owe a deep sense of personal gratitude.

We also wish to acknowledge the help of Shelley Hughes and Samuel Wilcocks of Music Sales (Chester/Novello) in finding photographs, producing scans from scores and in giving us permission to use them, some in reproduction from the composer's own remarkably clear manuscript – in itself a skill that may be diminishing as technological manipulation takes its place. Other photographs have come from the McCabe family albums with his permission to reproduce for the first time. Each article has been read and approved by John McCabe himself and his help in getting all the details correct has been invaluable.

It has been impossible to include an excerpts disc with this publication, but, as the discography shows, there are very many recordings to choose from to begin an exploration of this remarkable composer's work, or to refresh memories of previously heard works. The Guildhall School was proud to have hosted the recent McCabe Festival in 2006 and to have commissioned *Canyons*, the recording of which, performed by the Guildhall Brass and Wind and conducted by Peter Gane, is still commercially available.

George Odam

Head of Research and Staff Development

Guildhall School of Music & Drama, London

Contributors

Verity Butler graduated from the Royal College of Music with a Master's degree in Performance and the coveted Tagore Gold Medal for the most accomplished student. She now enjoys a varied freelance career combining recording work, educational projects and concert management with a busy schedule of concerto, solo, chamber and orchestral performances throughout Britain and abroad. Recent recordings include concertos with the Royal Ballet Sinfonia for Naxos' Marco Polo and Campion, and the City of Prague Philharmonic Orchestra for two ASV releases, together with two volumes of *Clarinet Kaleidoscope*, featuring lighter music for clarinet and piano, also for Campion. Verity is the Director of Cheltenham's acclaimed Pittville Pump Room Sunday Showcase Series.

Verity wrote her Master's degree thesis on the clarinet works of John McCabe and has since written for the magazine of the Clarinet and Saxophone Society of Great Britain and other periodicals.

Paul Conway is a freelance writer, specialising in contemporary and twentieth-century British music. He contributes regularly to *The Independent* and *Tempo* and has written programme notes for The Proms and Edinburgh Festival. His MPhil reappraised 'The Cheltenham Symphony' and he is currently writing a book on Arthur Butterworth's music.

Much of **Paul Hindmarsh**'s career in music has focussed on aspects of British music. After graduating from Birmingham University in the 1970s, he began an extended period of study on the music of Frank Bridge. His *Thematic Catalogue* (Faber, 1982) has become the standard reference work on this composer. Since then he has been the author of many articles and CD notes on Bridge's music, including the acclaimed orchestral music series from Chandos, for which he was also the music editor and programme consultant. Hindmarsh has prepared many new works by Bridge for publication, and has also adapted a number of theatre and radio works by Benjamin Britten for the concert hall, including *Johnson over Jordan* and *King Arthur*.

Since 1985, Hindmarsh has been a producer for BBC Radio 3, working on a range of programmes with an emphasis on British, choral and brass band music. He began the BBC Festival of Brass in the early 1990s and is currently artistic director of its successor, the Royal Northern College of Music Festival of Brass. Hindmarsh has commissioned over thirty new works for the brass band medium, either through the BBC or through the Brass Band Heritage Trust, which he founded in 1994. He contributed the chapter on the brass band repertoire of the twentieth century to *The British Brass Band* (Oxford University Press, 2000). Hindmarsh is also much in demand as a CD producer and programme-note writer. Current projects include *The History of the Brass Band*, with Elgar Howarth and Grimethorpe [UK Coal] Band, and an edition of the complete works of the composer Wilfred Heaton, whose biography he will be researching.

In 2005 Paul Hindmarsh was awarded the Iles Medal of the Worshipful Company of Musicians for his services to the brass band movement.

Since an auspicious US concerto debut at the age of seven, Gramophone Award nominee and international competition laureate **Tamami Honma** has forged a worldwide career, playing in Europe, Russia, the Middle and Far East and across seventeen states of the USA. She has appeared in some of the world's greatest musical institutions, from the Bolshoi Hall in Moscow to the Weill Recital Hall at Carnegie Hall and the Wigmore Hall in London, establishing her position as a leading pianist of the younger generation. In her formative years in the USA, Tamami had already received first prizes in the Stravinsky Awards International Competition and several others before she moved to New York to become a protégée of legendary pianist Byron Janis.

A participant in major festivals such as the Warsaw Autumn Festival, Aldeburgh Festival and the Gaida Festival, Ms Honma has made television and radio broadcasts in Europe and the USA with partners including the Lithuanian National Symphony Orchestra, the Kreutzer Quartet, the Vilnius Quartet and various American orchestras. Her commercial recordings have won high accolades, including a nomination for a prestigious Gramophone Award for her second Metier CD with violinist Peter Shepperd Skærved (MSV92029). Other recordings include music from Mozart and Chopin to Nigel Clarke (Metier MSV02024).

Honma also recorded McCabe's Second Piano Concerto with the St Christopher Chamber Orchestra for Dutton Epoch, and premiered his Eighth Study (*Scrunch*) at Carnegie Hall in 2002, and his Ninth Study (*Snowfall in Winter*) at St John's Smith Square, London in 2003. Both studies were written for her. Equally accomplished in traditional and modern repertoire, Honma often incorporates into her concert programmes world premieres of solo and chamber works written for her by distinguished composers from around the world. Tamami currently teaches at the Royal Academy of Music in London.

Head of Research and Staff Development at the Guildhall School of Music and Drama, London, **George Odam** was formerly Professor of Music Education at Bath Spa University College, in charge of postgraduate training courses in music education. He is a composer, writer and lecturer with interests across the arts. A composition student of Alexander Goehr, he also studied with Jonathan Harvey and Hans Keller and his works for young performers have been played throughout the UK, Europe and Australia. His book on music education in practice *The Sounding Symbol* (1995) has been widely acclaimed, and he is editor of the new Guildhall Research Studies series with Ashgate Publishing including *Seeking the Soul: The Music of Alfred Schnittke* (2002), Graham Johnson's *Britten, Voice and Piano* (2003) and *The Reflective Conservatoire* (2005). He is also co-author with Dr Jaume Rosset of *The Musician's Body: A Maintenance Manual for Peak Performance* (2007).

Guy Rickards is a freelance writer on music and regular contributor to *The Gramophone, The Guardian, Tempo, International Piano* and, from 2003 to 2006, *Nordic Sounds*. The author of two biographical studies – *Hindemith, Hartmann, Henze* (London, 1995) and *Jean Sibelius* (London, 1997) – he is working on a life-and-works study of Harold Truscott.

Tenor **John Vorrasi** has been a featured soloist in many concerts and liturgies throughout the country. He sang at Holy Name Cathedral for seven seasons and has been principal Cantor at Our Lady of Mount Carmel Church since 1985. A frequent soloist with the William Ferris Chorale, he has also appeared at the Spoleto Festival USA and the Aldeburgh Festival, and with the Chicago Opera Theater, the Virginia Philharmonic, the Tarvos Ensemble and the Chicago String Ensemble. He won critical acclaim for his performance as the Evangelist on the world premiere recording of Leo Sowerby's *Forsaken of Man* on New World Records. His recitals of contemporary music, often with composers such as Ned Rorem and Lee Hoiby serving as his accompanist, have been broadcast by the BBC, Radio Vaticana, WFMT and WNIB. He serves as Artistic Director of the William Ferris Chorale, an internationally acclaimed ensemble he founded in 1972 with composer–conductor William Ferris.

1

The early years

George Odam

orn in 1902, Frank McCabe, John McCabe's father, was a physicist working for a large telephone communication company, ATM (later ATE). In his early years he was part of the pioneering group with Marconi, as evidenced by a photograph in John's possession of Frank among a group of colleagues on Hampstead Heath near London in the late 1920s, celebrating the reception of transatlantic communication with a picnic. Tall, with brushed-back dark hair from a high forehead, in the style of the day, Frank was of the type who easily blended with a crowd, both in looks and dress. He was highly self-contained with a dry sense of humour, and appears (despite experiments in pottery and wood-carving in later life) to have been a stereotypical scientist with little interest in the arts or music. But his own early family life had been far from straightforward.

Opposite: John McCabe, c.1967.

Joseph McCabe, John's grandfather.

Joseph McCabe, Frank's father and thus John's grandfather, was of Irish/English stock and made a strong contrast with his son. Born the son of a Lancashire mill-worker in 1867, as a young man Joseph had taken his vows as a Christian monk at an Irish Roman Catholic monastery in Killarney in 1885, having entered an English seminary at the age of sixteen. As Father Anthony, over the next twelve years Joseph had risen through the monastic ranks, soon returning to England to continue his studies and then lecturing in a Catholic college in Forest Gate, Upton, West London. From 1893 to 1894 he studied philosophy and oriental languages at the University of Louvain in Belgium, returning to Forest Gate to his old post as lecturer. Appointed Principal of a Catholic college in Buckinghamshire in 1895, on Ash Wednesday 1896 he walked out, left the church, and from that point dedicated his life to

secularism and rationalism as a lecturer, journalist and author. He settled in the north-west London area of Golders Green, married Beatrice Lee (1881–1960) in 1900 and became a sought-after lecturer, writing and successfully publishing many books on such diverse subjects as astronomy, popular science, history and anti-religion polemics until his death in 1955, only three years before his grandson entered university. Beatrice and Joseph raised a family of four – Frank, Athene, Dorothy and Ernest – but the marriage was unstable and eventually broke up by mutual consent in 1925. John McCabe's only direct knowledge of his paternal grandmother, Beatrice (originally a hosiery worker's daughter from Leicester), is that she ended up living in self-imposed rural poverty on the South Downs, in a house surrounded by animals; he believes that she was an early and outspoken feminist. Given such an insight into his turbulent family life, Frank's self-possession and pursuit of scientific order perhaps comes as no surprise.

John McCabe expresses his relationship with his father as one of great respect, a phrase that also tells something of a distance between them. Frank hardly ever attended any of his son's performances, even those at school. However, he shared his own interests, fishing being one, with his son as well as he could. John has strong memories of a later fishing trip in a Lakeland stream with his father, when he had been given a fresh fish-head as bait and, much to his delight, had caught an eel. This created a memorable scene with his father and mother struggling to secure and dispatch the eel, finally cooking it and serving it for supper.

In complete contrast, John's mother, Elisabeth McCabe, was extrovert, energetic and artistic. A fine-looking and attractive woman, Elisabeth Herlitzius was born in Mülheim in the West German industrial region of the Ruhr in 1913 as a member of a large family. The Herlitzius family roots could be traced back to Sweden, Finland and even Spain, and Elisabeth was a talented amateur violinist who, throughout her days, bubbled with energy and interest in the world of the arts and life in general. Her uncle Franz Gottschalk, a zither player, had emigrated to the USA and eventually became a well-known orchestral conductor. Another Uncle Fritz Gottschalk owned a large music shop in Cologne, selling sheet music and instruments and specialising in violins. A photograph of this extensive emporium is in Elisabeth's photograph album, still in John's possession.

Notes on the back of this photograph in her handwriting tell the stark tale of the closure of the shop by the Nazis during the Third Reich, and the deportation of the family to what is described as a 'detention' camp. All this might suggest a Jewish family background, as does the family surname, but this has never been investigated. Photographs of Elisabeth's father and mother show a solidly middle-class couple. As far as is known, her father, Paul Herlitzius, had emigrated to Liverpool before the First World War, was interned during the war and continued to work there afterwards, to be joined by his wife and daughter in the early 1920s. Elisabeth could remember moving back and forth between Liverpool and Mülheim as a child and remembered the sadness of regular separation from her parents, which affected her insecurities in later life. She could remember the French occupation of the Ruhr and also the brief Communist government in the years leading to 1923.

It is certain that Elisabeth had many of the attributes of the stereotypical Jewish mother, and dedicated much of her life to her only child, becoming, in John's own words, a huge influence on him. Exactly when her family finally settled in Liverpool is not yet known, nor how and when she met Frank except that he attended German-language evening classes at ATM given by Elisabeth. An early album snap taken by Frank shows a *Uncle Fritz's music shop,* winsome Elisabeth, a daisy tucked behind one ear, gazing alluringly into *Cologne.* the camera. Elisabeth exuded charm and always was able to use her eyes to her advantage, never shrinking from engaging anyone that interested her in conversation. Whether her lisp was acquired or natural, it added to her strong personality and charisma, and it is perhaps not surprising that the more saturnine Frank fell for her.

Being married to a German wife was not the most comfortable of situations in England in the years immediately before the Second World War, and John's birth – in the then prosperous suburb of Huyton, Liverpool on 21 April – took place a short time before the declaration of war with Germany in 1939. John's first six years were lived under the periodic barrage of the blitz and the general privations of wartime life with food rationing and restricted travel. Frank continued his work in the important and nationally vital and secret area of the telecommunications industry, also acting as an air-raid warden within the community. For information and relaxation, the family would listen to the BBC Radio Home Service, with regular news, talks, comedy and feature programmes and often to the

John McCabe aged 2; with his mother, Elisabeth; with his father, Frank.

Third Programme, where the Reithian principles of culture for the masses encouraged the broadcast performances of new music as well as the established classics. As further family entertainment in the evenings, very likely at Elisabeth's instigation, they were able to enjoy listening to their extensive collection of shellac gramophone records, played, through Frank's professional interest and connections, on the latest technological equipment. One of John's earliest memories is of climbing out of bed late in the evening, and sitting half-way down the staircase to listen to the enthralling orchestral sounds of Brahms' Variations on the Saint Anthony Chorale coming from behind the living room door.

Towards the end of his second year, in the early spring of 1942, a chance accident in the home was to prove a profound experience, changing the direction of his life. An inquisitive child, John had assembled some favourite but somewhat inappropriate materials as the focus of his play on the hearth-rug by the welcome warmth of the living-room fire. Houses in those days had no central heating and often the fire burnt in the hearth all day, especially when it also heated the water. Elisabeth found her two-year-old son happily engaged in mixing ink with marmalade on the hearthrug, and, unsurprisingly, somewhat dismayed, she quickly removed the ink-bottle from his grasp, placed it on the nearby mantelshelf above the fire, then grasped the marmalade jar and returned it to the nearby kitchen cupboard.

Open fires were always protected by strong wire-mesh fireguards, and the safety-conscious McCabes had invested in a large one, bigger than those owned by other similar families. The young John obviously saw the wire-

4

mesh wall as a challenge and proceeded to climb the fireguard in search of the confiscated ink-bottle. Toppling over the fireguard, he fell directly on to the blazing coal fire, landing on his right torso and arm and setting light to his clothes. Elisabeth remembered returning to the room, minutes later, not summoned by cries of alarm, but startled by the reflection of flames on the opposite wall and the whimpering of her shocked and wounded child. Severely burned, John was kept sedated for a week to assuage the pain. In those years of austerity, the most effective anaesthetic available was cider, regularly administered in order to keep the dangerously ill child in a state of relaxation. John states that he owes his life to Dr Charles Garson, a doctor who had qualified in India and who practised in Liverpool at that time. Garson was a string player and took a great interest in his young musical patient, performing conjuring tricks to amuse him, and later John was to be presented with several of the same Doctor's miniature scores, which he still owns.

John McCabe in c.1945.

Over the subsequent weeks, months and years, John, whose immune system had been assaulted by the accident, fell victim to many illnesses including pneumonia, meningitis and mastoiditis, which affected his hearing and, at one point, left him deaf for a time. His formative years were therefore circumscribed by illness and spent mostly in the confines of the Huyton 1920s detached house and its garden, supervised by his mother. Attempts to integrate him into school were foiled by exhaustion and subsequent illness, and a three-week stretch was the longest he ever achieved during the primary years school phase, which in England was from five until eleven years. But although this only child, alone for most of the time with his mother in the home, had to make his own entertainment and construct his own education with his mother's help, John remembers the time as a happy one, in a house often full of children. Interestingly, as he later pointed out, the family snapshots show John always in the company of girls and women. He also felt that this period of constant battle with illness made him resilient and, in his words, tough but not an isolate, and he enjoyed the company of other children.

Two years or so after the traumatic accident, John was already reading, writing and drawing with enthusiasm. He was a voracious reader who, not unlike many other children in those days, did not need to learn to read at school because he had already acquired the skill at his parents' knees. Not surprisingly, books were a significant part of the family possessions, and the habit of reading, with the entrance into the world of knowledge

The early composer.

The McCabe house in Rupert Road, Huyton, c.1945.

and the imagination this afforded him, was to prove the foundation for a lifetime's practice. An artistic mother naturally provided her son with writing and drawing materials, although, interestingly, Elisabeth never in John's memory played her violin to him, despite her membership of an amateur string quartet. However, sheet music somehow came his way, and at five years old he became intrigued, as do many children of this age, by the shapes of western music notation. To a five-year-old, already accustomed to listening to full-length classical works, these musical symbols were just as interesting as the shapes of letters and words, and he naturally wanted to make up his own. With the attention of his mother never far away, these drawings were praised and encouraged and soon a music manuscript book with staves on each page was provided for him to experiment further. Not surprisingly, encouraged by his mother, the child followed this interest and was soon filling up sheets of manuscript paper with musical notation which were grandly named 'symphony' and given a key, like the examples he was used to hearing at home. Although most of these childish exercises were copies of music notation found around the house (for example, a six-bar précis of the melody from Tchaikovsky's Piano Concerto) John claims that he had a strong inner aural awareness of what he was writing, although he had no access to any musical instrument on which to experiment.

In post-war British society a child composer was seen as being remarkable and noteworthy enough to feature in the local paper, and a press photograph taken at about the age of six shows a diminutive McCabe seated at an upright piano with sheets of childish music manuscript on the music stand beside him. This piano was purchased by his parents and installed in the home in his sixth year, and he was immediately placed with a local piano teacher, Marjorie Madge, who was happy to take him on, since a pupil who had never touched a keyboard but who both read and wrote music as a hobby, and had an extensive and detailed knowledge of the classical repertoire, must have been an unusual and interesting challenge. It was only at this time that he began to write pieces of music with any real understanding. By the age of eight he was playing fluently and continued to write increasingly complex pieces. His piano teacher encouraged him to explore music on his own, not insisting on a preordained and orderly sequence of pieces, and John sees this as one of the greatest gifts that she gave to him. Throughout his childhood, McCabe remembers that he only spent his pocket money on records and music scores. At the age of eight he had bought the set of records of Alan Rawsthorne's Symphonic Studies (recorded in 1946) and he was to meet the composer the following year at the house of his next piano teacher, Gordon Green.

In late 1947 Elisabeth decided to seek professional advice on how best to continue her son's musical education and wrote a letter to Malcolm Sargent, then a nationally acclaimed conductor, and to John Barbirolli, principal conductor at the Hallé Orchestra in nearby Manchester. Sargent did not reply, but Barbirolli took the trouble to do so, advising that she should seek advice from Robert Forbes, Principal of the Royal Manchester College of Music. At the age of eight, John was taken for an audition with Forbes in Manchester during which he was also seen by the keyboard professor, Gordon Green. Forbes was of the opinion that the young McCabe had no musical talent, but Green, fascinated by the many pages of compositions that were also presented as well as identifying latent talent in his playing, accepted John as a private pupil and placed him forthwith under one of his star pupils, Sheila Dixon, who lived in Liverpool and who became engaged to and eventually married Oliver Vella, a cellist in the Liverpool Philharmonic Orchestra. One of the first compositions that John acknowledges as a significant piece is an Adagio for Cello and Piano, written with these people in mind, and performed by them as an encore at a local recital.

The age of nine appears to have been an important year in John's development, and it was during the summer of 1949 that Elisabeth and Frank, following medical advice, decided to take their son for the summer months to the countryside, for fresh air and exercise. They were able to rent Godrill Cottage in Patterdale in what is now the county of Cumbria, at the heart

The young John McCabe with his cat, Clifford.

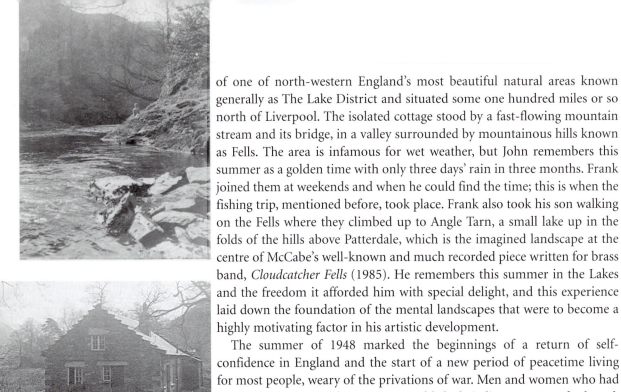

of one of north-western England's most beautiful natural areas known generally as The Lake District and situated some one hundred miles or so north of Liverpool. The isolated cottage stood by a fast-flowing mountain stream and its bridge, in a valley surrounded by mountainous hills known as Fells. The area is infamous for wet weather, but John remembers this summer as a golden time with only three days' rain in three months. Frank joined them at weekends and when he could find the time; this is when the fishing trip, mentioned before, took place. Frank also took his son walking on the Fells where they climbed up to Angle Tarn, a small lake up in the folds of the hills above Patterdale, which is the imagined landscape at the centre of McCabe's well-known and much recorded piece written for brass band, *Cloudcatcher Fells* (1985). He remembers this summer in the Lakes and the freedom it afforded him with special delight, and this experience laid down the foundation of the mental landscapes that were to become a highly motivating factor in his artistic development.

The summer of 1948 marked the beginnings of a return of self-confidence in England and the start of a new period of peacetime living for most people, weary of the privations of war. Men and women who had fought, had returned home to re-establish their lives or start afresh and, having also endured the problems of the severest winter for many years in 1947, the threads of a new life were beginning to be rewoven as the summer sun seemed to shine more brightly. Customs and ceremonies of the old ways began to re-emerge after wartime suspension, and in Patterdale that year the May Day festival was revived. This rustic celebration, welcoming the beginning of summer, often featured processions through villages with branches of early flowering bushes, and the traditional dancing round the maypole by women and children. The McCabe family were already in

Top: The grounds of Godrill Cottage in Patterdale, 1948; John seated on a rock.
Above: Godrill Cottage in Patterdale, 1948.
Below: May Day at Patterdale, 1948; Frank in the centre.

Patterdale in May 1948 and took part in the celebrations. The family album contains a snap taken by Frank of this ceremony and a local guide-book, still in John's possession (see left), includes exactly the same scene with the same people dancing, but taken from the other side where Frank can be distinguished standing back in the crowd, having taken his snapshot. The fact that John McCabe was to become a champion of British music in later life may partly be traced back to his encounter with its folk culture at a time when he felt newly released from his battles with illness and rejoiced in the beginning of a new and healthier life.

It was later in this year, back in Liverpool, that Elisabeth took her son to see his first opera. Benjamin Britten's *Peter Grimes*, a story of social injustice amongst nineteenth-century Suffolk fisherfolk and featuring the physical abuse of a child of about John's age, may possibly seem a strange choice for the introduction of a child to opera. Elisabeth knew of the excitement that the first performance of the work had created in London two years before, and was possibly eager herself to see and hear the work on tour by the Covent Garden company. She obviously thought that it would be an excellent introduction to opera for her son, and, indeed, John remembered this occasion vividly and spoke of the lasting and favourable impression that the music and the operatic experience had on him. *Peter Grimes* became one of his favourite musical works, and one of which he remains a life-long and firm champion. As the public examination (the '11+') taken nearing eleven years by all school children, qualifying them for entrance into secondary education, approached, the McCabe family hired a private tutor, the wife of a local church organist, to prepare John for the test. He remembers these sessions with pleasure and took to his studies so well that when an inspector from the school system called to check on his progress he was able to submit a very positive report.

His piano technique rapidly consolidated and his parents gave him a copy of the Rachmaninov 32 Preludes as a present for passing his 11+ examination and gaining a place at the well-known and highly respected local grammar school for boys, the Liverpool Institute. His transition into regular schooling was marked at first by continuing bouts of illness, but slowly, from this time onwards, John's immune system recovered and the illnesses, although continuing for several years with sudden and equally quickly passing flu-like symptoms, began to recede as he matured towards adolescence. It was also in 1951 that the family moved house to 29 Mount Street, in an elegant if then somewhat faded row of late eighteenth-century houses leading up the hill towards the Anglican cathedral and also to the location of the Philharmonic Hall. Gordon Green, his piano teacher, together with his wife Dorothy, lived in Hope Street, diagonally opposite, and their house was a centre of attraction for artists and musicians. The painter Austin Davies, who painted a portrait of the young John McCabe at fourteen, lived in the basement of the Greens' house, and the house was a meeting point for instrumentalists from the Liverpool Philharmonic Orchestra, visiting musicians such as Josef Krips and Wilhelm Kempff, artists such as George Mayer-Marton, and many local supporters of the arts. The young McCabe would gravitate towards the Greens' house whenever he could and a particular friend of the family was Fritz Spiegl, then a flautist in the Philharmonic Orchestra, who gave the aspiring young musician his own father's dinner jacket – made in Buenos Aires and by then somewhat green with age – for McCabe's first public appearance. Elisabeth and Fritz Spiegl would sometimes speak German together and this, perhaps, formed a special bond in these days immediately following the end of the Second World War. Spiegl's sense of humour and love of the ridiculous affected the young McCabe, who remembers well the original April Fool's Day concerts at the Liverpool Philharmonic Hall that Spiegl invented and organised, and which eventually inspired Gerard Hoffnung to imitate them so success- fully in London. McCabe remembers well the famous occasion when the programme featured the Cuban National Anthem, which was a single rifle shot, and also the occasion where John Pritchard, then resident conductor of the Liverpool Philharmonic Orchestra, walked with dignity across the front of the waiting orchestra, on to the rostrum, and, in the same manner, then left the platform on the opposite side. It was at Green's house that McCabe first met the composer Alan Rawsthorne, whose music he already knew well through his treasured recording, broadcasts and occasional live performances. It was during one of Rawsthorne's visits that McCabe took a fragile shellac disk of Rawsthorne's Bagatelles, in its paper slip-case, to the composer, who autographed it for him (now, alas, lost). Gordon Green and Alan Rawsthorne had been music students together with the composer and conductor Constant Lambert and the pianist James Gibb, and all had remained good friends.

The Rachmaninov Preludes gift gives an insight into McCabe's level of achievement as a pianist by the age of eleven. Green had given him Oscar Beringer's Studies to work on to build his technique, and McCabe remem- bers that he was always treated as an adult by his teacher. He had received weekly lessons from Green since the age of eight and the lessons were often wide-ranging with references made to other arts, especially painting and to the broad musical repertoire. It was through Green that McCabe gained his first insights into the Beethoven String Quartets and also was introduced to the music of Soviet Russia at the Anglo-Soviet Music Society in Liverpool at the Bluecoat School Arts Centre. Green was politically very left-wing, as were many artists of that era, and through Green he met and talked with the composer Kabalevsky and the violinist David Oistrakh, whom Kabalevsky was accompanying. The weekly lessons took place in Green's house always on two pianos ('He always played the better one himself', McCabe noted) and the young pianist was often presented with difficult sight-reading chal- lenges. One that stuck in his memory was the 8th of Bartók's Bagatelles, whose chord progressions and bitonality affected him strongly. McCabe treasures the copy from which he sight-read at that lesson and plays the work still with a continuing sense of wonder and delight.

Entry to full-time secondary education marked a waning and finally a pause in McCabe's composing output. The last of the many so-called 'symphonies' had been written in 1951. They had always been written straight into full score, in the innocence of youth, and McCabe explained that he felt that he didn't know enough about harmony and counterpoint, as Green revealed more to him of music's inner workings. He felt that, maybe for most of the time, he had merely been creating patterns in musical notation without enough understanding of technical matters, and now they no longer satisfied him. When he entered the Liverpool Institute, more musical opportunities were open to him and McCabe first began to learn to play the violin, but after two years transferred to the cello, which he studied for the next four years. His interests widened as he reached adolescence and he also became increasingly passionate about cricket and films – two passions that still remain to this day. It was not unknown for McCabe to leave school without permission to visit local cinemas where he first saw films such as *The Third Man, Blithe Spirit, The Overlanders, The Cruel Sea*, and the Ealing comedies such as *Kind Hearts and Coronets* and *A Passport to Pimlico. The Sound Barrier*, with its score by Malcolm Arnold, and *Scott of the Antarctic*, with its score by Ralph Vaughan Williams, left lasting impressions on him, both visually and musically. In his final two years at secondary school he undertook to write and produce his own film magazine and joined a local film society to which interested older students were invited. He experienced new films of many types – some from other countries such as Russia, Germany, Japan, France and Italy – but the American Hollywood Western became the genre that most fascinated him both structurally as films and also in the way that the Western musical genre was being established having been formed in the late 1930s arising out of the work of composers such as Grofé and then Aaron Copland. He remembers the impact made on him by actors such as James Stewart, and it was John Ford's *She Wore a Yellow Ribbon* and *Shane* (which he saw three times) that left lasting impressions.

McCabe remembers his lower-school music teacher as a man who told jokes rather than being able to motivate his students to study, and he was followed by a quick succession of other similar teachers. It was not until 1955 – when he was in the upper school, or 'sixth form' as it was commonly known, and had begun studies in music for the Advanced Level General Certificate of Education public examinations – that McCabe began again to write music himself. Since the study of music at this level was not available in the school (a not uncommon situation), McCabe received intensive private lessons outside school in order to catch up and prepare for the examination, success in which was necessary for university entrance. These were given by Bridget Fry, wife of Fritz Spiegl, who lived nearby. It was the school's policy then not to support Advanced Level studies in music so it was mostly through the encouragement of his chemistry master, Laurie Naylor, a keen amateur violist, that he began again to compose, although, at that time, composition was not an option for submission in the public examinations. Naylor had started a chamber ensemble and a school orchestra in both of which McCabe played cello – indeed was the only cellist – and a brave performance of Schubert's 'Unfinished' Symphony sticks in his memory, since the main melody of the first movement was solely his. It was Naylor who in 1957 also engineered for McCabe to write the incidental music for a school production of Sheridan's *The Rivals*, and ensured a performance of his somewhat gloomy but well-shaped Passacaglia for Two Pianos at the Rodewald Chamber Concert series. This was followed by a Divertimento for Flute, Oboe and Strings and a Fantasia for Organ. Incidental music for a Victorian theatre production at the Bluecoat School Arts Centre and also the score of a *Holiday Overture* completed the works written in this schoolboy period.

At the age of fourteen or so, McCabe had come to the attention of William Jenkins, who was then Music Adviser to the Liverpool City Education Committee and conductor of the Merseyside Youth Orchestra, and the McCabe family were encouraged to apply for a bursary available to talented youngsters as a Music Studentship. Indeed, Frank McCabe had already declared that if his son failed in gaining this award, his lessons with Gordon Green would have to cease. Fortunately John McCabe was successful, and the award was renewed annually until he finished his secondary schooling. McCabe was also recruited into the Merseyside Youth Orchestra in which he played percussion and, when the score demanded it, piano. Not a trained percussionist, McCabe tackled instruments such as cymbals and bass drum with perhaps more enthusiasm than technique. Since the repertoire chosen by Jenkins tended to be conservative there was little need for the more complex and exotic percussion instruments that might have been more challenging to play. McCabe remembers performing as soloist in Turina's *Rapsodia Sinfónica* and as orchestral pianist in Don Gillis's Symphony Number Five and a Half, then a very popular work, Bizet's *L'Arlésienne* Suite and Edward German's *Welsh Rhapsody* (reflecting Jenkins's Welsh ancestry), in which McCabe remembers playing bass drum, cymbals and tambourine. His first professional engagement was playing the first movement of the Beethoven Third Piano Concerto with the Liverpool Philharmonic Orchestra under Trevor Harvey at a concert in the Liverpool Philharmonic Youth Education Concert series, given to audiences of older school children. This also led to his first solo appearance in a concert series featuring young performers from various countries, in which he, representing the home city, played the Mozart C Minor Fantasia (and received his first newspaper review by a local journalist who found that his performance contained 'too much interpretation').

It was with an increasingly rich musical background and experience that McCabe decided to apply as a student on the Bachelor of Music degree at Manchester University that ran its courses in performance jointly with the Royal Manchester College of Music, which at that time stood only a few hundreds of yards away from the main university campus. As he joined the university's music department – under its idiosyncratic Professor and former pupil of C.V. Stanford, Humphrey Procter-Gregg – in the autumn of 1958, McCabe suffered the final attack of his childish flu-like condition, so that he missed the first weeks of the course. His aspiration at that time was to be an accompanist and rehearsal pianist and, although composition was part of his course, the university department – strongly influenced by the highly conservative Professor himself, who taught composition – did little to encourage him; the Professor tried to discipline him as he did all other composition students, with enforced writing of pastiche in dance forms such as minuets. Peter Maxwell Davies, who had just left the same department where he underwent the same routines, had left a distinct aura behind him, at least by reputation. The advice received by all Procter-Gregg's composition students of 'four bars a day', however, was good and, overall, studies in the university music department were of the strictly traditional kind such as harmony, counterpoint, history and set works. McCabe played percussion in the university orchestra and also, making best use of his sight-reading ability, accompanied rehearsals of the university chorus and of opera. The set works studied in those years included the Verdi Requiem and Haydn's String Quartet in E Flat Op. 76 No. 6, part of which work would reappear in McCabe's later writing in a new guise.

His lessons with Gordon Green continued, now under the aegis of the Royal Manchester College of Music, where Green remained a piano professor, as part of the joint course. Elisabeth's relationship with Frank had slowly been deteriorating for many years over McCabe's school period, and she chose to take an apartment in Altrincham, a pleasant south Manchester suburb, where she and her son could live during the week and where it was intended that Frank would be a weekend visitor, although this rarely materialised. As life went on over the next three years, Frank receded in influence and in contact with the rest of his family and eventually lived in the lower half of the Mount Street house, with Elisabeth in the upper, when she moved back there after her son's university course was completed. Half-way through his university course, a somewhat ridiculous confrontation with the Professor, Humphrey Procter-Gregg, was quite unintentionally provoked by McCabe being invited and programmed to play one of his compositions at a concert at his old school – a piece which had not first been vetted and approved by the Professor. Procter-Gregg was eccentric and domineering and very much inclined to irrational behaviour and thereafter refused to give McCabe composition tutorials. The degree programme allowed him a choice of composition and instrument or instrument only, so McCabe unsurprisingly chose the latter, successfully graduating in 1960 as a pianist.

After gaining his degree, McCabe continued his piano studies at the Royal Manchester College (RMCM) as a postgraduate and sat his Associate of the Royal Manchester College of Music examination, which required him to sit a paper entitled 'rudiments of music'. Circumstances dictated that he was late for the examination and rushed through the paper, consequently failing in the rudiments of music. The failure was considered an aberration by the College tutors who marked it and knew him, and they still awarded him the qualification. He had started on a course at Manchester University Education Department that would have qualified him to become a teacher of music in the state-school system, but one prolonged experience as a trainee teacher under the deadening mentorship of the resident music specialist in a local grammar school strengthened the unfortunate memories of his own schooling, and was enough to put him off classroom teaching for life, and he withdrew. Fortunately, at about the same time, at the suggestion of his college professors, he was invited by Manchester's Hallé Orchestra to play the solo piano part in a run-through performance of Christopher Headington's Variations for Piano and Orchestra, and this successfully took place in January 1961. He joined the RMCM as a full-time postgraduate student, playing for singing lessons given by the tenor Heddle Nash, and accompanying the mezzo-soprano Meriel Dickinson. During this period he was also able to play a Bartók Piano Concerto with the RMCM orchestra.

During the summer vacation of 1959, before his final university year, he and Elisabeth had, once again, retreated up to Patterdale, back to the cottage they had rented since he was nine and which held such happy memories for him. During two weeks of this holiday, McCabe sketched out the short score of his Violin Concerto, the work that marked the beginning of his life as a professional composer. The work was scored in spare time over the next two years and was eventually submitted to the Society for the Promotion of New Music and awarded a rehearsal run-through and performance with orchestra. The work, played by the then Hallé leader, Martin Milner, and which contains a Passacaglia movement, was much influenced by Brahms' Fourth Symphony, Beethoven's C Minor Variations for Piano and, importantly, the Chaconne from Rawsthorne's First Piano Concerto. The performance was given a favourable review by Noel Goodwin, critic and assessor for the SPNM panel, and with this performance McCabe's composing career was launched.

From the opening section of the Violin Concerto, 1959, transition from slow opening to Allegro moderato. Manuscript, including conductor's markings.

2

The professional years

Guy Rickards

In 1961, by the time that McCabe had decided against teaching, it was already apparent that his best career path lay as a performer; if not purely as a soloist, then certainly as a chamber musician, accompanist and opera repetiteur, with time at the weekends to compose. His piano playing had improved dramatically during his three years at university and his performance of the late Schubert A Major Piano Sonata in his graduation recital had convinced his tutor that a career as a performer was indeed viable. In his postgraduate year at the College he had taken part in a good number of recitals and chamber concerts as well as acting as accompanist for singing lessons given by Ena Mitchell and Heddle Nash. He had planned a series of concerts, featuring a good number of contemporary works, in which he often took part, one of the most memorable being that given by Peter Pears and Benjamin Britten. The recital included songs by Purcell, Debussy, Webern and two of Britten's cycles, and McCabe acted as page-turner. This gave him a chance to observe Britten at close quarters and he noticed that the latter usually did not mark fingerings on the scores but rather wrote in instrumental indications, such as 'horns', 'strings', etc., confirming that he thought in orchestral terms even while playing the piano, just as McCabe was doing himself.

With a slowly growing portfolio of performances to his credit – from local recitals to Bartók's Third Concerto with the college orchestra and a run-through of Christopher Headington's Variations for Piano and Orchestra with the Hallé – McCabe acquired a career as pianist, not by design but partly as a result of his being prepared to play anything and having a talent for learning pieces quickly. In 1962 he gave his first recital in London, for the Park Lane Group, playing two thorny contemporary American scores, then still very new, which have gone on to become clas-

Facing: Notturni ed Alba, extract, opening soprano entry.

sics: Copland's Variations and the Sonata by Elliott Carter. A career in the opera house, however, did not take off despite his involvement in some of Manchester College's productions, for example *L'Italiana in Algeri*, *Parsifal* and *Fidelio* – for which, at the request of the College Principal, Frederic Cox, he arranged some of Beethoven's instrumental music as recitative to replace the spoken dialogue.

At the College, McCabe had resumed composition studies under Thomas Pitfield, a highly regarded teacher from whom McCabe learned much, but to this day a woefully underestimated composer. (McCabe later repaid the compliment by recording several Pitfield scores.) In 1962, McCabe received early recognition when he won the Royal Philharmonic Society's composition prize with his Five Elegies for Soprano and Chamber Orchestra, which received its premiere the following year in Liverpool. Also in 1963, he approached the Bavarian composer Karl Amadeus Hartmann – whose *Concerto funèbre* had made a great impression on him when played in Liverpool – to see if he could study with him in Munich. Hartmann, another undervalued composer, was highly respected as an administrator, particularly of the ground-breaking concert series *Musica Nova*. However, he did not teach but suggested to McCabe that he enrol at the Munich Hochschule für Musik for the 1964–65 academic year under Hindemith's former pupil Harald Genzmer, with regular review sessions with Hartmann along the way. Hartmann, alas, died in December 1963 but McCabe – after a two-month German course (which, sadly, did not prepare him for the Bavarian dialect) – spent a valuable year in Munich nonetheless. The benefit came not from Genzmer's tuition but from the social and music-cultural environment: he was able to visit the opera with far greater regularity than had been possible in Britain and was able to see a good number of the operas of Richard Strauss and Werner Egk, although a major disappointment was the replacement of Henze's *König Hirsch* – then a repertory item – by a Verdi work. Opportunities for piano practice were limited as his digs (in an old Gothic building resembling the witch's house in *Hansel and Gretel*) were quite a way out of the city so that by the time he could get into town the limited number of instruments available were always taken. As a result, he eventually ceased his piano lessons with Rosl Schmidt but returned periodically to Britain to give recitals – and, at Christmas 1964, a BBC broadcast. (On this same trip to London, he directed the Portia Ensemble at the Wigmore Hall in the premiere of his own Symphony for Ten Wind Instruments, a rare outing as a conductor, an area of music-making not at all to his taste.) In learning a new work he would work out the fingerings and learn the physical movements required on a table in his digs, marking out the keys on paper, then apply his knowledge on a real instrument when rehearsing back in Britain.

Munich also gave him the opportunity to compose and he was beginning to make a name for himself in the north-west of England. The First Violin Concerto had been successfully premiered by Martin Milner, the leader of the Hallé Orchestra (and for whom McCabe also composed *Musica Notturna*), and this same orchestra also gave several performances of the Variations on a Theme of Karl Amadeus Hartmann, which he had written in the Bavarian's memory in 1964. In the next year, McCabe was commissioned, at the suggestion of Maurice Handford, to provide a work for the concert at which Sir John Barbirolli returned with the Hallé to the Cheltenham Festival after several years' absence. The result was the First Symphony, *Elegy*, and provided McCabe with his first taste of national success. Barbirolli was so impressed that he insisted the BBC broadcast the work (there had previously been no plans to do so and the Violin Concerto had only achieved regional cover), although the subsequent recording on the Pye label was eventually conducted by John Snashall. McCabe had also found a publisher by this time – Novello – following the publication of the Variations for Piano (1963) in a series selected and edited by another Manchester University graduate (and former pupil of Gordon Green), John Ogdon. All of McCabe's subsequent output has appeared under the Novello colophon.

On his return to Britain in the summer, McCabe returned to the Royal Manchester College, where he gave occasional lectures, but that September he received a telephone call from Alun Hoddinott that proved, at least in the short term, life-changing. Hoddinott was at the time a lecturer (later Professor of Music) at the University of Cardiff. He was a respected composer and McCabe had played several of his works, including the first two piano sonatas and a nocturne. Although the two men had never met they had corresponded and Hoddinott clearly knew the measure of McCabe as a performer. Hoddinott was also in a fix because the pianist in residence at the University, Patrick Piggott, had unexpectedly left (on the agreed one month's notice) to work for the BBC. McCabe was invited to take his place in the year-long season of recitals, lectures and chamber concerts (including one every fortnight with the University string quartet), and for the next three years McCabe based himself in Cardiff (where he composed his First Symphony), learning and playing – sometimes with precious little lead-time – some 76 chamber scores, dozens of recitals and giving occasional lectures to up to eighteen piano students (though he was not their official tutor). The experience was immensely rewarding both professionally – he was automatically selected to broadcast for BBC Wales and his concert-giving increased – and personally: one of his students was Hilary Tann, who has become a noted composer in her own right. She and John fell in love and married in 1968, in Ynysbwl, following her graduation. That same year, the couple moved from Cardiff (McCabe had given Hoddinott ten months' notice, however) to Southall in West London.

The year 1968 saw the creation of two works of considerable import for the composer but which have not enjoyed the exposure they deserve. The first, and at the time his largest, work was the children's opera *The Lion, the Witch and the Wardrobe*, setting a libretto by Gerald Larner derived from C.S. Lewis' famous children's novel. Scored for two adult soloists, nine children and a large chamber orchestra, the opera was premiered in April 1969 at Chetham's Hospital School as part of the Manchester Cathedral Festival. However, the opera subsequently fell under a copyright restriction following the acquisition of the rights to Lewis' book by Walt Disney, the agreement for which forbade any other theatrical presentations – including operatic ones. The terms previously extended to Larner and McCabe had been phrased vaguely and, one or two sanctioned outings aside, permission for performance in recent years has been withheld. The other composition was his second harpsichord concerto *Metamorphosen* (the first, *Concertante*, had been penned three years earlier), which signalled a breakthrough for McCabe in its use of the orchestra. The important lessons he gained in creating this score were put to good use in the next ones, but *Metamorphosen* itself remains an unknown quantity. It has only ever been performed once (in 1972), with the composer as stand-in soloist after the intended performer – a Baroque specialist – withdrew because he had little understanding of contemporary music and felt unable to do the work justice. In the meantime, McCabe began the composition of a series of large-scale piano studies to which he has been adding at various times since. The first to be written were *Capriccio* and *Sostenuto* in 1969, quickly followed in 1970 by *Gaudí*, in honour of the great Catalan architect, and *Aubade*.

The immediate first fruit of this improved awareness of what the orchestra could achieve also marked his first major national success as a composer, the song cycle *Notturni ed Alba* (1970). A commission for the Three Choirs Festival, it was premiered in Hereford Cathedral by Sheila Armstrong and the City of Birmingham Symphony Orchestra conducted by Louis Frémaux in a concert sandwiched between works by Tchaikovsky and Brahms. This radiant score made an enormous impact and was quickly taken up by London-based orchestras, so much so that when James Loughran wanted to programme it at the Royal Festival Hall with the Hallé Orchestra, it was politely turned down because it had already been heard there several times that season. McCabe followed this up with his Second Symphony in 1971, commissioned by the Feeney Trust for Frémaux and the Birmingham orchestra again, who duly premiered it that September. The following year, Frémaux recorded the symphony and *Notturni ed Alba* (with soprano Jill Gomez) for EMI.

One of the main reasons for McCabe's departure from Cardiff was that he was finding it increasingly difficult to fit all his musical projects into the available time. He was receiving commissions for new works increasingly – not least his First Piano Concerto, for the City of Southport's centenary in 1966–67, and *The Lion, the Witch and the Wardrobe* – and his performing diary was becoming ever more crowded. In 1969 he was a piano prizewinner in the prestigious Gaudeamus competition in the Netherlands and six years later would receive a Special Award from the Composers' Guild of Great Britain for his services to British music. McCabe had already started to write record reviews (mainly for the periodical *Records and Recording*) whilst still at Cardiff and this activity increased on his arrival in the capital. He had also made his first recording, relatively early in his career, accompanying the singer Marni Nixon in songs by Gerard Schurmann, Goehr and

John Barbirolli with Elisabeth and John McCabe, Cheltenham Festival, 1966.

Ives. This was followed by a series of discs for various companies, including music by Brahms and Satie (the latter re-released on CD in 2005). An LP of twentieth-century music – including the Copland and Webern Variations, Nielsen's Chaconne and works by Rawsthorne, Schoenberg and his own Five Bagatelles (1964) – was released by Pye but a disc for them of Haydn sonatas never saw the light of day for reasons that remain unclear.

McCabe had been introduced to some of Haydn's sonatas while still a student by Gordon Green and he was immediately captivated. Not only was this repertoire almost entirely untouched by any other player at the time, which appealed greatly to McCabe the performer, but Haydn's methods of motivic development and alternating variation struck a chord with his composer side, being elements that fascinated him and which he began to deploy in his own music. Although the Pye disc miscarried, a release of three sonatas a couple of years later for EMI proved successful and prompted Decca in 1974 to undertake the enormous project of recording McCabe performing all 55 extant sonatas (no. 28 in McCabe's own completion), to which were added several sets of variations and other smaller pieces, plus an arrangement of *The Seven Last Words of the Redeemer on the Cross*. The issue, once completed, was rightly hailed as 'one of the great recorded monuments of the keyboard repertoire' and remains available – and selling – to this day. Haydn's influence persisted into McCabe's own compositions over the ensuing few years, initially with the Third Symphony, *Hommages*

McCabe with Alun Hoddinott.

(1977–78), taking the E flat String Quartet he had analysed with Procter-Gregg as its springboard. (In September 2005 this connection was spotlighted at a BBC concert in Watford when the quartet and symphony were performed side by side; in the same concert McCabe gave a vivid interpretation of Haydn's Eleventh Piano Concerto in D.) McCabe's Fourth Quartet (1982) and *Haydn Variations* (1983) were written in honour of the 150th anniversary, celebrated in 1983, of Haydn's birth, and he later wrote a BBC Music Guide to the sonatas, published in 1986.

Although in terms of his career the move to London was immediately beneficial, McCabe's personal circumstances changed very quickly. His marriage to Hilary broke down and they separated in 1970, divorcing two years later. Hilary moved to the United States in 1972 to start a degree course at Princeton University, subsequently remarried and has since made a successful teaching and composing career from her base in the Adirondacks. Following Hilary's departure, McCabe applied himself to recording, working frequently with the producer Bob Auger, a former assistant of whose – Monica Smith – was working on the editorial staff of *Records and Recording* and who had interviewed McCabe for his early studio projects. In 1971 McCabe asked Monica to write the text for a new choral work he had been commissioned to write for the next Three Choirs Festival, at Worcester in 1972. The result was the cantata *Voyage*, the second largest work he had written to date, for five vocal soloists, chorus and orchestra. Working together on this project and a ballet for the Northern Dance Theatre, *The Teachings of Don Juan* (1973), for which Monica prepared the text from Carlos Castaneda's book, brought composer and librettist closer together. They wed in 1974 and are still happily married today.

That same year, McCabe was commissioned to write a new orchestral work by the Hallé Concerts Society and used this as an opportunity to satisfy a project he had long had in mind to write a work inspired by the stained-glass windows created by Marc Chagall for the synagogue in Jerusalem University's Medical Centre. McCabe has described the windows, which he had seen photographs of only, as 'one of the most exciting, moving visual artworks of the century' and is emphatic that the result, *The Chagall Windows*, premiered in January 1975, is 'not programme music … [but] above all an abstract work'. It received considerable attention when it became the subject of a television documentary. In 1973 McCabe had written a couple of short items, *Madrigal* and *Arabesque*, for use as background music to accompany the TV signal for Granada TV as well as the theme music to that company's drama series *Sam* (over the next few years he would write over a dozen more for Granada, the BBC, Thames

TV, Hammer House of Horror and even a Michelin tyre advert) and the Manchester-based station was the ideal choice for such a documentary. Granada even flew the composer to Jerusalem to experience the windows 'in the glass', which helped him clarify certain aspects of the work's structure, as he remarked in a note for the work's commercial recording. 'The essential element of continuity, enhanced by Chagall's use and contrast of dominant colours, is exemplified by the placing of the twelfth window next to the first. This sense of unity within diversity, and of continuity, is something of deep importance to me as a composer.'

In the meantime, McCabe was extending his range of activities further, with two monographs, one on Bartók (a BBC Music Guide), the second on Rachmaninov (for Novello). Two theatrical ventures followed, the first being a large-scale chamber opera (running to almost two hours, making it still one of his three longest works), *The Play of Mother Courage*, with a libretto adapted by Monica from the Grimmelshausen book. It was commissioned by Opera Nova and premiered by them in Middlesbrough

in October 1974, conducted by the redoubtable Iris Lemare. In 1975 came his first full-length ballet, *Mary, Queen of Scots*, to a two-act scenario by Noel Goodwin and commissioned by the then Scottish Ballet. This received its premiere in Glasgow in March 1976 and has enjoyed several revivals. (McCabe subsequently extracted two orchestral suites and a pair of dances for harp and strings from the score, as well as re-using material from it as his Fifth Piano Study.) Despite this success and those of the Second Symphony (as *Shadow-Reach*, to a scenario based on Henry James' *The Turn of the Screw* by the Irish Ballet Company) and *The Chagall Windows* (as *Die Fenster*, to choreography by Rosemary Helliwell for Stuttgart Ballet), it would be almost twenty years before McCabe was commissioned to write another full-length ballet, producing one of his greatest successes in the process.

McCabe's career is notable for pursuing two strands – one as performer, the other as composer – with neither predominant. His success as composer began to be overtaken by that of pianist, led primarily by his recordings, not least the Haydn sonata cycle. The timing of this change of focus in public perception was ironic in that during 1976 he experienced something of a compositional epiphany. While never an out-and-out serialist, McCabe had deployed elements of Schoenberg's twelve-note method in his music to varying degrees over the years, always within a tonal – if free-tonal – basis. During 1976, while writing a setting of the Stabat Mater, he realised that decisions regarding the music should come from him, not from someone else's abstract formula. Although he has used dodecaphony when it has suited him to do so since then, from that time on his music has enjoyed complete freedom from any ideology or method. This is immediately apparent from his Third Symphony (1977–78), which includes a series of homages to composers of special importance to his own music. As mentioned above, the work is fundamentally influenced by a Haydn string quartet but casts its evocative net much wider. The very opening is a homage to Szymanowski and later on are quotes from or allusions to Nielsen (the *Luciferiske* Suite), William Schuman (whose Piano Concerto McCabe later recorded for Albany), Richard Strauss (the *Alpeinsinfonie*), Vaughan Williams and Walton (the First Symphony and Hindemith Variations). Written for the Royal Philharmonic Orchestra, this sumptuous score – almost a concerto for orchestra in its richness and instrumental élan – is still awaiting its first recording, as is another RPO commission from the following year, *The Shadow of Light*, a nocturne written to commemorate the bicentenary of William Boyce's death.

As a travelling virtuoso he began to go further and further afield, with several trips to the United States and Australia (to both of which countries he has returned frequently and enjoyed great success), as well as a tour of the Middle East, funded by the British Council, that took in Turkey and Syria: his Sixth Piano Study, *Mosaic* (1980), was inspired by the decorations in Damascene mosques. These experiences, allied to an innate joy in landscapes, prompted a series of intriguing musical responses in him with the creation of a string of ecologically inspired works. First came the *Desert* series, starting in 1981 with two works for wind ensembles, *Lizard* and *Horizon*. Two further works followed, and in 1984 the first of three pieces entitled *Rainforest* was written. These series between them include recorder solos, a piano trio and a chamber trumpet concerto, and to them should be added several other items such as the unaccompanied vocal sextet *Scenes in America Deserta* (1986) and a double-bass solo,

Pueblo (1987). The series eventually came to a halt with *Canyons* for wind ensemble in 1991 (although the composer did consider calling his 2006 Horn Concerto *Rainforest IV*, but eventually decided against it[1]). In the meantime, however, McCabe the composer had been restored to wider public notice with two resounding public and critical successes. The first of these, in 1983, was with his Concerto for Orchestra, commissioned by the London Philharmonic (after McCabe was selected by a committee of the players themselves) and premiered by them to great critical acclaim conducted by Sir Georg Solti, who took the work to Chicago the following year. The Concerto is unusual in McCabe's output in that part of it – the start of the first main section, after the opening fanfare-like episode – came to him in a dream. Two years later, McCabe scored an even greater hit with his brass band piece *Cloudcatcher Fells*, a remarkable homage in sound to the holiday landscape of his childhood. Written as a test piece for the 1985 National Brass Band Championship, the work has become a staple of the band repertoire and been recorded more than any other of McCabe's works (seven times).

In 1983 (during which year his father Frank died), McCabe embarked on a new and, as it turned out, very time-consuming addition to his career, the result of another telephone call, this time from his long-time cello partner, Julian Lloyd Webber. The latter's father, William, had been the Principal of the London College of Music and had recently died. The College was well known for its production of music teachers but was not perceived as having a high profile and the governors had been persuaded that McCabe would be the right man to rectify that. McCabe was not convinced, having no real experience in this area although he had been serving as President of the Incorporated Society of Musicians (1982–83). He agreed to talk the matter over with them – as a result of which he was offered the post and accepted! For the next seven years, in often very trying conditions, McCabe succeeded in halting the College's decline.

When he arrived he found that musical standards had been steadily falling when compared to the other London music colleges and he was able to bring some modern thinking and practical musical expertise to bear. Over the next few years he expanded the teaching staff, although he did not himself teach while there, and widened the variety of courses, including starting a jazz arrangement course – the College had boasted a big band for some years but had no jazz tuition – as well as a film music course, and instituted a recording studio, sponsored by Yamaha. He revitalised the College's core concert-giving by using his contacts to bring in a more varied range of conductors and musicians and planned year-long series of concerts designed

1 After the first performance McCabe decided to retain the original title of the Horn Concerto (*Rainforest IV*).

26

to expand the students' knowledge and experience of music. One year featured Australian music, another a triple theme of Nordic works, music by the sons of Bach and Vaughan Williams' concertante pieces. Perhaps the most memorable was the American year, with 21 concerts including performances of the second symphonies of Howard Hanson and Walter Piston, plus a movement of John Corigliano's Oboe Concerto. McCabe had given the UK premiere of Corigliano's Piano Concerto a few years earlier and Corigliano visited the College; he also requested that the College be invited to provide students to march behind James Galway at the premiere of his *Pied Piper Fantasy*.

McCabe has described his period at the College as 'a very exciting time' in which he 'learned a great deal about administration, budgets and the minutiae of planning fire escapes'. He even had to deal with concerns over the College ghost, allegedly one Harry Johnstone, caretaker in the 1920s and 1930s, who habitually walked the halls a few inches above the floor (the level of which had been lowered in the 1950s). Despite calls for an exorcist to be brought in, McCabe determined to leave this benign spirit in peace. This may have been due to the opposition he was subjected to by some of the living occupants, who were unenthusiastic about both his innovations in the College and his methods. Matters came to a head with regard to the premises in Great Marlborough Street, which were in a very dilapidated condition bordering on unsafe. The problems with the building predated McCabe's appointment and, unaware of a damning building report, he endeavoured to have the fabric repaired. Such short-term patching deferred the hard decision and McCabe became convinced that the best course was a move to an alternative location in Ealing as part of what would become Thames Valley University. The opposition to the move hardened but after a period of some tension the move finally took place in 1991.

By that time McCabe had resigned as Principal, due not to the strictures or pressures of the post per se but rather the increasing conflict he felt between his career as a musician – he had been made a CBE in 1985 in recognition of his services to British Music – and administrator. He had continued to compose, scoring notable successes with two works partly inspired by books: the unaccompanied *Scenes in America Deserta* for the King's Singers in 1986 (from Reyner Banham's book of the same name) and orchestral tone poem *Fire at Durilgai* (from Patrick White's novel, *The Tree of Man*). The tone poem is also derived in part from McCabe's 'fascination with the Australian landscape' and its night sky, though it is not a 'desert' or 'rainforest' piece, as well as the notion of fire itself, with all the autobiographical resonances that might be expected. It 'represents an expression of something which, inevitably, has had a deep effect on my own life – I only wish I knew precisely how the significance and nature of fire itself has affected my subconscious'. The BBC Philharmonic Orchestra toured *Fire at Durilgai* in Britain during 1989, including a triumphant Prom performance, and abroad. The lure of becoming a full-time professional musician again proved too hard to resist when he received an invitation to tour Australia for three months, playing concertos and giving recitals at the Melbourne Summer Festival and in Queensland – including a performance of de Falla's *Nights in the Garden of Spain*, which he had long wanted to play. Feeling that his work at the College was done, he left in 1990.

The tour included, ironically, a month at Melbourne University as Visiting Professor of Composition, a post he relished. Two years after this he received a joint commission from the Australian Broadcasting Company and BBC for a new symphony, which would become his fourth: *Of Time and the River*. This was written partly while he was active in another short-term academic appointment, as Visiting Professor at the University of Cincinnati, between September and October 1994. Composing was made easier by his acquisition of a laptop computer and an early version of the Sibelius score-writing software, which he has used ever since. At Cincinnati he also worked on his Oboe Concerto and a new ballet commission. His lecturing duties involved a series of 24 lectures, the main theme of which was tonality in the twentieth century. His analyses included a wide array of works including Britten's opera *The Turn of the Screw* and Simpson's Ninth Symphony. As it turned out, his lectures had to be curtailed in number owing to his having to fulfil various contractual engagements, so he substituted a recital at which he played Hindemith's *Ludus Tonalis* and the Webern Variations, Op. 27, which latter piece he had already toured in a series of lecture-recitals. His performance of the Webern was hailed as the best he had heard by a member of the La Salle Quartet, whose recordings of Webern remain benchmarks to this day, who was in the audience. In between these two professorships, McCabe had been active again in the recording studio, with a series of projects that attracted great critical attention and praise: the original Piano Sonata version of Bax's First Symphony for Continuum in 1992; a disc of Howells' *Lambert's Clavichord* and *Howells' Clavichord* for Hyperion the following year and, for the same company, *Ludus Tonalis* and the *1922 Suite* in 1995. With Murray Khouri he recorded the clarinet sonatas by Brahms and Hans Gál.

The ballet commission McCabe worked on while in Cincinnati was his first such since *Mary, Queen of Scots* in 1975. The subject was historical again, this time *Edward II*, with a scenario, based on Christopher

Marlowe's great play, by David Bintley for Stuttgart Ballet, who had staged *Die Fenster* in 1980. If the subject of a medieval English king might seem strange for a German company and audience, it must be remembered that Marlowe's play is familiar in Germany due to Brecht's translation-cum-performing edition (which has since been translated back into English and toured in Britain). The ballet was staged to great acclaim in 1995 and has since been revived by that company. In the same year, McCabe enjoyable another high-profile international success when *Of Time and the River* was premiered by Vernon Handley in Melbourne. A few months later, David Atherton gave the first British performance at the Royal Festival Hall. Although linked with a book – here Thomas Wolfe's – the symphony was not inspired by it directly. Trains, train journeys and the interplay of different tempi lie at its heart: '"A symphony must travel" said Bob Simpson and I agree with him. The book reflected a lot of the interests that concerned me.'

McCabe found working with Bintley a most rewarding experience and he was greatly encouraged when Bintley took up the post of Artistic Director of the Birmingham Royal Ballet in 1997 and revived *Edward II* as one of his first productions. The first British performances were a huge success, perhaps the greatest of McCabe's career as a composer, certainly since that of *Notturni ed Alba* 27 years earlier, and garnered several awards – including the 1998 Barclay Theatre Award – and other nominations (including for a 2000 Laurence Olivier Award). Bintley proposed another subject, although one of semi-mythical rather than purely historical character: King Arthur. Bintley's conception was even more ambitious than that for *Edward II*: a diptych, of two full-evening ballets (each around two hours in duration), the first (1999), *Arthur Pendragon*, tracking Arthur's rise to power, the second (2000–01), *Morte d'Arthur*, his fall. The first ballet, billed by Birmingham Royal Ballet prosaically as *Arthur: Part 1*, was premiered in January 2000; its successor (as *Arthur: Part 2*) the following year. In the meantime McCabe had returned to the score of *Edward II* and extracted several key episodes to form his fifth symphony in 1999, although not numbered as such. McCabe now prefers to give his symphonies descriptive titles as did Andrzej Panufnik, whose *Sinfonia mistica* is an especial favourite. As he told the present writer recently, 'I had got a bit fed up with using numbers and I got to thinking about the Panufnik symphonies; the names identify them better'. Although the first three symphonies retain their numbers in his official catalogue, those from *Of Time and the River* onwards are identified by their titles; thus the 'fifth' is simply *Symphony: Edward II* while his most recent is styled *Symphony on a Pavane* (2006). With the music from the *Arthur* ballets, however, McCabe has contented himself with extracting a single suite (2000) – recently issued on the Dutton Epoch label – but as it is styled 'No. 1' a second may be expected in due course. The tone poem *The Golden Valley* (2000) also shares some of its material with the *Arthur* ballets.

Other satellite works spun out from *Edward II*, finding a place on the concert platform, such as the clarinet–violin–piano trio *Fauvel's Rondeaux* (1995–96) and the Cello Sonata (1999). The latter was composed to a commission from the Presteigne Festival, where McCabe has in recent years enjoyed a continuing association, and was the fulfilment of a long-held wish. That same year, another project long in the planning came to fruition when OUP published his fine biography, *Alan Rawsthorne: Portrait of a Composer*. In 2004, McCabe was Composer-in-Residence at the Three Choirs Festival in Gloucester, with several works being performed including *The Golden Valley*, the *Salisbury Service* and several piano works. McCabe also took part in a composer's workshop with Robert Saxton, whose piano *Chacony* he has recorded and which he performed in a Festival recital as the opening item in a particularly wide-ranging programme, featuring sonatas by Haydn and Beethoven, Ives' *The Alcotts*, Ravel's *Valses nobles et sentimentales*, Teruyuki Noda's *Berceuses* and two of his own studies: *Evening Harmonies* and *Scrunch*. He also contributed a variation (the first) to a joint commission, *Orchestral Variations on Down Ampney*, the other contributors being Saxton, James Francis Brown, David Matthews and Judith Bingham.

Opposite: Horn Concerto
(Rainforest IV), final bars.

John and Monica McCabe.

30

John McCabe remains as active as ever as he approaches his seventieth birthday. Since 2000, he and Monica have been living in Sittingbourne in Kent, where he has founded and runs a local music society. Their first concert was staged in 2004 and they continue to put on several each year. He believes firmly that this type of activity is essential in order to give something back to the community in which he lives and is similar to the work he has done previously with the Royal Philharmonic and Performing Rights Societies, the Association of Professional Composers (as Chairman, 1985–86) and the Musicians' Union. He tours regularly, as always wearing coloured (usually red, but never black) socks, a habit – not a superstition, he insists – from very early in his career. He continues to record: six of his own works for a British Music Society CD in 1998, works by composers from north-west England (ASC Classical), Saxton's *Chacony* and chamber pieces (NMC, 2000), Ireland chamber music (ASV, 2004), a two-piano disc with Tamami Honma for Dutton (including his *Basse Danse* and Stravinsky's *Agon*) in 2005, plus the complete Rawsthorne piano music (for Dutton, issued in 2006), among others. Two discs of music by John Joubert will be released in spring 2007 by Somm (the three piano sonatas) and Toccata Classics (song cycles and instrumental works).

The flow of works from his own pen remains undiminished as the recently completed Symphony on a Pavane and Horn Concerto (*Rainforest IV*), premiered respectively in January and February 2007, confirm. Piano music has become, perhaps curiously given his lifelong career at the keyboard, 'terribly important' to him, as can be heard in his ever-lengthening series of substantial studies. Each new addition pays homage in some way to a figure from the past: Dukas in No. 7, *Evening Harmonies*, and Domenico Scarlatti in No. 8, *Scrunch* (both completed in 2001), Debussy – obliquely – in No. 9, *Snowfall in Winter* (2003, written for Tamami Honma and commemorating a visit to Vilnius), and Ravel in the Tenth, *Tunstall Chimes* (2004). This last is named after a Kentish church but bears resonances of the Frenchman's Sonatine, part of McCabe's staple repertoire. Bell-sounds recur in the Eleventh, *Epithalamium* (2006), which takes as its starting point the two great chords in the Coronation Scene from Mussorgsky's *Boris Godunov*; it will be premiered by Malcolm Binns in the summer of 2007. And there is much more to come, for he has ideas for around 30 more compositions, including three or four string quartets, more symphonies and several more piano studies. Not being one to compose for his bottom drawer, or talk about works before they have been completed, all that is needed are the appropriate commissions to make them happen. Fortunately, the demand for his music shows no sign of running dry.

Opposite: John McCabe, 2007.

3

Symphonic and concertante works

Paul Conway

The superbly crafted Variations on a Theme of Hartmann (1964) is the earliest clear indication of John McCabe's potential as a symphonist of the front rank, taking into account the thirteen symphonies he had written by the age of eleven. It is stamped with several of the composer's most indelible fingerprints, including the influence of jazz, atmospheric use of glockenspiel, vibraphone and celesta, and agile, emancipated writing for tuba (his symphonies frequently wield this traditionally staid instrument in the nimblest of passages).

The 'theme' derives from the sombre opening of the Fourth Symphony by Karl Amadeus Hartmann (1905–63), and McCabe's piece, written while he was studying in Germany, is a celebratory tribute to the Bavarian composer. One year previously, William Walton had gradually transformed a dour excerpt from Paul Hindemith's early Cello Concerto into a typically exuberant Waltonian creation in his Variations on a Theme of Hindemith (1963). Similarly McCabe appears to become more himself as the Hartmann Variations progress.

Without preamble, the theme is presented at the outset: an arch-like melody of expressionistic intensity for strings (Hartmann's symphony is scored for string orchestra). A harp *glissando* signals the start of the variations, an Elegia, restating the theme on cellos and bassoons, and later violins, decorated by a carillon of xylophone, cymbal, piano and harp. In the following Scherzo, a woozy waltz is initiated on horn punctuated by side drum and pizzicato lower strings. Two violent tutti eruptions seem like flashes of anger at its befuddled state. Oboes, trumpets, trombones and tuba are omit- *Opposite: Symphony No. 1,* ted from the following lyrical Intermezzo, whose lavish use of glockenspiel, *opening.*

35

vibraphone and celesta conjures up a psychological inner landscape of a kind McCabe explores further in later works. In the variation's evocative central section, swaying strings envelop a technically challenging horn solo. Trenchant and metrically fluid, the ensuing Capriccio, scored for brass, piccolo, double basses and percussion (including bongos), is a welcome burst of exuberance, delighting in wrong-footing the listener with its constantly changing time signatures. There is more than a touch of Malcolm Arnold in the jazz-band brass and percussion writing and scampering piccolo lines earthed by hulking tuba counterpoint.

At this stage, the work's only significant break occurs, effectively dividing the piece into two halves of approximately equal duration. The next variation takes the form of a chaconne for full orchestra, though its title, Sarabande, suggests an archaic dance. A passionate solo for bassoon sets in motion a mournful, slow fugal passage over a muted passacaglia tapped out on *staccatissimo* piano and *pizzicato* basses. More extended than previous variations, it gradually builds up to a sustained, drum-led climax, ushering in a Fugue with Epilogue. The jazzy fugue subject begins in the brass, later joined by percussion, the remaining instruments not participating until much later. Considerable energy is accumulated, until, at the emotional peak, the mood switches dramatically in a stunning *coup de théâtre* from ebullient high spirits to anguished intensity as an impassioned restatement of the climax of Hartmann's theme materialises. This apparition quickly fades to a sustained note, accompanied by a tapping side drum, and, after a brief pause, the work closes with a single tutti *fortissimo* crash. The composer used such a 'parting shot' gesture again to end two later key orchestral works, *Notturni ed Alba* (1970) and *The Chagall Windows* (1974).

Variations on a Theme of Hartmann is John McCabe's earliest major orchestral work in which it is possible to discern his own individual voice. Paradoxically, this can be heard chiefly in its eclecticism (embracing serial, jazz and pop techniques), a quality that has served to enrich rather than dilute the composer's personal language ever since. Other foretastes of the McCabe style include crescendos of repeated figures in the Scherzo and Capriccio variations, presaging McCabe's later assimilation of aleatory and minimalist techniques, and the last variation's sudden change in temperament, a forerunner of numerous unexpected character shifts in later McCabe works. The very form of the piece has also been a regular source of inspiration in the composer's writing: his development sections from symphonies to string quartets are distinguished by continual variation techniques, their material in a constant state of transformation.

As the work progresses, its increasing exuberance and sense of adventure suggest that, just as Brahms and Elgar wrote celebrated variations before embarking on their symphonic odysseys, so McCabe is flexing symphonic muscles and widening his orchestral palette prior to tackling his own first symphony. A more tangible link is provided by the scherzo second variation, which shares a side-drum rhythm of four notes with the symphony's central dance movement.

After the accomplished Hartmann Variations and the Symphony for Ten Wind Instruments (1964), with its wide-ranging scoring and intricate thematic working out, the time was right for McCabe to face the challenge of his first orchestral symphony. Symphony No. 1, *Elegy* (1965), although not a traditional four-movement structure, is avowedly symphonic in language and development. The solemn opening processional dominates the *Lento moderato* first movement, entitled Prelude. Under a dry, ticking glockenspiel, reminiscent of the opening of George Lloyd's Seventh Symphony (1959) (also a tragic, death-haunted work), a slowly evolving melody emerges from the depths of the strings. An important *staccato* figure first heard on flute is developed, introducing a dramatic central section characterised by chiming brass ostinati, as desolate as the echoing horn calls in the Scherzo from Mahler's Fifth Symphony, though with more of the cemetery bell than the Alpine cowbell in their morbid tolling. The implacable opening material returns, its sepulchral tread eventually faltering, unresolved.

McCabe with John Snashall at the recording of his First Symphony.

The ensuing *Allegro molto* dance employs the preceding movement's material in a quicker tempo, a favourite McCabe device. Its darkly insistent *ostinato* establishes a jazz-like feel, abetted by side drum and plucked double bass. On repetition, the theme becomes irascible, curdling into fierce martial dissonances and the movement ends violently, the antithesis of its cool opening. McCabe's vivid *Totentanz* is brutish and short, a hypnotically compelling Day of Judgement to a syncopated beat, orchestrated with admirable economy and precision. Peter J. Pirie's description of the Scherzo from Vaughan Williams' Sixth Symphony as a 'speakeasy in Hades' has more resonance in this context.[1]

1 Peter J. Pirie, *The English Musical Renaissance* (London: Gollancz, 1979), p. 186.

The substantial Finale, the 'Elegy' of the subtitle, begins as an *Adagio* with thick tutti chords and a grieving lament first articulated on bassoon. This slow introductory section leads to a quick *Allegro vivo* dance, based on a speeded-up version of the first movement's flute motif, with an accompanying figure from the Prelude, also up-tempo. The tuba's melancholic *ostinato* establishes a mood of impending crisis, leading to a devastating climax, superimposing several previously heard thematic blocks. The movement then reverts to its initial *Adagio* tempo and the disturbing sound of the ticking glockenspiel. In the sparsely scored coda, a sinuous violin solo (the fiddler, traditional leader of the dance of death, perhaps?) precedes a return of the tolling bells from the central section of the Prelude, now muffled and distant. A clarinet solo recalls the symphony's opening before the work is snuffed out on a single *pizzicato* note.

Ear-catching orchestration, resourceful re-fashioning of material and perfectly judged sense of architectural symmetry make this first symphony tremendously satisfying. With the raging central scherzo as a kind of 'Dies Irae', the piece could be seen as McCabe's *Sinfonia da Requiem* and perhaps Britten's fine example, written in 1939–40, provided inspiration. The overall character is a lament on life's passing, a remarkable choice of subject for a First Symphony, often designed as a young composer's showy calling card.

If McCabe's *Elegy* Symphony was composed in the wake of a brilliant and promising orchestral work, his next contribution to the genre was immediately preceded by one of his most successful, critically acclaimed compositions. *Notturni ed Alba* (1970), for soprano and orchestra, was commissioned by the Hereford Arts Association and first performed in Hereford Cathedral as part of the Three Choirs Festival. Like Mahler's *Das Lied von der Erde*, it is a truly symphonic song-cycle: both parts of that description carry equal weight in one of McCabe's most richly lyrical and intricately worked-out scores. The four medieval Latin poems set by the composer all deal with one of his preferred themes – various aspects of night. Whereas McCabe's chamber work *Musica Notturna* (1964) is a nocturnal evocation of a great city, *Notturni ed Alba* is a much more individual response to the hours of darkness.

It forms a structural and emotional arch from an objective, instrumental depiction of a sunset via the soloist's expression of a deeply personal psychological journey back to the relative detachment of a powerful orchestral evocation of dawn. Typically, two phrases heard at the beginning of the piece prove critical to the work's later development: the soprano's descending opening line incorporates a seven-note series that furnishes material throughout the work, and the related opening horn phrase is also of crucial importance, whether hammered out by brass in the purely orchestral Phantoms episode or transfigured into the work's imposing, luminous peroration. A solo oboe provides another key theme in the form of an undulating, sensuously chromatic line, preparing the listener for the arrival of the singer.

Once the voice enters with the first song ('Fluxit labor diei'), its humanising influence draws the listener into the world of the poet/singer, expressing the growing feelings of anguish as night approaches. The second verse brings a quickening of tempo and a significant contribution from the flutes. The original *Andante* tempo is restored for the third and fourth verses, after which the oboe's winding phrases are deepened by cor anglais, preparing the way for the stealthy arrival of Phantoms, a fleeting, inventively scored scherzo, set in motion by a fully fledged fugue for untuned percussion and replete with gambolling tuba and spectral flutter-tongued flutes. After this masterly display of orchestration, there is a delicately scored, ardent lovesong ('Te vigilans oculis') in which the poet wishes a loved one was close.

This tender section is violently interrupted by arrival of the third song (Somnia) and its vivid depiction of a nightmare marked 'Agitato'. For the only time in the piece, the singer is given *parlando* passages, adding to the sense of dislocated unease incited by spare but taut orchestral writing.

In the final section, Alba (Aubade), there is a gradual release of tension as the singer radiantly heralds the coming of dawn. The sense of the poet's attainment of inner peace is movingly conveyed in the soloist's final, upwardly striving phrases. They contrast with the increasing intensity in the orchestral postlude's massive crescendo culminating in a glorious, climactic sunburst. A decisive final chord brings a conventional last-ditch gesture of order to a brilliantly wilful and wayward work, whose impressionistic half-lights illuminate a nocturnal world of ambiguity and suggestion.

Intimate, sensual and emotionally complex, *Notturni ed Alba* is one of

the very few John McCabe works where his love of Ravel finds expression, not least in its coruscating, fastidious and jewelled instrumentation: McCabe seems to be exulting in the variety of sounds at his disposal. Among the array of exotic percussion instruments required are Japanese wind chimes, claves, guiro, whip, maracas, crotales, bongos and temple blocks, all amounting to a true equal of the other orchestral sections. It is also important to note that, although the material is developed with the assurance of a proven symphonist, the singer's role is that of a genuine soloist: perhaps the most impressive feature of this enigmatic and alluring work is McCabe's vigorously resourceful use of a large orchestra to accompany, enhance, provoke and develop the solo line without ever distracting from it. *Notturni ed Alba* is a gem that shines very brightly indeed in the McCabe catalogue, consolidating his prior achievements in the field of orchestral writing: as McCabe himself has remarked, it is the work in which people 'perceived' he had found his own voice.[2]

Notturni ed Alba shares some characteristics with McCabe's next orchestral work, the Symphony No. 2 (1971). Both are cast in single movements, alternating fast and slow sections, and require a large orchestra. Something of the song-cycle's emotional intensity fires the later work, but the brutal, menacing atmosphere is unique to the symphony. Symphony No. 2 is scored for full orchestra, including a large percussion section, piano, celesta, harp and, among the various woodwind doublings, an oboe d'amore, an unusual choice of instrument, to which the composer was soon to confer solo status in a concerto. The single continuous movement with alternative tempi, typical of the composer's chamber music of the period, strives to achieve unity through contrast. Impetuous mood changes vary the material common to all sections, which derives mainly from the opening bars: a brief, desolate phrase on three flutes and harp, along with a simple descending run on bass clarinet. With these slender, fragmentary phrases, McCabe constructs the entire 22-minute edifice. As Harold Truscott noted of this opening, 'not even Sibelius … ever wrote anything like this'.[3]

Although sober and expansive in mood, the marking of this opening section is *Vivo* and the undercurrent of a faster tempo is always present – a truly Sibelian achievement McCabe was to develop in a later symphony. The underlying lively tempo surfaces in an explosive recurring figure, unleashed in a string of savage outbursts. After a terrifying culmination, the *Andante* second section, also inaugurated by flute, is relaxed and atmospheric, a picturesque evocation of calm stasis. A central *Allegrissimo* scherzo-like episode begins in jocular, dance-like mood, but clouds over ominously. The substantial *Lento* fourth section starts with a highly expressive horn solo

2 John McCabe in conversation as part of an interval feature during the Radio 3 broadcast of his 60th birthday concert from the Philharmonic Hall, Liverpool, 21 April 1999.

3 Harold Truscott, 'Two Traditionalists: Kenneth Leighton and John McCabe', in Lewis Foreman (ed.), *British Music Now: A Guide to the Work of Younger Composers* (London: Elek, 1975), p. 150.

41

before lower strings drive the material to an emotional peak. A subdued recapitulation of the horn solo, now on oboe d'amore, leads to a sustained chord. A questing theme for violins takes the music into the Finale, marked *Vivo*. This barbarous last section surveys the previous material in delirious 'fast forward', spitting out brief snatches of earlier motifs as the texture becomes increasingly dense. The music builds up to the most ferocious climax of the symphony, echoing the percussion rhythm at the outset of the piece. In the aftershock, the flutes return to their important initial phrase, ostensibly bringing the work full circle. Yet the impressive journey the composer has taken his listeners on ensures that when the opening material returns at the end it sounds entirely different, transformed by our experience.

The symphony was based upon McCabe's emotional reaction to Sam Peckinpah's film *The Wild Bunch*, and he has written passionately about this influence.[4] Even the form of the symphony (alternating sections within one continuous movement) and the use of leitmotifs were influenced by the Western film's structure. However, the symphony is non-programmatic, never consciously describing specific incidents in the film. Perhaps something of the brooding, elemental power of *The Wild Bunch* is reflected in this music's violence (even slow, quiet passages simmer with latent aggression). Significantly, it is the only existing McCabe symphony without a subtitle – knowing what really lies behind it would lessen the considerable impact of this devastating *tour de force*.

In contrast, the title of his next symphonic masterpiece, *The Chagall Windows* (1974), is so indicative of specific extra-musical associations that the work's essentially symphonic nature has tended to be overlooked. This highlight of the McCabe canon, which he has described as 'a work I have grown to think of as a single-movement symphony',[5] was commissioned by the Hallé Concerts Society and first performed in January 1974 by the Hallé Orchestra under James Loughran. The original idea of writing the piece dates back to the early 1960s when the composer saw photographs of Marc Chagall's stained-glass windows for the Synagogue at the Medical Centre of the Hadasseh-Hebrew University, Jerusalem. At the time of composing the work, McCabe was flown out to Jerusalem, to see the windows, by Granada TV as part of a documentary they were making about the composition.

The windows depict the twelve sons of the patriarch Jacob, and thus the Twelve Tribes of Israel, following a chronological plan from Reuben, the first born, to Benjamin, the youngest. This sequence is observed in the score, which is not simply a series of descriptive episodes. Although some details in the windows are echoed in the music, and the character of each

4 John McCabe, 'The Film Behind the Symphony', in Peter Dickinson (ed.), *Twenty British Composers* (London: Chester, 1975), pp. 38–44.

5 Reprinted in the booklet notes for the 1999 EMI CD release of *The Chagall Windows*, also featuring *Notturni ed Alba* and the Second Symphony (7243 567120 27).

Opposite: The Chagall Windows, Reuben, *extract.*

42

section stems from McCabe's response to Chagall's artistic realisation of the subject matter, the piece is ultimately conceived in terms of an abstract symphony. As if to emphasise this, there are no fewer than two well-defined large-scale slow movements: the first three sections make up a *Largo* of cumulative tension and weight, and similarly sections five to seven form another substantial slow movement. Gong strokes, reverberating against various orchestral diminuendos, occur at the end of Judah, at the end of Gad, and at the close of the work. Their appearance at key moments calls to mind Sibelius's similar use of a recurring magisterial trombone figure in his compact, organically conceived one-movement Seventh Symphony of 1924. A further significant formal point is tempo, in that the overall balance shifts from an initial predominance of slow tempi to an emphasis on quick ones as the music progresses.

The opening section, Reuben, the first-born, acts as a prelude, presenting the main motifs of the score, notably a ruminative, melancholic descending figure on violins. Reuben's window is blue, as is that of the ensuing Simeon, which McCabe casts as a sombre Nocturne. Set in motion by undulating upper woodwind, it is dominated by a restless, tormented figure (introduced on sorrowing cor anglais accompanied by muted brass) representing the anguish of Jacob's curse. McCabe avoids any danger of monotony in offering three slow movements in succession by cranking up the suspense with each movement: Levi, depicting the priestly guardians of the Torah, features gradually spreading brass chords decorated by woodwind and tuned percussion and is cast in the form of a long crescendo. This third window is yellow and radiant.

Judah, 'the lion's whelp', releases the work's considerable accumulated tension in its first fast section, dominated by a pounding main theme on timpani, piano and lower strings, second cousin to the strongly rhythmic theme that launches Michael Tippett's Second Symphony. There is a fleeting reference to the tolling horns from McCabe's *Elegy* Symphony (1965): this time, the horns are muted, perhaps to emphasise that this momentary allusion is a distant memory. The echoing chords are later mirrored in divided violins, a marvellously eerie passage in a score teeming with invention and dazzling sonorities. Towards the end of this extended 'Allegro Deciso', trumpet fanfares sound a musical transliteration of the name CHAGALL.

After the climax, a glissando on harp and piano sweeps into Zebulun ('an haven of ships'), whose music is a softer, more glowingly iridescent red than that of Judah. For this sea-faring tribe, the music is flowing and melodic, with a choral theme in cellos, horns and bassoons decorated by

Opposite: The Chagall Windows, Zebulun, *extract.*

44

richly divided strings. Just before the close, there is a sharp reminder of the pounding figure that opened the preceding movement (a further brief reference is made much later in the piece at the end of Naphtali: such cross-references of material between sections lend weight to *The Chagall Windows* being regarded as an organically conceived symphony rather than an episodic tone poem).

The music then sinks to the first of the work's two distinct points of repose, and a cadenza-like passage for solo cor anglais leads to Issachar, the first pastoral tribe, depicted by a verdant green window and marked by a horn theme and chordal passages in woodwind and strings, punctuated by celesta and harp. Appropriately, this section depicting a pastoral tribe features the work's most English-sounding music: the haunting opening of Vaughan Williams' Eighth Symphony is invoked in the celesta and harp's interjections. A sinuous piccolo solo might be heard as a more stratospheric *Lark Ascending* or a parody of shepherd's pipes. This hesitant cadenza-like passage introduces Dan, 'the serpent by the way'. A winding cello theme (foreshadowed by the previous piccolo solo) and intertwining brass clusters drip with serpentine tension and menace. A stunning aleatory passage for full orchestra, delivered triple *forte*, peters out into a pause, charged with anticipation, before Gad, a warrior tribe, bursts in.

This second fast section, thoroughly exploring the extensive range of percussion, bristles with violent changes of scoring and dynamics. At the end, the music winds down to the work's second point of repose for Asher, another pastoral piece, scored for strings and celesta, strongly harmonic in impulse, with soloists decorating the gradual growth of the music. The melancholic, descending main theme, initially heard on first violin and later half-remembered on celesta, keenly resembles Edward's principal motif from McCabe's ballet music for *Edward II*, written some two decades later. Asher ends in a widely spaced string chord leading to Naphtali, 'like a fleet hind', a flickering, gossamer-textured scherzo. This is another of McCabe's ingeniously scored quick movements with prominent roles for bassoons and stopped horns sandwiched between twitching upper woodwind and spacious, sustained string chords. The impression is one of pent-up energy. Suddenly, the music sweeps upwards to herald Joseph, the blessed; the brass, largely absent from the preceding two sections, returns in full and the strings slowly build up a wide-ranging theme, which lies behind the whole score, but is only now revealed in full. With a climactic change to a faster tempo for Benjamin ('a wolf that raveneth'), the various threads of the work are knitted together in a very satisfying overview of the work's main material, culminating in a musical representation of this tribe's heroic ferocity; the CHAGALL fanfares from Judah return just before the close – a final chord of epic heft and finality.

The Chagall Windows is a pivotal work in the McCabe orchestral canon. A logical culmination of organically conceived, closely argued works such as the First Piano Concerto and the Second Symphony, it also looks forward twenty years to the Fourth Symphony in its concern with matters of tempo relationships. It is one of the composer's most underrated achievements and perhaps the remarkable dearth of recent performances can be traced to its deceptive title: far from being a slavish depiction in sound of each of the Chagall windows, like some gaudy aural souvenir, it works successfully as a tightly constructed one-movement symphony, whose subtle thematic development has perhaps been overshadowed by its undeniably compelling painterly aspects.

In complete contrast to its numbered predecessor, Symphony No. 3, *Hommages* (1978), is one of the most radiant and haunting of John McCabe's orchestral works. The subtitle refers to quotations from Haydn (the sublime slow movement from the Op. 76 No. 6 string quartet forms the basis of the central *Adagio*) and Nielsen (two chords from his Suite for Piano of 1919 are used throughout the symphony). The symphony also alludes to other composers such as Walton, Richard Strauss, Shostakovich, William Schuman and Szymanowski. The buoyant opening movement, marked *Flessible*, is a free, fantasia-like treatment of an open sonata form wherein much of the material is unique to this movement. Two elements heard at the start are crucial to the whole work: the intense, soaring opening theme, closely related to the Haydn quartet material, caught on the wing by first violins, and the contrasted woodwind chords heard almost immediately after, derived from the Nielsen Suite.

The *Adagio* second movement, which overlaps the first, is entitled 'Fantasia', like the Haydn quartet movement it comments on. Different sections of the orchestra share the quotation, a hovering, ghostly presence, always dimly audible through the textures – a deeply poignant effect, like a fading precious memory, constantly overwhelmed by more earthly concerns. The soaring theme from the previous movement reappears as does the rhythmic motif in a spectacular tutti, but it is the transfiguration of the Haydn melody that lingers in the mind. The choice of quotation seems unusual for a composer so immersed in Haydn's piano music, yet the Fantasia from the Op. 76 No. 6 quartet is perfect for McCabe's purpose. In the Haydn original, one of that composer's most remarkable inventions, the opening fragile, chorale-like theme is repeated in various remote keys as if trapped, destined to transform itself in endless modulations, each reappearance more tender than the last. The restatements are interspersed with ascending scalic figures, seemingly reflecting on the theme's plight. It feels fitting for the restless spirit of Haydn's sublime quartet to reappear embedded within the Third Symphony of John McCabe, who, through his performances, has been acting as a medium for Haydn's work for many years. Significantly, this same Haydn quartet was a set work for the final examinations that the composer sat at Manchester University in 1960 and had been the focus of analysis seminars.

The Finale, an artful fusion of fugue and variation form (a favourite McCabe device, exemplified by the Finale of the Hartmann Variations), grows imperceptibly out of the slow movement, which it overlaps. Starting as a *Moderato*, it increases in tempo and intensity, building to a final shattering climax over which the horns ring out the symphony's glorious opening theme, affirming its relationship to the Haydn quartet movement and the fugue subject. Drained of energy, the music fades into silence with a whirring string figure and a side drum rhythm. The basic tonality, tangible throughout, is E, and the whole work is reinforced by a strictly observed scheme of key relationships.

Luminously scored and a worthy tribute to its symphonic forebears, John McCabe's Third Symphony completely assimilates earlier composers' styles, without compromising its own unique voice. One of this immensely attractive work's main achievements, apart from finding something new to say about tonality, is that, although in three movements, its sections are absolutely indivisible, a challenge McCabe had not undertaken in this way before.

Symphony *Of Time and the River* (No. 4) (1994) is one of the composer's most powerful and concentrated large-scale works. The basic structural concept is that of a symphony in two parts, the first beginning with quick, dynamic music yielding (often imperceptibly) to slower tempi and ending in a bleak, slow passage, and the second part starting with a suspension of forward motion gradually accelerating to return eventually to the opening music and finally whirling out from it. This arch-like use of tempi is matched by a strong tonal scheme moving from the opening's unambiguous D to the remote region of A flat (as far removed from D as possible in harmonic and tonal terms) at the end of Part One and from the stasis of A flat at the start of Part Two to a resumption of the emphatic D major tonality after the quicker music has established itself.

The opening bars mould apparently simple material into something arresting and genuinely symphonic. Over a long-held pedal D on timpani, cellos and double basses, the clarinets and violas weave wisps of theme interrupted by a key falling motif in lower strings accompanied by timpani thwacks and a rising figure on trumpets and trombone. Creating a sense of symphonic scale and scope, this introductory passage highlights another important facet of the work: its preoccupation with time and different tempi occurring simultaneously. Hence, while the opening sustained D anchors the work in that key, the fizzing clarinets and violas generate a genuine *Allegro deciso*.

The inertia at the start of Part Two is offset by imaginative scoring: suspended cymbal played with a cello bow and eerie flute *glissandi* over a soaring held chord from *divisi* violins catch the ear, and, at one stage, the strings are spread into no fewer than twenty separate staves! Chiming tubular bells and grim brass chords alternating with strings are fleetingly reminiscent of the *Elegy* Symphony. Then follows a sparkling section with scurrying violins and woodwind underpinned by whirring vibraphone, celesta and harp in the midst of which the first bassoon carves out a slower tempo. An increase in speed and intensity signals the opening music's return. The strings become a positive blur above a brass chorale and, after a terminal climax, the piece collapses into a micro-coda (a mere six bars long!) in which A flat reappears, posing a final question (a quizzical version of a theme heard initially on oboe in Part One), lest we forget the Symphony has explored darker regions, as personified by the A flat music, as well as the optimism of D major.

Its strong sense of time passing and the different levels on which this works led McCabe to call the work *Of Time and the River* after the novel by the American writer Thomas Wolfe, which explores similar concerns. The accustomed impressive array of percussion instruments is always used sparingly and the score frequently introduces a genuine feeling of spaciousness: the very opening explores the orchestra's outer edges, recalling in this respect the ninth symphonies of Gustav Mahler and Malcolm Arnold. Careful balancing of key relationships and architectural symmetry makes the piece immensely satisfying for players and listeners alike. McCabe's supreme achievement is to have created such an exciting and original-sounding Fourth Symphony: anyone new to it could be forgiven for assuming it was the composer's First, so vital and fresh are its ideas.

Begun in 1994 and completed in April 1997, Symphony *Edward II* (No. 5) is derived from John McCabe's hugely successful ballet score of the same name, and employs extracts the composer felt went well together. It requires a large orchestra with a spectacularly wide-ranging percussion section: suspended cymbal, clashed cymbals, side drum, tenor drum, bass drum, three tom-toms, wood-block, whip, anvil, tam-tam, xylophone, glockenspiel, vibraphone, marimbaphone and tubular bells. Harp, piano, celesta and electric guitar also contribute distinctive timbres. From such an extensive orchestral palette, McCabe fashions one of his most colourful and thrilling creations.

The first movement (*Adagio–Allegro, poco pesante*) starts with the ballet's opening music depicting the funeral cortège of Edward I and proceeds with material connected with outdoor sports to the civil war music from Act One, including the graphic representation of the Grim Reaper stalking England. The symphony opens with a brief flourish over the solemn progress of the cortège represented by tenebrous timpani strokes. Over these relentless beats floats a memorable chant-like dirge in triplets, strikingly scored for horns and viola. After the funeral procession has run its course, an important theme emerges with a falling three-note motif on flute and oboe. It is taken up by piccolo, clarinet and trumpet, before the *Allegro, poco pesante* section bursts in with a brutal timpani barrage punctuated by offbeat staccato stabs from the lower woodwind and strings and interrupted by antiphonal writing for strings and brass. A *molto pesante* section with heavy timpani blows recalls Tybalt's death in Prokofiev's *Romeo and Juliet* ballet score. A jazzy, *ostinato*-laden *Allegro vivo* episode stands out, its violent off-beats as explosively portentous as the Prologue, Mambo and Rumble movements from West Side Story's *Symphonic Dances* by Leonard Bernstein. Tom-toms and side drum command an extended starkly rhythmical passage before a single massive tam-tam stroke signals the end of an uncommonly physical first movement, dance steps energised into motor rhythms.

The following Romanza (*Lento espressivo*) begins and ends with material from a love duet in the form of a pas de deux for Edward and Gaveston from Act One of the ballet. Delicately scored, this movement is graced by a ravishing main theme, starting with the falling three-note motif from the previous movement, on oboe over a sea of divided solo strings alternating hushed chords. A second equally rich melody is shared between strings and horn over which upper woodwind gurgle ecstatic arabesques. After a brief central *Andante* passage taken from a brief, passionate interlude for Isabella and Mortimer from Act Two, the *Lento espressivo* returns with its second theme now lavished upon the tuba (unlikely casting for a romantic scene; the instrument darkens the texture, ominously). The movement ends with gently fading upper string chords, tinted by glockenspiel.

The grim portent of the previous movement's rumbling tuba is manifested by the Scherzo (*Maestoso e deciso*), which seizes upon the gently alternating divided string chords from the start of the Romanza, turning them into a sulphurous brass discourse. This music is taken almost note-for note from the end of Act One, Scene Two of the ballet, where the Barons express their defiance. A second theme, characterised by the unexpectedly sinister sound of fuzzy electric guitar, begins with an inversion of the falling motif that opened the Romanza. A central *Vivo* section, a nightmarish, clodhopping Trio in ever-changing time signatures, adds to the unease. Lower woodwind punch out the ungainly theme punctuated by woodblock and side drum thrashed by wire brushes. In a reprise of the Scherzo proper, the brass chords return, underpinned by piano ostinati, closing the movement in a mood of smouldering discontent.

The *Andante con moto* Finale concentrates on material from the ballet's closing sections: the dialogue between Edward and Lightborn, which gradually becomes more menacing as Lightborn is revealed as Edward's assassin; the final, vicious pas de deux for Isabella and Mortimer; and the funeral of Edward II, followed by the music for the young Edward III alone on the throne of England. The movement begins quietly with the strings. An ominously persistent motif, perhaps suggesting Fate knocking at the door, appears on oboes and is transferred to the timpani where its insistent repetitions assume terrifying proportions. With the arrival of an *Andante, calmo* passage, string *glissandi* triads slide with sinister urbanity, around which wispy ascending and descending woodwind themes weave a tracery of increasingly complex lines. A dramatic triple *forte* bridge passage leads to an *Adagio*, whose writhing woodwind and string figures, pointed up by snarling brass fanfares, express the lustful cruelty of the pas de deux. A huge climax is reached with strings and glockenspiel oscillating sevenths. With a terrifying inevitability the funeral music for Edward II turns out to be the same as that used for Edward I: thus, the symphony (and the drama) turns full circle, McCabe finding a fresh, psychologically apt, use of the traditional symphonic structural device of reintroducing earlier material at the end of a work. In the closing bars, menacing string octaves underpin hypnotic woodwind ostinati. Reinforced by brass, timpani and percussion, this material intensifies, reaching a final towering climax, peremptorily severed.

McCabe has taken some of his ballet score's most gripping passages and fashioned from them a symphony of considerable dramatic power. He brilliantly subverts traditional archaic devices such as chants, chorales, cantus firmus and canons to convey a claustrophobic sense of menace and foreboding. The use of motifs, important in ballet as in opera to aid characterisation, unifies movements formally, whilst sustaining a coher-

* The Wind Chimes should be very delicate, such as small pieces of metal or glass

ent symphonic development throughout the work. No prior knowledge is needed of the story of Edward II to appreciate the stark tragedy, as well as the love story, that unfolds. Where the First Symphony was predominantly elegiac in its contemplation of mortality, the Fifth rages against the dying of the light – the sense of loss in the final bars is palpable.

Symphony on a Pavane (Symphony No. 6) (2006) was commissioned by and dedicated to the London Philharmonic Orchestra. It is based on the Fifth Pavane and Galliard from William Byrd's *My Ladye Nevills Booke*, a piece which has long been part of McCabe's repertoire as a pianist. The Pavane is never heard in full as a direct quotation, but provides the melodic and harmonic basis upon which the new work is built. As the slow movement of Haydn's String Quartet Op. 76 No. 6 pervaded the slow movement of McCabe's Third Symphony, so Byrd's keyboard piece is an unheard presence throughout the Sixth.

Lasting just over twenty minutes, the symphony is in four movements played without a break, linked together by three sections, called 'Dissolve': a term borrowed from the film technique for dovetailing one scene with another. The bold and brilliant *Allegro vivace* first movement makes much play of a four-note motif sounded on the brass; the second movement is a poetic, moderately paced scherzando spotlighting the woodwind section; whilst the eloquent, Arcadian *Largo* third movement is graced by exotic bird calls from the piccolo and a moving solo for the rarely heard bass oboe supported by eerie string *glissandi*. The boisterous finale includes a reference to the opening of Byrd's Pavane, heard on the brass at the climax of the symphony. In the closing bars, the work fades away in a characteristically enigmatic ending: a man of his time, McCabe chooses to ask difficult questions rather than serve up easy solutions.

Scored for double woodwind, four horns and two each of trumpets and trombones, tuba and strings, the orchestra required is not especially large, but there is a key role for celesta and the percussion includes an important part for rototoms (sometimes requiring two players) rather than timpani, lending the symphony an exotic quality, reminiscent of Michael Tippett's last orchestral work, *The Rose Lake* (1995), and contributing to a distinctively modern reinterpretation of Byrd's original. The work shares with McCabe's *Edward II* Symphony (No. 5) a celebratory juxtaposition of the archaic and the contemporary.

Extrovert and good-humoured, the *Symphony on a Pavane* exhibits elements of an orchestral concerto, in that it keeps each instrumental section busy; this is especially apt as the London Philharmonic gave the world premiere of McCabe's Concerto for Orchestra, and the memorable opening

Opposite: Symphony on a Pavane, opening.

53

* Strings: Non-synchronized, fast full bows, getting slower with the diminuendo

brass fanfares of that 1982 piece are called to mind in the symphony's first movement. A triumphant return to the form McCabe reveres most, his Sixth Symphony finds the composer at his most ebullient and genial, the life-affirming product of a questing, fastidious and instinctive symphonist.

Though his symphonies represent the apogee of John McCabe's large-scale orchestral achievements, it is the concerto, more than any other form, that has consistently engaged his interest as a composer, and there are representative examples at every stage of his development. Though products of the same fertile imagination, the McCabe concertos are sharply defined; their individuality springs from the composer's unerring grasp of each solo instrument's inherent character and potential. Considering his outstanding abilities as a pianist, it is unsurprising that he has written most for keyboard and that, in many instances, he was the soloist at their first performances.

The Concertante for Harpsichord and Chamber Orchestra (1965) is scored for wind quintet, trumpet, string quartet and two percussionists, who play a variety of instruments, including xylophone, glockenspiel, vibraphone, temple blocks and tubular bells. The harpsichord part, although its proportions and difficulty justify solo status, is more closely integrated with the development sections' chamber-music style than is usual in traditional solo concertos, hence the title 'concertante'. The harpsichord's distinctive timbre is used effectively, enriching the outlandish array of percussion.

Cast in three movements sharing most of the thematic material, the Harpsichord Concertante includes serial and aleatory passages, always operating within a tonal idiom. The first movement, Elegia, is slow throughout and falls into two sections. The first (*Adagio*) develops by blocks of contrasting material eventually combined in a climax, whilst the second (*Lento*) is a more straightforward and linear Arioso. The central Capriccio is in rondo form: the *ritornello* is a short slow section, two quick sections forming the body of the movement. Unlike the preceding movements, the brief concluding Toccata is in quick tempo throughout (*Allegro moderato ma vigoroso*), apart from a fleeting reference back to the Elegia before the close.

Brittle and spiky, with the discernible influence of Stravinsky in neo-classical phase, the Harpsichord Concertante belongs to a distinctive and immediately attractive group of early works (including the *Elegy* Symphony and First Piano Concerto) where the composer experiments freely with sounds and textures.

Chief among its many fine qualities, Piano Concerto No. 1 (1966) makes great interplay of the solo instrument and percussion: McCabe is one of the

Opposite: Concerto for Orchestra, final bars.

55

few composers since Bartók to exploit fully the piano's percussive as well as lyrical properties. The percussion section is extensive; requiring three players, it comprises side drum, tenor drum, suspended cymbal, cymbals, xylophone, glockenspiel, vibraphone, gong, three bongos, Chinese block, crotales, tambourine, castanets and tubular bells. The four movements divide into pairs, each played without a break.

Typically, the slow first movement's opening bars supply the concerto with all its thematic material. A gong stroke initiates a mysterious ascending theme from the lower strings: rich, poised and built on arches of fourths and sevenths. A variant of this for harp ushers in the soloist's entry on an enigmatic trill, as the clarinet gives out another important theme in its highest register. This opening passage is recapitulated in condensed form, with interjections from the soloist in the form of an important sextuplet motif, and the rest of the movement gradually works out this initial material. Similar in mood to the first movement of McCabe's *Elegy* Symphony, the fabulously exotic sounds of this opening prelude-like *Largo* will appeal to anyone who responds to William Mathias's tone poems *Vistas* and *Laudi*, for example.

A very brief Scherzo, marked *Vivo*, is dominated by scurrying piano figurations (in semiquavers almost throughout) spun over a theme inimitably given to tuba with percussion interpolations. Rhythmically vital and harmonically adventurous, this tersely brilliant toccata-like movement contrasts satisfyingly with the decoratively languorous opening movement.

The third movement (*Lento*) returns to the mood and tempo of the concerto's beginning. It starts with a daringly lengthy passage for orchestra only, based on a variation of the clarinet tune from the first movement, and gradually intensifies until the arrival of a cadenza, ruminative rather than flamboyant, and integrated thematically with concerto's main material. A quicker, dance-like section precipitates another climax, followed by a slow epilogue.

The Finale (*Giocoso–Danzato–Giocoso*), rondo-like in form, bursts in with indomitable strides (a sunlit positive take on the first movement's brooding, dark opening theme) shared between timpani and piano. Like the Finale of Vaughan Williams' Eighth Symphony, it spotlights the percussion section, with side drum, tambourine, castanets, vibraphone and xylophone all making their mark. Full brass provides the main contrasting material, with an erratic but pronounced rhythmic shape. These two tunes alternate in quiet scoring, leading up to the main rondo theme's return. The opening material of the concerto reappears near the end, followed by a fleeting aleatory passage for violas and cellos: the use of this technique,

Opposite: Piano Concerto No. 1, opening, fourth movement.

57

both here and in the Harpsichord Concertante, is worth noting, for, along with the use of serialism in the Hartmann Variations and the Harpsichord Concertante, it signals that, even at this comparatively early stage, McCabe is open to employing any stylistic device provided it suits his purpose and is right for the music. After the piano's brief cadenza-like passage, the coda is concise and decisive. The closing pages are emphatic, not triumphalist: this is an essentially contemplative work, an evocative study in timbre.

The *Miniconcerto* (1966) is an occasional piece, written for a light-hearted Royal College of Organists concert and scored, intriguingly, for organ, percussion and 485 pennywhistles played by the audience. It has a relationship with Walton's *Spitfire Prelude*, with tongue firmly in cheek, but also with great affection. Inspiring the tantalising thought of a genuine, large-scale McCabe Organ Concerto, the *Miniconcerto* might be fun to hear, but more substantial works from this composer need championing as a priority.

Another light piece, the Concertino for Piano Duet and Orchestra (1968) was dedicated to Christopher Latham and the orchestra of Frensham Heights School. It is cast in a single twelve-minute movement, with a measured introduction and two slower episodes breaking up its predominantly quick pulse. The various sections are linked by close thematic cross-references, much of the material stemming from the initial slowly played scale figure. Although there are no formal cadenzas, a passage for the duet soloists and percussion, the latter improvising in short bursts, partially fulfils that function.

McCabe never writes down to his players. The adventurous piano writing, with scrunchy dissonances as well as beguiling melodies, makes the Concertino enjoyable and rewarding for the two young soloists, while typical McCabe rhythmic and harmonic felicities tickle ears of all ages.

Rafael Puyana was the intended soloist for the first performance of Metamorphosen for Harpsichord and Orchestra (1968), but he was unable to fulfil the engagement, so, in his one major appearance as harpsichord soloist, John McCabe deputised. A good example of the composer's predilection for several conjoined movements, the work's elaborate scoring predicts the rich ornamentation of works such as *Notturni ed Alba*. Also noteworthy is a rare overtly political gesture from the composer: a chorale-like theme expresses his sorrow at the crushing of the Prague Spring in 1968 (another contemporaneous example is the substantial, heartfelt slow movement of *Concertante Music* (1968), inspired by McCabe's reactions to Martin Luther King's assassination).

Scored for flute, oboe, clarinet, bassoon, horn and piano soloist, the Concerto for Piano and Wind Quintet (1969) is in five continuous movements, preceded by a *Maestoso*, introducing the main thematic and harmonic material. The following movements' element of display, and the solo prominence given to every instrument in turn, earn the title 'Concerto'. So, though the piano part is of virtuoso standard, it is also a concerto for all five players. Garrulous, quicksilver woodwind writing, including flutter-tongued flutes, was developed in subsequent orchestral works such as *Notturni ed Alba* and the Second Symphony, whilst the brilliant ensemble writing for a small group of instrumentalists is echoed in McCabe's next work featuring piano soloist.

Piano Concerto No. 2, subtitled 'Sinfonia Concertante' (1970), is scored for Classical-sized forces (no timpani or percussion) made up of (i) piano solo, (ii) a concertante group of nine instruments and (iii) small orchestra. The material is thus worked out on three levels: solo, concertino and orchestra. The concertino aspect of the scoring plays a highly important role throughout the work (hence its subtitle). All three musical entitles combine, develop and juxtapose the ideas in a satisfying variety of textures.

There are seven continuous sections: *Maestoso/Andantino lirico – Allegro vivo – Lento – Vivo – Lento – Con moto – Allegro*. In contrast to the atmospheric opening of its predecessor, it begins with a bold, unequivocal statement incorporating cadenza-like flourishes and superimposed orchestral chords. The temperature drops, and in the extended *Andante lirico* passage the soloist introduces a long melodic line that feeds material for the rest of the work. A brief *Allegro vivo* follows: McCabe's scherzo-like movements are always a special pleasure, and this Puckish gossamer-scored example is particularly delightful. The first of two substantial slow movements (*Lento*) starts with an intense piano line, leading to a more painterly variation of some of the work's main ideas: the consummate scoring chills with its penetrating *ponticello*, *tremolo* strings and flutter-tongued flutes. Another scherzo (*Vivo*) skips by, sporting an emphatic, pounding middle section. The second *Lento* movement opens with a measured section for concertino ensemble followed by a more opulent passage for full orchestra (so includes all three musical entities). The opening bars return, ushering in the *Allegro* Finale, a distinctive combination of rondo and variation forms with a toccata texture. It begins softly but, with the main theme's arrival in striding octaves on the piano, forges ahead to the orchestral return of the work's opening chords, bringing this compact and skilfully layered piece to a vividly turbulent conclusion.

McCabe habitually tackles forms afresh, ensuring each individual example is genuinely unique, and his Piano Concerto No. 3 *Dialogues*

(1976, revised 1977) differs from its predecessors in many ways. Its two substantial movements are dominated by the exacting solo part, but also engage in a number of dialogues. These take many forms: those between soloist and full orchestra prevail, sometimes involving members from an orchestral section (for example, at the start of Part Two, where the piano and two horns have an extended conversation; soon afterwards a similar exchange occurs between piano and three clarinets). In addition, there are contrasts between harmonies, unique to specific instruments. Occasionally there are struggles between two or three chords. Also, most importantly, there is a complex rhythmic dialogue in the music, such as the scherzo-like *Vivo deciso* section in Part One where the basic triplet rhythm is constantly interrupted by quick duplets in the piano part. On another level, the rhythmic dialogue extends to matters of pace and pulse, so although much of the work is written in a leisurely tempo, not all of it sounds as slow as it really is (such as in the closing *Allegro moderato*, where the scurrying string *fugatos* generate momentum but woodwind and brass lines reveal the underlying pulse to be much steadier).

Piano Concerto No. 3 stands Janus-like in John McCabe's output: the plentiful percussion, used with great imagination and flair (especially in Part Two), looks back to earlier orchestral pieces exploring that orchestral section, whilst the practice of suggesting different tempos simultaneously anticipates the Fourth Symphony, and brief aleatory passages presage more substantial engagements with the technique in the Third Symphony and Concerto for Orchestra. Unlike the composer's two previous piano concertos, this is a grand, barnstorming work, the soloist requiring enormous stamina and seemingly playing without a break. It was written with the 'virtuoso' technique of dedicatee Ilan Rogoff, the Israeli pianist, in mind, and its heroic stature extends to its duration – at just under forty minutes long, it is nearly twice the length of Piano Concerto No. 2.

John McCabe's expertise as a pianist of international stature informs every bar of his keyboard concertos. It is a measure of his significant achievement as a composer that his three large-scale piano concertos are distinguished by brilliant orchestration as much as the fine quality of the soloist's material.

McCabe's wind concertos enhance his output with their subtlety, acute awareness of instrumental colour and sense of fantasy. His first, the Concerto for Oboe d'Amore and Chamber Orchestra (1972) is in one continuous movement in three main sections: a slow introduction, a vigorous central scherzo and a measured conclusion, ending with oboe d'amore alone. Mildly aleatoric passages for orchestral players and numerous cadenza-like episodes for soloist are integrated into the overall formal structure. Chords derived from Richard Strauss's *Metamorphosen* underlie the whole concerto, transformed throughout and never in their original form, creating the reservoir for the work's themes and harmonies. A fairly large chamber orchestra is required, with strings often divided extensively, most notably in the concluding *Lento* section where the vertiginous writing, with liberal use of harmonics, recalls Elisabeth Lutyens' stratospheric violins in her memorable score for the film *The Earth Dies Screaming* (1964). An inventive, poetical showcase for a distinctive-sounding instrument rarely afforded such prominence, the concerto strongly merits revival.

Unusually for a McCabe orchestral work, the Clarinet Concerto (1977) dispenses with most of the percussion, though this is countered by imaginative use of timpani throughout (in the very opening pages, the timpanist has an extended duet with the clarinet). The first movement introduces themes associated with a particular instrument or group. The most important idea appears at the outset on horns and the ensuing clarinet subject is also significant. After various themes are contrasted and juxtaposed, sometimes appearing on different instruments, the movement reaches a climax, in the wake of which the *Andante* second movement begins. For this passionate, sorrowing threnody, the orchestra is reduced to strings with timpani and harp, anticipating the Oboe Concerto's scoring. The third movement reprises material from the opening *Moderato* in condensed form whilst the Finale, marked *Vivo*, alternates soloist and tutti in the manner of a more traditional concerto, deriving all its material from the first movement (again distributed amongst different instruments). The *Andante*'s lament is recalled wistfully and, after a final reference to the horns' opening motif, the music dies away to nothing.

Closely knit and tautly argued, the Clarinet Concerto adopts some ideas and concerns of the more expansive Third Piano Concerto with its conversations between soloist and orchestral sections. It is as much a test of musicianship as technique.

As the title suggests, *Rainforest II* (1987) is the second of a series of pieces inspired by the atmosphere and landscape of rainforests. As in its predecessor, the rainforest in question is Australian. In four continuous parts in a predominantly slow tempo, the piece is launched and rounded off by a trumpet solo; when the strings enter, they construct a downward figuration of the work's basic chord (a cluster built up of superimposed thirds). This section's relative freedom gives way to a more strictly notated slow passage heralded by a contemplative, ornamental trumpet tune – the work's basic theme. After the faster section's climax, the slower pulse returns, alternating phrases from soloist and full string statements, leading to the trumpet's final solo fading into oblivion. The trumpet part works successfully with the string sound, taking full account of the music's harmonic denseness. With no programmatic or pictorial intent, McCabe has composed one of the least consciously brilliant and virtuosic trumpet concertos in the repertoire, characteristically choosing instead to probe the soloist's musicality.

The longstanding idea lurking behind the Double Concerto for Oboe and Clarinet (1988) is a phrase from the Prelude to Act One of Erik Satie's incidental music to the play *Le Fils des étoiles* (*The Son of the Stars*), a piece in McCabe's repertoire as a pianist. The concerto is both a free fantasy on the Satie quote (a simple phrase consisting of four notes followed by two chords) and a genuine double concerto (the soloists nearly always play together, exchanging ideas rather than alternating as happens in most examples in the form). As in the Oboe d'Amore Concerto, there are frequent cadenza-like sections throughout the work and even these are mostly double-cadenzas. The piece juxtaposes forward momentum and stasis, looking forward to similar contrasts in the Fourth Symphony.

Like the Piano Concerto No. 2, the Double Concerto divides into seven continuous sections (*Largo – Vivo – Andante – Allegro – Lento – Allegro Deciso – Lento*). The overall form is that of a large slow movement punctuated by quicker interludes. An extended opening *Largo* alternates between slightly minimalist orchestral build-ups and solo cadenza passages, a technique common to all the slow movements. The *Vivo* and *Allegro* sections highlight the fantastic elements of the work, whilst the *Allegro deciso*, the most substantial interlude, has a recurring passage like a variant of Morse code. The concerto closes with a slow passage where the soloists recall a vital phrase from the earlier *Vivo* and are gradually overwhelmed by the orchestra's repeated pulsating chords. These diminish and the work tapers into silence, the soloists required to hold their playing positions a moment after the piece has finished. Prefaced by a line from W.E. Healey ('Night with her train of stars'), the score mixes fantasy, nocturne, minimalism and traditional concerto elements with bewitching charm.

Confounding expectations, John McCabe's Flute Concerto (1990) is one of his biggest and most volatile works. Rather than exploiting the lyrical nature of the solo instrument, this concerto demands brilliance of tone and extreme virtuosity from both soloist and orchestra.

In one continuous seething movement, it falls into four main groups of sections including a *Vivo* episode combining no fewer than three scherzos! The sea, whether calm or in full flood, inspired the concerto, accounting for its sparkling and occasionally tempestuous nature. Spray from waves

Opposite: Horn Concerto (Rainforest IV), extract.

62

19
Fl. 1
Fl. 2
Ob. 1
Ob. 2
B♭ Cl.
Bass Cl.
Bsn. 1
Bsn. 2
Susp.Cymb.
l.v.
Mar.
dim.
Hp.
Hn. Solo
* Quasi vivace
poco liberamente
1. Solo
Vln. I
Vln. II
Vla.
Vc.
Db.
22
To Piccolo
T.-t.
hard stick
half
tutti
cresc.

* As before

breaking on the shore suggested the work's opening bars: the chiming glockenspiel is important, not just for its distinctive sound, but because it carries the work's harmonic basis and an essential melodic component. A large orchestra is treated with chamber-like sensibility, strings frequently subdivided and individual instrumental lines featured in all orchestral sections. The three orchestral flutes are spread out across the platform, playing off the soloist, echoing and engaging in dialogues, a dramatic effect beloved of Thea Musgrave. The concerto's ending is particularly affecting: after a towering tutti climax has subsided, the solo flute keeps repeating a simple, folk-like melody heard earlier in the piece, as if distractedly attempting to recapture vanished memories.

The Oboe Concerto (1994), in one movement divided into four main sections, is scored for timpani, harp and strings, a combination that complements the solo writing's frequently song-like nature. Behind the work is an image of a bird in flight, sometimes in slow motion, swooping down, circling or floating in the sky, and this vision informs much of the concerto's character with its chattering main motif, based on a repeated note. This motif, varied constantly throughout the piece, brings it to a close.

Unlike the Flute Concerto, this work deliberately brings out the solo instrument's lyrical character. Beautifully crafted, it is the most relaxed and immediately appealing of the McCabe woodwind concertos and, at around fourteen minutes, one of the most compact and cogently argued. Far from hampering his creativity, the reduced forces stimulate the composer's imagination, especially in his inventive treatment of the strings.

Completed in 2006, the Horn Concerto (*Rainforest IV*) was inspired by numerous concerts in which John McCabe took part performing with the great horn player Ifor James. Two other major influences on the piece are sound of jazz horn in the 1950s and 1960s (especially in West Coast jazz) and the contemplation of rainforests.

The concerto takes the form of a slow introduction and epilogue framing three contrasting main sections, all played without a break. The beginning and ending of the piece share the same material, distinguished by eloquent solo writing, recalling Britten's Serenade for Tenor, Horn and Strings of 1943, especially in the *Adagio* introduction, where the horn is hand-stopped. This substantial solo provides the basis of the material for the ensuing main sections. The first quick section, a lively and sophisticated Scherzo and Trio, is very clearly influenced by jazz: the strings are silent, save for violas in the Trio section. A lyrical, 'English'-sounding slow section follows with restrained brass. Restless shifts of tempo in a second quick movement increase the tension, building up to a strenuous, emphatic tutti made up of three chords (which underpin the whole work), leading to the epilogue.

Airy and luminous, the score requires a slightly reduced symphony orchestra (two each of horns, trumpets and trombones) with few percussion instruments, though there are important roles for timpani and marimba, whose hypnotic, fateful ostinato is a compelling invention. The whole orchestra is seldom heard together: the elusive, will-o'-the wisp character of much of the piece derives from an almost chamber music transparency.

The dancing quality of the deft and engaging Horn Concerto (*Rainforest IV*) gives it the feel of a divertimento. McCabe exults in the bright, clear tones of the solo instrument and has taken great pains in his orchestration to ensure that it can be heard, not least in his markedly restrained use of orchestral brass. The concerto's lightness of touch does not in any way denote superficiality: it is in many ways an intensely personal work, not least in its evocative juxtaposition of specific urban and natural soundscapes very close to the composer's heart.

McCabe's first concerto for a stringed instrument is also the first orchestral work he still acknowledges. Violin Concerto No. 1, Op. 2 (1959) is a nostalgic piece affirming a love of British music, especially Vaughan Williams, who had died the previous year. Its subtitle, 'Sinfonia Concertante', the first of several such indications in McCabe's output, signals that, although the solo part has virtuosic elements, the orchestra is equally important to the musical development. Sketched during a Lake District holiday, the concerto and its general outline were inspired by T.S. Eliot's poem *The Hollow Men*, an early example of a work of art providing the catalyst for a McCabe project. A fascinating document of the creative ideas of the twenty-year-old composer, it anticipates a persistent interest in the passacaglia and, especially, the variation form: the short Capriccio is the only movement untouched by it. Another foretaste of things to come is the large, but judiciously applied, percussion section. Despite the atypically orthodox structure (the four movements include a scherzo, slow movement and rondo finale) and some uncharacteristically overloaded tutti climaxes, the First Violin Concerto's melodic fecundity and charming, Baxian nostalgia secures its place in the McCabe catalogue.

In contrast, the *Concerto funebre* for Viola and Chamber Orchestra (1962) is a compact, darkly brooding thirteen-minute work. Completed on 16 April 1962, it was written for a violist friend of the composer who never played it; the piece had to wait some years before its première. Hearing Hartmann's *Concerto funèbre* for violin and strings in Liverpool at one of

John Pritchard's *Musica Viva* concerts suggested the title to McCabe and possibly influenced the work's emotional tone. Its restrained character extends to the scoring: two oboes, two horns and strings. The six succinct and direct movements (Prefazione – Elegia I – Notturne – Elegia II – Cadenza – Elegia III) have a mournful quality well suited to the dark sonorities of the solo instrument, which dominates the work.

The Chamber Concerto for Viola, Cello and Orchestra (1965) has never been performed and remains something of an experiment, being scored without violins. It was written for two friends of McCabe, fellow-students at the Royal Manchester College of Music who had moved to London to play in different orchestras, and they never managed to secure a performance. The influence of big-band jazz (still one of McCabe's pleasures) can be detected here and there, especially Gil Evans. At an estimated duration of 35 minutes, it is one of the composer's most substantial concertos, making its lack of performances and recordings all the more frustrating – this is a prime candidate for rehabilitation.

Violin Concerto No. 2 (1980) was written as a mark of John McCabe's admiration of the musicianship of Erich Gruenberg, with whom he has appeared in violin and piano duos. As in McCabe's previous violin concerto, the overriding character is one of lyricism, though expressed here with less opulent romanticism.

In the *Moderato* first movement, the swooping main theme (with soloist supported by a tintinnabulation of percussion) contrasts with more astringent material; this dichotomy of mood gives the movement its main impetus. The second movement is entitled 'Dances', and these take many forms: balletic, as in the violin and oboe d'amore duet in the first slow section; and folk in the later, faster sections, including Spanish, Norwegian and Polish examples, the latter being a whirling 'Oberek' demanding virtuosity from both soloist and orchestra. The *spiccato*-driven vigour of the *Con moto, poco pesante* third movement powers towards the solo cadenza, which recalls previous material and calms the music for its *Lento* finale. Cast in the form of a passacaglia on a series of four opening chords, this concluding movement is concerned with the contrast between the melodic solo part and the harmonic nature of the orchestral writing. The airborne opening theme of the concerto returns to close the work, the last of many cross-references between the movements. As in the Third Symphony, there is a strong key-centre underlying the music, the home key being F sharp.

Though the concerto lasts around forty minutes, the listener is never aware of its length, nor does it feel like a 'warhorse', but rather an exquisite exploration of tonal colours, including some beautiful melodies. There are several connections with the First Violin Concerto (both are in four movements, feature passacaglias and stress the lyrical side of the solo instrument) but this work breathes the same confident air as the more contemporaneous Third Piano Concerto and Clarinet Concerto, exploiting the soloist's technical ability, tempered by strong melodic impulses.

The subtitle of *Les Martinets noirs* (2003), 'Concerto for 2 Violins and String Orchestra', defines it very precisely: as in the Double Concerto for Oboe and Clarinet, the two solo violins form a duo partnership, never playing separately and always sharing their material and virtuosity. Written for the Amsterdam Sinfonietta (to whom it is dedicated), the string orchestra's role is also notably technically demanding. There are three movements (*Allegro scorrevole – Adagio – Allegro scorrevole*) played continuously, the third being at exactly the same quick tempo as the first. The central *Adagio*, the most extensive of the three movements, exploits the full range of string sonorities.

Like his Oboe Concerto, the inspiration came from the composer's love of birds: 'Martinets noirs' is the French name for swifts, and one of the composer's annual summer treats is to sit in the garden and watch them wheeling about in the stratosphere and then swooping down around the trees and chimney pots before returning to the heights. Fiendishly virtuosic and ingeniously scored, *Les Martinets noirs* successfully captures the swifts' swooping grace, making one hungry for more McCabe string concertos: they bring out his lyrical and Romantic side, satisfyingly marrying formal command with brilliance of utterance. The forthcoming concerto for cello, his favourite string instrument, is keenly anticipated.

Before considering the composer's two officially designated concertos for orchestra, three other significant, organically conceived works merit attention. Characteristically, these substantial pieces refuse to be categorised easily – more symphonic than an average tone poem, they could be said to present a fusion of symphony and concerto for orchestra. Whatever their structure, the most important point is that they are quintessential McCabe.

The Shadow of Light (1978) was commissioned by the Royal Philharmonic Orchestra to celebrate the bicentenary of the death of William Boyce. McCabe uses material from works by Boyce (symphonies or overtures, plus one trio-sonata movement), set in the context of a large-scale nocturne, featuring a series of dreams of characteristic events or dances of Boyce's time, prefaced, linked and concluded by 'dream' music, connecting psychologically with the orchestral ritornello from Britten's Nocturne of 1958. McCabe's dream music charts one of his most haunting inner landscapes as drowsy string glissandi encircle remote horn calls and muted trumpet figures, followed by tousled descending woodwind phrases pluming like ectoplasm in the night air. All-pervasive, the dream music is also heard in various forms underpinning several set pieces.

In the Pastorale, which contrasts woodwind against the 'dream' back-cloth, is there just a hint of a wistful phrase from Rawsthorne's *Street Corner* Overture in the flutes' initial statements? The score culminates in a brilliant Fugue, using two of Boyce's fugue subjects and accruing brief reminiscences of earlier parts of the work, and a Quodlibet, which recalls most of the earlier sections. A traditional, affirmative conclusion seems unlikely in the context of such as veiled and multi-layered work and, inevitably, the dream music gradually resumes control as the visions of the past recede.

Only an instinctive eclectic such as McCabe could absorb so much of another composer's works into his own and still produce a strongly characteristic piece, whilst miraculously preserving the essence of Boyce's original music, which acts as a benign 'presence' throughout the piece. In this respect, *The Shadow of Light* is directly related to McCabe's Third and Sixth Symphonies, also inhabited by the spirits of other composers (Haydn and Byrd, respectively). Significantly, McCabe frequently plays both composers in his concert programmes: the traditional role of performer and interpreter has been extended in the creative process to that of re-interpreter, McCabe acknowledging his influences by building them into the very fabric of his compositions.

Although commissioned as a heartfelt tribute by one composer to another, *Shadow of Light* also shows signs of darker qualities. It was written at a time when McCabe appears to have been deeply concerned with opening up psychological inner vistas, a preoccupation shared with the contemporaneous Third Piano Concerto (1977) and Third Symphony (1978). Consequently *Shadow of Light* is not entirely the celebration it purports to be; its overall effect is unsettling and occasionally vaguely sinister and perhaps this can best be explained by the derivation of the title from Swinburne's *Atalanta in Calydon*: 'Night, the shadow of light/And Life, the shadow of death.'

Rainforest I (1984) was commissioned by the Chamber Music Society of Lincoln Center, New York. It is one of many fine examples of McCabe works inspired by landscape. The title refers specifically the subtropical rainforest of South Queensland, in Australia and, by implication, to the stark contrast between this kind of topography and the Scottish-glen-like scenery in the heights of the Great Dividing Range or the very different bush landscape to the west.

Instrumental forces are divided into three small groups: a string quartet, a piano trio and an ensemble of flute, clarinet and glockenspiel, which sometimes work together as one large group but more often divide into separate ensembles with their own characteristic thematic material. The piece is played without a break, but falls into three main sections, the first and third being slow.

The preludial *Andante* begins in the heights with ticking glockenspiel joined by solo violin harmonics and piano. During its descent, it is joined by flute and clarinet, before the entry of the string quartet. Gradually, the main chord of the whole piece is assembled and textures thicken as solo lines intertwine and various instruments combine and connect with each other.

A soaring solo flute introduces the central Scherzo, a teeming *Allegro* soundscape alive with buzzing insects in the strings over a hopping piano bass line. Clarinets interject an important theme developed in the first Trio, which alternates between two tempi (*Moderato* and *Andante*). The *Moderato*'s material is hushed and fluid in character, contrasting with the archaic *Andante* theme, its Scotch-snap rhythms a possible allusion to the Great Dividing Range landscape. The second Trio is based on a perpetually revolving series of dance-like rhythmic figures in the piano trio group. Just before the return of the *Allegro*, the solo piano's recurring phrases remind the listener of the 'tape-loop' figure from the Concerto for Orchestra (1982). A solo for glockenspiel, delivered at full tilt and again based on a recurring pattern, ushers in the concluding *Lento*.

At the close, the process of steadily mustering the work's main chord during the first few minutes is mirrored, with permutations, by rising scale figures on the strings. The piece ends, as it began, with single repeated glockenspiel notes.

In its interplay with different-sized groups of instruments, *Rainforest I* shares some of the concerns of the Second Piano Concerto 'Sinfonia Concertante' of 1972, whilst its gestures in the direction of minimalism would be developed in the Double Concerto for oboe and clarinet of 1987. A kaleidoscopically textured work, *Rainforest I* takes full advantage of the variety of forces at its command, switching between intimate chamber music delicacy to sonorous tuttis and sometimes acting as a kind of concerto with constantly changing soloists. Once again, though it has a strong pictorial element, the work's structural and developmental concerns generate the most interest as McCabe assiduously takes every opportunity to express himself anew through his unusually flexible ensemble.

Fire at Durilgai (1988) was inspired by Patrick White's book *The Tree of Man*, which includes a spectacular description of a bush fire. Two additional elements lie behind this impulse – McCabe's fascination with the Australian landscape and a childhood accident when the composer was badly burnt in a fire – but there is no sense of trauma in this essentially jubilant, bravura piece. The ebb and flow of fire, its gradual build-up of structure within a context of continual enlargement and the unpredictable twists and turns it takes, despite a clearly perceptible and logical pattern, are reflected in the work's formal workings.

McCabe has described the piece as falling in the tradition of the symphonic poem (Sibelius's *Pohjola's Daughter* was an especial influence) but he makes no attempt to write music evoking the sounds of a fire. Instead, *Fire at Durilgai* is an expression of the composer's fascination with the inexorable development that fire represents and, to a lesser extent, its changes in direction.

The piece beings with an intensely atmospheric slow section, inspired by the vast Australian night sky – massive, illimitable string chords outline both the harmonic material of the work and the work's basic, scalic melodic outline, whilst crotales chime out a simple repeated figure perhaps suggesting twinkling stars in the Australian night sky, but their insistent reiterations, crackling with portent, imply a psychological aspect. Sinuous flute arabesques evoke birdcalls. In a deft whetting of the listener's appetite, several interruptions of music in a faster tempo provide foretastes of the work's large-scale central scherzo.

This scorching scherzo transfigures the introductory section's material, elaborating and recasting it with protean energy. A larger harmonic process underpins the tumultuous surface action, and this simultaneous exploration of contrasting tempi suggests links with Sibelius as well as pointing forward to McCabe's own Fourth Symphony *Of Time and the River*. After the scherzo has pursued its wayward and yet strangely inexorable course and erupted into a colossal climax, a sustained harmonic on double bass (a typically unexpected piece of instrumentation) instigates a measured final section, formally balancing the work's slow introduction, in which a gigantic crescendo gradually builds up into a massive final chord of almost tangible dimensions. Chiming tubular bells make a telling counterpoint to the opening section's twinkling crotales before this monumental last chord is suddenly and sharply cut off, as if the music has ultimately imploded.

Clearly and cleanly scored, *Fire at Durilgai* is one of John McCabe's most purely exciting and dramatic works – a born composer of ballets is much in evidence as the inexhaustible, driving rhythms of the miraculous central scherzo point forward to the scores of *Edward II* (1995) and *Arthur*, parts one and two (1999, 2000). Obsessive refashioning of fragmentary motifs into a state of perpetual variation showcases the archetypal McCabe process of thematic transformation, heightened and perfected. Its form – a quick movement encased within two slow movements – is shared with the composer's *Elegy* Symphony and the *Sinfonia Elegiaca* and Symphony No. 10 of Andrjez Panufnik, and there is a strong case for *Fire at Durilgai* also to be regarded as a one-movement symphony: once again the power of McCabe's symphonic logic and the conviction of his abstract structures dominate the descriptive content even in one of his most overtly programmatic works. Above all, *Fire at Durilgai* exemplifies how the composer seems able to reinvent himself in his large-scale orchestral works, finding new means of expression and ensuring the modern orchestra's sonic possibilities are expanded and enlarged with each new score.

Twenty years separate John McCabe's two orchestral concertos. The brief and uncomplicated Concerto for Chamber Orchestra (1962) derives all its thematic material from the declamatory tutti opening statement, or its quieter answering phrase. The five different sections – Introduzione (*Allegro Moderato*); Capriccio (*Allegro*); Scherzo (*Giocoso*); Notturno (*Andante – Lento*); Toccata – develop these ideas in contrasted moods and at diverse tempi, behaving like separate movements, although the work is continuous. The title 'Concerto' emphasises the use of solo instruments, a major impulse behind the piece.

The initial call to attention, similar in mood and manner to that of Haydn's Symphony No. 95, is arresting enough, but its wide intervals to some extent defy effective development, though the insouciant Scherzo makes the most conspicuously successful attempt. Although the orchestra is small (one flute, two oboes, two bassoons, two horns and strings), prophetically, the percussion section, which only really comes into its own in the Finale, is comparatively ample (cymbals, suspended cymbal, side drum, tenor drum, temple blocks and triangle).

John McCabe's Concerto for Orchestra (1982) takes inspiration from single-movement examples by Hindemith (1925) and Kodály (1939), rather than Bartók's more celebrated 1943 work. The choice of title highlights the free treatment of form and the special role orchestration plays in its development. As in other McCabe pieces, it moves on two planes of tempi, having a slow-moving theme surrounded by quicker, more complex decoration, all derived from a common origin – a passacaglia. The score's notable features include the prominence of brass throughout and concentration on certain sections or groups of instruments at a time: the whole orchestra only plays in the Finale.

The five-movement format derives from Schumann's *Faschingsschwank aus Wien* for piano, a McCabe favourite, though in Schumann's case the movements are separate and not continuous. To emphasise the connection, the middle sections of the Concerto for Orchestra share the same titles as in the Schumann, though the order is changed. The arch-shaped structure reaches its apex in the central *Romanze*, and everything afterwards is a reflection of preceding movements' ideas. The work is continuous, transitions between movements stealthily effected. Especially memorable is a 'tape loop' repeating piano figure, which ushers in the Scherzino and rounds off the piece more memorably than any blatant cadence.

No brash showpiece, McCabe's Concerto for Orchestra masterfully combines his symphonies' impressive formal logic and structural mastery with his concertos' virtuosity and imaginative orchestration. Perhaps its exceptionally rich scoring benefited from the experience of creating such previous celebrations of colour as *The Chagall Windows*, *The Shadow of Light* and the profoundly resonant Third Symphony. The Concerto's myriad rewards ensure orchestras worldwide will continue to take on its prodigious challenges.

John McCabe's orchestral music, a significant proportion of his oeuvre, embodies the very essence of his creative talents. His acknowledged 'first love' as a composer,[6] it provides a perfect introduction to his distinctive soundworld. In particular, symphonies and concertos span his career, authentically charting his artistic progress. Directly communicative, they invariably revitalise and personalise the genres, never content merely to replicate earlier models. In most cases, seeds of the works' main material are contained within the introductory bars, lending them an acute sense of embarking upon an epic voyage. It is a measure of McCabe's achievement that the ensuing journey never disappoints the listener.

6 McCabe, 'The Film Behind the Symphony', p. 38.

4

The wind chamber music

Verity Butler

John McCabe's exceptional gifts have brought him wide recognition in many diverse areas of musical life. In addition to being a greatly admired and widely played composer, he has an equally active career as a solo pianist and is also acclaimed as a critic and writer. His prolific compositional output covers every genre and displays the versatility of his wide-ranging musicianship; even within the narrower confines of his wind and brass chamber music he encompasses a diverse range of works, from pieces for a single solo instrument lasting only a minute to full-scale 30-minute chamber works for larger ensemble. His writing is always sensitive to the needs of performance, and shows an innate understanding of the nature and quality of each individual instrument, and the blending of the instruments within the group.

Writing, unashamedly, from a clarinettist's perspective, it seems hardly surprising that an instrument embodying as many diverse qualities as the clarinet should prove to be an appealing stimulus to such an imaginative and versatile composer as John McCabe. Many of his chamber works feature the clarinet, and it is the primary participant in his first four pieces featuring a wind instrument.

During the early 1960s he wrote a number of folksong arrangements, several using clarinet as well as voice and piano, and a group of these was first performed in 1963 on a tour of Scotland that McCabe gave with Catriona Gordon and Barry Gregson. There were originally four songs but they were so successful in the first concert that the next morning McCabe wrote 'Hush-a-ba, Birdie' to use as an encore that evening! When they later came to be published as Three Folksongs for Soprano, Clarinet and Piano, there were several arrangements left over, two of which were rewritten later to produce a set of Five Folksongs with Horn instead of clarinet. McCabe enjoys utilising folksongs, describing it as 'a bit of a sport' and 'almost like writing pastiche'. He has said, 'I do treat the task really as a kind of art song; in other words, without in any way trying to disturb the natural proportions of the tune, I try to echo in my setting the emotional feeling behind the words, just as, perhaps in a more complex way, one does when setting poems'. He has certainly achieved his aim in the Three Folksongs. The American song, 'Johnny has Gone for a Soldier', is quite beautiful, with a few slight rhythmic dislocations. 'Hush-a-ba, Birdie' is the simplest setting, with some canonic treatment of the tune between voice and clarinet. The lively 'John Peel' always brings a smile to the faces of an audience, in particular due to the clarinet and piano making reference between verses to several traditional nautical songs.

Three Pieces for Clarinet and Piano, extract.

2 IMPROVISATION
Bossa Nova

The Three Pieces for Clarinet and Piano, first performed by Keith Puddy and Vivian Troon at the 1964 Cheltenham Festival, undoubtedly form his best-known work for the instrument to date, now firmly established as a major work in the clarinet repertoire. The pieces incorporate many different moods: the first consists of a recitative-like introduction followed by a lyrical *Adagio* movement, the second, *Improvisation (Bossa Nova)*, has a strong Latin-American feel, and the last combines a lyrical, rhapsodic section and a three-part *fugato*, culminating in a brilliant coda. There was a specific period early in his career when McCabe made much use of serial techniques. This work is actually a twelve-note piece, the three pieces being bound together by a twelve-note row common to all the movements, but the overall flavour of the music is actually rather tonal. In his serial works at this time McCabe often used his note row to generate certain elements that were fairly strict, then combined them with others that were not so strict. For example, he would devise a chordal accompaniment, based on the row, to a melodic line simply designed to fit with these chords. He also frequently used it to create patterns, selecting a group of notes from the row and repeating them in fast pattern work. Following the examples set by Stravinsky and other former composers, McCabe does not necessarily use the whole of the row at any one time. For example, the opening phrase of the Three Pieces outlines a row containing only nine notes, and it is not until the end of the third phrase that the missing three notes have all been added. He has also been open to changing a few notes 'when they sounded better' and frequently repeats groups of notes.

In the first two movements the titles indicate something of the mood of the music, with the sub-titles showing the technical background. The first, *Nocturne: Aria*, is a night-piece using an aria-like texture, contrasting melodic phrases on the clarinet with irregular chordal patterns in the piano, leading to a climax and a final, dissolving melisma for the clarinet. The second, *Improvisation: Bossa Nova*, is improvisatory in a jazz-like sense and uses the rhythm of the Brazilian dance-form bossa nova, with its typical 3, 3, 2 pattern, which was especially popular during the early 1960s. Its composition was influenced by the composer hearing a record of Stan Getz playing the bossa nova standard *Desafinado*. It includes some fairly complex rhythmic interplay between the instruments – it is mostly in 5/4 metre and is marked *con moto*. The final *Fantasy* is more extensive and has several sections, alternating between writing for the two instruments in a co-operative fashion and separating them so that each has its own material, joining once more as equal partners in the final section. It contains some fine examples of rhythmic contrapuntal writing and creates sheer excitement, calling for bravura technique from both players to generate propulsive energy and concluding with a flourish.

Several of McCabe's earlier large-scale works also employ twelve-note technique, including *Notturni ed Alba* and *The Chagall Windows*. However, in 1976, whilst working on the Stabat Mater, McCabe consciously abandoned twelve-note serial writing as he felt that he should not be relying on formulae to produce ideas and that he should concentrate on his ability to 'walk freely without the aid of a crutch'. However, he acknowledges that it taught him a method of working, a mental approach to the material, that he still uses. Certainly elements of the technique have remained with him. The use of small melodic cells as sources for development is one of the most obvious trademarks of his writing. This has led to several consistent features which are central to his musical language, such as the use of ostinato, canon, imitative counterpoint, transposition, repetition and inversion. These can all be seen as elements of variation technique; McCabe enjoys both writing and playing variations.

Considering the quality of his writing for the instrument it is perhaps surprising that McCabe has no specialised knowledge of the clarinet. He recalls that 'we used to have clarinets at home. My father played it a little bit when I was a child', but doesn't acknowledge this to have made any lasting impression, placing greater emphasis on the fact that he just happens to know a lot of clarinettists! His clear understanding of the character and capabilities of the clarinet are immediately evident from his writing for the instrument, and are nowhere more clearly demonstrated than in his Bagatelles for Two Clarinets, written in 1965. The eight movements are really in the nature of studies, exploiting different modes of attack and styles of playing, and also different musical characters. Both instrumental parts in this work are equally demanding, giving each player the opportunity to display their command of the instrument. The writing is ideally suited to the clarinet, indulging many of its natural abilities, and the Bagatelles clearly demonstrate both the clarinet's agility and its expressiveness, amalgamating many different styles. The first movement makes use of aggressive accents and a *fortissimo* dynamic, while the second is an *Andante* lament calling for careful control of the softer dynamics. The third movement demonstrates the instrument's capability to play notes fast and fluently, in a 15/8 *Allegro giocoso*. The quaver movement is almost incessant, beginning as a quiet murmur then reaching three waves of crescendo and diminuendo, the second ranging from *pp* to *ff*. The wittily titled *Fugatississimo* is another example of exemplary rhythmic contrapuntal writing reverting to the harsher accents and staccato of the first movement,

followed by an extremely atmospheric and lyrical *Adagio* fourth movement, which exploits the clarinet's sustained legato. The ensuing bossa nova in 6/8 time immediately transforms the character, written in a totally new vein with its jazzy syncopated style, incorporating many large leaps in the accompanying figuration. The seventh movement is aptly entitled *Crescendo*, as it does just that – beginning *pp* and finishing *ff*. Again the clarinet's facility is exposed in a continual flurry of semiquavers divided between the parts. The final movement is a *Fantasy* recalling themes from previous movements. It briefly reintroduces many of the technical aspects heard before: extremes of dynamics, beautifully lyrical legato, aggressive accents and light staccato.

Michael Kennedy once described John McCabe as 'a recognisably individual talent controlled by a fertile imagination'.[1] However, there can be no doubt that his music is eclectic. It draws on many contemporary styles and techniques – clear traces have been left by jazz big bands, sixties' rock drumming and serial thinking as well as by several prominent composers. He has even described himself as being parasitic, but he claims that all composers are eclectic to some extent, drawing inspiration from a variety of sources:

1 Sleeve notes to HMV recording of *Notturni ed Alba*, ASD 2904 (see Discography).

> If you're influenced by anything you're parasitic and you're bound to be influenced. I'm influenced by jazz for instance and by particular sounds in other works which I transform when I use them. I'm sure that people can't actually tell where I got some of my ideas from because they have been completely transformed, by being used in a totally different medium.

An early influence in the formation of his idiom was Alan Rawsthorne, for whom he has great admiration. It has also been said that his early basic materials derived from such composers as Stravinsky and Hindemith, that Hartmann is among the composers who have influenced him most and that it is not difficult to deduce his admiration for Bartók, Vaughan Williams and Britten. It may be true that he draws on elements of these composers' styles, but he always uses them with a relevance to the contemporary context in which he is writing. He stands apart from any recognisably English tradition and from the newest international trends.

McCabe describes himself as a mainstream composer, an integrator rather than an exclusivist, and as a progressive. He believes that any composer's style must be instinctive: 'The kind of person you are affects your interest in other kinds of music … and affects the composers you actually

78

take from in the sense of getting inspiration from or being influenced by …
But I do believe that in the long run the greatest progress is made by the
composers who integrate the discoveries of others.'

Robert Maycock, writing for the *Musical Times* in 1989, describes
McCabe's development of style as being gradual rather than in leaps and
bounds, and showing a shifting balance of preoccupations. McCabe himself recognises this thread of development. He believes that his music has
become more complex, although the actual materials that he is using are
sometimes simpler but integrated into a more complex structure of layers.
The wind chamber works can also be seen to mirror this development,
beginning with the Three Folksongs, set simply and tastefully in pleasant
modal style, and graduating to the more complex textures of works such as
Lizard and *Fauvel's Rondeaux*.

John McCabe draws inspiration from a wide variety of sources, from
art and literature to more abstract aspects of nature. The Movements
for Clarinet, Violin and Cello (which date from the same period as
the Bagatelles for Two Clarinets, being written in 1964 for the Gabrieli
Ensemble, and revised in 1966) were inspired by *The Sound and the Fury*
by William Faulkner. This book is written in four parts, with the same
events described from four different viewpoints, and the true sense of the
earlier sections is only revealed at the end. The original impulse behind
Movements was to write a work that would be rounded off at the end and
only complete as a whole rather than each section being complete in itself:
'a work which would make sense more when you have reached the end of
the piece. There are clear sections but I hope that they balance out and
make sense when they are balanced out.' Movements is composed using a
free variation technique to develop the ideas, and is also a fine example of
another important feature of McCabe's music, that of mirror images. The
work is broadly palindromic in shape, the last three movements being a
mirror image of the first three, and the central *Adagio* is also a palindrome
in its own right. The arch plan of the piece is immediately obvious, the
Adagio demonstrating an expressively free clarinet line, supported by the
violin and cello. Each pair of movements with the same tempo indications
shares the same musical content, and movements three and five are an
extremely strict mirror image of each other in all three parts. Symmetry in
general is a notable element of McCabe's composition, found in different
guises: for example, many of his rhythmic motifs often fall into symmetrical patterns. However, in this piece the listener is never made to feel that
this is a mere intellectual exercise – rather that the piece is more akin to a
divertimento in its overall texture and mood.

The years from 1967 to 1969 saw the composition of four major wind chamber music works, firstly moving away from the prominence of the clarinet in favour of the horn in the Dance-Movements for Horn, Violin and Piano of 1967 and the oboe in the Oboe Quartet of 1968, with the Concerto for Piano and Wind Quintet and the Sonata for Clarinet, Cello and Piano following a year later. All four of these works are typical of the pieces of this period, and indeed of a large proportion of McCabe's music, in that they are written in a single-movement framework, in which the various sections together add up to one single indivisible unit rather than being a succession of movements that just happen to be played without a break. The progression of the composition therefore rests largely on the element of contrast within the movement, whether it be a fast or slow tempo, a serious or lighter feeling or the use of ebb and flow of dissonance. This is seen clearly in the Dance-Movements for Horn, Violin and Piano, a fully fledged trio for the three instruments written in 1967 for the Ifor James Horn Trio, and first performed by them at the Wigmore Hall, London, in that year. The four full-length movements are closely related and the changes of tempo and mood are simply changes of emphasis rather than complete switches from one separate piece to the next. The melodic material is common to all four movements, given a preludial character, rising to an intense climax, in the first movement and treated with a constantly fluctuating rhythmical shape in the scherzo-like second movement. The third movement, *Andante con moto*, is a tribute to the American jazz musician Charles Mingus, and incorporates a *Maestoso* introduction and coda framing a series of increasingly hectic or frantic variations on a ground-bass theme generating from the left hand of the piano. The finale has a brief central slow section but is mainly an exciting, fast and virtuosic *tour de force* for all players.

The Oboe Quartet of 1968 was commissioned for the Cardiff University College chamber concerts, and is dedicated to McCabe's old friends and colleagues at the College. Here the one-movement framework incorporates six sections within a self-contained unit (*Vivo – Lento – Fantastico – Lento – Agitato – Lento*), the variations of speed, texture and mood being part of the gradual progression of the structure of the whole. Throughout the piece the textures are basically light, and the scoring is seldom very full. Two motifs of great importance in the development of the music are announced at the beginning, featuring a cluster of semitones and the interval of a tritone, both of which add a certain sharp edge to the pervading general lightness of colouring.

The work features much in the way of side-stepping chromatic passages diffusing sustained string chords, seen first in the vigorous opening

Vivo, and adapted in the following *Lento* and in particular in the 'extended cadenza' marked *Tempo di fantastico* which links into the final *Lento* passage. There are elements of free composition included too; in the *Agitato* the strings are required to race up and down a chromatic mode in free time marked *frantico* and *presto possible* whilst the oboe plays declamatory figures and multiphonics above, and in the first *Lento* section groups of notes appear in brackets in the oboe part indicating that they 'should be played within the limits of the crotchet beat as symbolized by the brackets; the position of the notes within the beat is roughly indicated by their position in the brackets'. The quicker movements surround an expressive central *Lento* in which the strings, for the first time, assume the leadership of the ensemble. The first, marked *Fantastico* as an indication of atmosphere, is a scherzo-like section which has occasional forceful outbursts and is full of cross-rhythms. The *Agitato* begins with quiet *misterioso* scurryings but soon bursts out into a violent climax. This leads into a final extended cadenza for the oboe and the work ends with a brief contemplative codetta for the strings.

The Concerto for Piano and Wind Quintet was completed in 1969, commissioned by the Birmingham Chamber Music Society and first performed by the composer with the Venturi Ensemble in February 1970. In it McCabe set out to write a genuinely virtuosic piece exploiting the public impact of a concerto, rather than that of a chamber music work, as demonstrated by the dynamism, and sense of discussion or argument between the two protagonists, the piano and the wind quintet. The virtuoso nature of the writing includes cadenzas for horn and clarinet as well as important solos for all the instruments. The piece is written thematically along very concentrated lines, the main melodic material of the work from which most of the themes and harmonies are largely derived being introduced in the opening *Maestoso*. It employs the cyclic style of structure of which the composer is so fond, with the work's opening flourish returning at the end of the finale to close the piece in a mood of defiance.

Three of the four main movements use elements of rondo form. The first movement is a fast rondo, with much changing of time signatures and decoration of the main subject group. The third movement is a scherzo of very light, scurrying textures with the piano's main subject treated with rondo-like repetition in which it is expanded further on each appearance. The finale merges rondo form with a kind of fugue in which the theme is varied on each entry. The second movement, in contrast, is slow and reflective in feeling, and includes another notable feature of McCabe's composition, the occurrence of the 'sound effect' of clusters, found here

in the piano part with the instructions 'Clusters, played with the flat palms of both hands, placed on the white keys; the fingers should be splayed out to catch as many black notes as possible. The top and bottom notes of each cluster are indicated.' The movement is bridged to its adjoining movements by the related horn and clarinet cadenzas respectively, with a short slow movement for the wind quintet alone forming the link into the last movement.

In the same year McCabe composed the Sonata for Clarinet, Cello and Piano, commissioned for the 1969 Macclesfield Arts Festival for the De Peyer-Pleeth-Wallfisch Trio, to whom it is dedicated. It is again cast in various linked sections which together make up a continuous movement, and as with the preceding concerto the thematic material is derived principally from the opening of the piece, in this case a clarinet solo. The development of this theme thereafter is defined by the different characters of the three instruments, their special characteristics being emphasised by the differing approaches to the thematic material. McCabe chose the title 'Sonata' rather than 'Trio' because he felt that 'this approach, intent on separating the instruments somewhat rather than trying to combine them as far as possible, would be more in keeping with a less traditional, though equally abstract, title: the intention has been to keep each instrument's individuality while letting them all work with roughly the same tunes.'

The Sonata calls for an extremely wide range of dynamic contrast. Even within the opening improvisatory phrase of the piece the clarinet is required to crescendo from *pppp* to *ff* and then diminuendo *a niente*. This pattern of dynamic tension and relaxation is continued in the following bars until a forceful *fff* is called for in all three instruments at the *poco agitato*. The Sonata is characterised by contrasts, employing extremes not only of dynamics, but also of tempi and tessitura. This work can again be seen to fulfil McCabe's interests in both 'making of a single entity through diversity' and the writing of works which 'come full circle at the end'. The Sonata concludes with a sombre clarinet cadenza in the style of the opening. These passages call for immense control, and this – combined with the light, quick tongue and fluent finger-work required for the *Allegro* and *Vivo* sections of the composition, and the essential ability to encompass many varied moods into a coherent musical whole – results in a clarinet part that is very demanding.

When writing for specific performers McCabe is not so much inspired by people's characters but by their musical technique and the sound they produce. This concept of sound is extremely important to him: 'It's the sound of the instrument that always gives me the ideas – that is to say,

Opposite: Concerto for Piano and Wind Quintet, opening.

always defines them. Even when I write a little sketch, even when it's just a few notes, I will actually indicate the instrument which is playing right from the start because it's part of the character of the sound.'

McCabe has a particular interest in colour and atmosphere in music; the Sonata for Clarinet, Cello and Piano, for example, contains much in the way of interesting sonorities. The piece is written for the A clarinet, undoubtedly because of its richer tone quality, and demonstrates McCabe's clear appreciation of the beauty of the clarinet's expressive vocal line in the haunting melodies of the *Tristamente*. The piano part incorporates two common techniques for producing pitches inside the piano: striking the string with rubber beaters and plucking the strings with the fingers. These features are also employed in the *Tristamente* section and in the brief *Andante* preceding it, and along with cello harmonics provide an atmospheric accompaniment to the clarinet's mournful melodic line. The complete piece is extremely effective, blending diverse sonorities and styles.

McCabe has a fascination for exotic sonorities, particularly from the percussion. This is, of course, especially evident in his orchestral music, but it is also apparent in the chamber works, especially those forming part of the *Desert I* and *Rainforest* series, written after seeing desert scenery in California and the Middle East, and also having visited the Australian countryside. The first of the series, *Desert I: Lizard*, for example, contains some extremely effective percussion writing. *Lizard* – composed in 1981 for flute, oboe, clarinet, bassoon and percussion – was inspired by the lizards the composer encountered in Redlands, California. He has offered the following preface to the score: 'The title derives from my fascination with both desert country and its fringes, and this particular piece stems from the kind of sudden movement of lizards, which seen to go from total immobility to an extremely fast rate of movement without any intervening stage of acceleration. The various sections which go to make up this piece are not necessarily a pictorial portrait of this point, but it was the basic impulse underlying the formation of the melodic material.'

Rainforest I includes important parts for two wind instruments, the flute and clarinet, and McCabe returned once more to the wind in *Desert IV: Vista*, for solo recorder, which followed in 1983, first performed in May of that year by John Turner. This is a *tour de force* for one player performing on both tenor and sopranino recorders. Often written without time signature, it utilises several popular traits of contemporary wind writing including quartertones, pitch bending and audible intakes of breath through the instrument. The piece moves through several widely contrasting sections within its one movement of seven minutes' duration.

84

McCabe's next piece for a wind instrument was again a solo, the *January Sonatina* for solo clarinet, written in January 1990 at the request of Philip Rehfeldt of the University of Redlands, California. It is one of a collection of 33 short unaccompanied works included in the *Etudes for the Twenty-First Century Clarinettist* compiled as a Festschrift for the 64th birthday of the composer Barney Childs, on 13 February 1990, from his friends and former students. The first performance was given in America by Philip Rehfeldt, the British premiere given the following year by Verity Butler at the Purcell Room, London. The piece is in one movement lasting about five minutes, blending together a variety of musical and technical challenges within its three sections: *Slow*, a lyrical opening – *Presto possible*, alternating very quiet and fast-flowing melismas with stuttering figures – *Fast – Rhythmical*, a dance-like finale. The ability of the clarinet to play long notes in a gradual crescendo is one of the characteristics of the instrument that McCabe finds particularly appealing. He exploits it not only in the Sonata and the Three Pieces, but to a greater extent in the *January Sonatina*. As with *Vista*, McCabe did not find any particular problems in writing for a single melody instrument. In making up for the absence of an underlying harmony and the presence of other instruments to create texture, he introduces a very strong character of ideas and many contrasts. Two other characteristics of the clarinet that are particularly appealing to McCabe are clearly in evidence in the *January Sonatina*, those of rhythmic incisiveness and the ability to play very, very fast, very quietly – 'it's an instrument which can "burble" wonderfully!' The rhythmic vitality of the final section is ideally suited to the clarinet, as are the fast repetitive flourishes of the *Presto possible*.

This rhythmic vitality in his writing is extremely important to McCabe, and the Dance-Prelude of 1971, despite its brevity and lightness of mood, demonstrates both this, and several other points of style, particularly well. Originally written for oboe d'amore and piano, but also existing in a version for clarinet, this short introduction and rondo was written for a Royal Gala Concert at the Empire Theatre, Liverpool, in 1971 in the presence of Her Majesty Queen Elizabeth II, the composer giving the premiere of the work accompanying Jennifer Paull. The piece is fairly light in character, the opening lyrical *Lento* followed by a jazzy, rhythmical *Allegro giocoso*. It is also written fairly strictly along twelve-note rules, the composer recalling that 'it was, in a sense, a challenge to write a piece that would be pretty much light music while using a contemporary technique. In other words, the rigorousness of the technique is disguised by the lightness of the music.' Ostinati, canons and variation devices form an important part in developing the apparently simple material. The first section incorporates an ostinato with canonic entries of the same pattern in augmentation in the outer lines, and the *Allegro giocoso* contains further canonic entries and imitative counterpoint along with further use of ostinato with a frequent repeated rhythmic pattern. McCabe often uses incisive rhythmic motifs that characterise particular movements in this way, giving them obvious unity. The whole of this *Allegro giocoso* is highly rhythmic, incorporating much syncopation and staccato, with accents often highlighting the rhythm against the main metre. This rhythmic impetus is typical of McCabe's writing, generating energy and forward movement and giving the effect of spontaneity. Rhythm is vital to him and it is probably the motivic rhythms of his work that hold most responsibility for the direct appeal of his music.

There is much music of immediate appeal to be found in McCabe's 'lighter' works. Within the realms of his wind chamber music these may be considered to include not only the aforementioned Three Folksongs and Dance-Prelude but several more recent pieces. In 1980 he composed two sets of pieces suitable for Associated Board Grades V–VII, for the series edited by Richard Rodney Bennett. The Dances for Trumpet and Piano are perfectly characterised melodic miniatures, ideally written for the technical requirements of the situation, and showing a wide range of styles from jazz influence to traditional forms as indicated by their titles – *Polish Dance, Ballad, P.B. Blues, Halling, Highland Habanera, Siciliano* and *Jigaudon*. The Portraits for Flute and Piano are exactly that: seven character studies or 'portraits' of a particular musical style, with the music in several cases being a deliberate pastiche or a tribute to another composer. In 1994 McCabe composed an affectionate 60th Birthday present for the composer Anthony Gilbert, in the shape of a short piece for treble recorder and piano *Not quite a tAnGo*. As the title suggests, it is cast as a witty variation on the traditional tango pattern, and it covers much dynamic and articulate contrast within its brief one-minute duration! A further light work for recorder followed in 2000: *Domestic Life*, again written for a 60th birthday, this time for Margaret Turner, in its original version for treble recorder and piano. An edition for recorder and string orchestra (with xylophone) appeared the following year, at the suggestion of John Turner, who has since recorded the work as part of his English Recorder Concertos CD with the Royal Ballet Sinfonia conducted by Gavin Sutherland for ASV. *Domestic Life* is an arrangement of tunes from an 'entertainment', *This Town's a Corporation Full of Crooked Streets* for voices and ensemble, written in 1969. The original work was based on texts that were all connected with Liverpool, including Liverpool children's rhymes and poems by Adrian Henri, Roger McGough and Brian Patten, and the music is written in a very light style that is almost Merseybeat. Three of the original tunes are represented, which all come from the same movement of the 'entertainment' and are here combined into a single movement. McCabe writes in his programme note for the piece 'It was fun to write music after a manner which became part of the Liverpool scene shortly after my own schooldays had finished, and the piece is essentially a very light *pièce d'occasion*'.

In complete contrast The *Goddess* Trilogy for Horn and Piano is a major work in every sense; a set of three pieces for horn and piano, based on the idea of the Great Goddess in ancient Celtic mythology, whose three sister-aspects are Arianrhod, Blodeuwedd and Cerridwen. The three separate movements are designed to be performed either individually or as a single work. The first piece, *The Castle of Arianrhod*, was written in 1973 for an American tour by Ifor James and the composer, the remaining two movements, *Floraison* and *Shapeshifter*, following in 1975, with the whole trilogy receiving its first performance at the Three Choirs Festival, Worcester, in 1975. The composer's own programme note provides much insight into the piece and its Celtic mythological background:

Arianrhod, whose name has been translated as 'She who turns the Silver Wheel of Heaven', is the goddess of birth and initiation – her Castle is the place where the mighty dead, chieftains and heroes, go after death to await reincarnation, and it has also been linked with the Milky Way constellation. The musical idea underlying the piece is that of the decay of a musical sound and its rebirth, perhaps in another form – thus, each section rises to a climax which disperses, the musical material reassembling for the start of a new section. The opening flourish returns to make a violent conclusion. *Floraison* (literally, 'flowering' or 'blossoming') depicts the flower maiden and love goddess Blodeuwedd (which means 'bloom maiden'), who is also an owl goddess of wisdom. She is made of nine kinds of flowers, and in one pagan ritual her husband was sacrificed, ascending after death into the skies in the form of an eagle. It is the lyrical flowering of the increasingly elaborated melodic lines that forms the basic musical impulse for this piece, which is cast in the form of a passacaglia with nine free variations. The image of a flower gradually opening and closing governs the shape of the music, with its intense growth towards the climax and then a return at the close to the opening ideas. Cerridwen, the death goddess, was variously a white sow (devourer of human flesh), a screaming black hag, and giver of the 'inspired arts' through necromancy, divination and 'speaking with tongues'. She was a shape-changer (hence the title of this piece), who pursued the miraculous child Gwion (representing perhaps the changing year). Formally, this work is a rondo, mostly quite quick and using a free variation technique and a good deal of inner changing of the motifs, and at the close it recalls the opening flourish from *The Castle of Arianrhod*.

John McCabe's two most recent major wind chamber works are based on musical material from previous compositions, and both have recently been recorded, together with the Concerto for Piano and Wind Quintet, by The Fibonacci Sequence for an excellent CD of McCabe's chamber music available on the Dutton Epoch label. The immensely attractive Postcards for Wind Quintet, written in 1991, is a reworking of the eight Bagatelles for two clarinets dating from 1965. The idea of thoroughly rewriting this work had been in the composer's mind for some time, and with a commission from the Vega Quintet, to whom the work is dedicated, he produced this exquisite set of miniatures for wind quintet, which was first performed at the 1991 Huddersfield Festival. The basic musical material is the same as that of the Bagatelles, but much decorated, elaborated upon and expanded, resulting in a more substantial set of pieces. Only the *Bossa Nova* could be considered to be an arrangement, the remaining movements being recomposed, with some ending up as much as twice as long and others remaining almost the same length but considerably altered. The title of 'Postcards' was chosen to change the emphasis from simply a set of bagatelles to something more indicative of the nature of the pieces. These are, in a sense, short messages 'sent' from various musical forms and styles; brief postcards from different genres, with the final Fantasy developing references to several of the previous movements.

John McCabe.

Fauvel's Rondeaux for clarinet, violin and piano (which also exists in a version for clarinet doubling bass clarinet) was composed in 1996 and dedicated to the Verdehr Trio. The work takes the form of a gigantic rondo, with the opening music acting as the ritornello material, and the episodes which constitute the main part of the work forming the substance of the music. The trio was inspired by, and to some extent derived from, McCabe's ballet *Edward II* (choreographed by David Bintley), which was first performed by the Stuttgart Ballet in 1995. In the ballet, the character of Fauvel is the leader of a troupe of entertainers, including jugglers, acrobats, clowns and musicians, which provide a kind of commentary – sometimes ironic, sometimes savagely direct.

McCabe himself gives the following description of the stimulus behind this work:

> The origin of this idea lies in the medieval Roman de Fauvel, in which a donkey (Fauvel) becomes Lord of the World, a kind of Lord of Misrule – the political and religious satire, often scurrilous and crude, allowed an expressive extension of the world of the English and French courts in the ballet, and directly related to Edward's tragic fate in that his assassin enters as Fauvel, with an ass's head, and reveals himself as Lightborn, the murderer, only after a short while. In the trio, various sections from the ballet are drawn upon, including some crudely playful dances performed by the troupe of wandering players – the final, intensely chromatic section is taken from the evil *pas de deux* performed by leading conspirators against Edward, his wife (now his widow), Isabella and her corrupt lover, Mortimer. The contrast between the playful nature of the court entertainment and the gradually darkening world of conspiracy, lust and power-mania, which slowly develops during the ballet, is the kind of changing character that has long fascinated me and it was this that I wanted to explore further in this trio. There are, of course, substantial sections which are different from anything in the ballet, but much of the material of these is derived (respectively, as it were) from the music of the final *pas de deux*.

McCabe writes very quickly, preferring to work without the distraction of people around him and away from the piano. He finds it easier to see the structure of the music working at a desk rather than at the piano, and also avoids writing music which is conceived pianistically and which is therefore not ideally suited to other instruments. He is aware that as a performer there is always the danger that he is going to be too much influenced by the pieces that he is playing at the time. Consequently he tries to keep his careers as a pianist and composer as separate as possible, but he does not regard either as the more important: 'I think the two disciplines, which involve totally different ways of actually thinking about music, refresh each other … . It is an essential thing for a composer to have another musical discipline to work in.' The composer believes that being a pianist is an advantage to his composition, in that it gives him a particular contact with audiences that he would not have otherwise. He feels that being a performer, making the music himself and communicating directly with the audience, is a great benefit. He also thinks that it makes him more practical than he might otherwise have been: 'I've got a bit bolder as the years have gone by, but I am aware that the people who have got to play it are also human beings!'

McCabe's writing for wind instruments is often very demanding, but the writing is always well within the realms of practicability and the works are highly rewarding to the performer. In the performance of his wind chamber music all aspects of the technical demands of instrumental playing are encountered. Yet the ultimate role of the performer must surely be to give an interpretation that is not only accurate but musically expressive. These sentiments are equally echoed in McCabe's own attitude to performance; he believes that music is basically about communication:

> I do believe that music should convey something to its listeners and its performers, or should stimulate them to make it convey something to them. But a composer's job is to put his or her thoughts into the most appropriate and clear format so that the essential nature of the thoughts can be as compelling as possible. That's why I put such stress on the structural aspect of the thing. I never like discussing what music actually means, because I believe that music means many things, or at least different versions of things, to different people, and it is dangerous and even false to try to impose a literal interpretation of it on others.

Certain elements in McCabe's writing demand particular attention when preparing for a performance. The rhythmic quality is perhaps the most exciting aspect of his music, so any successful performance must have a strong sense of rhythm. McCabe stresses that a natural feeling for the rhythmic flow is essential and also that the marked accents are often crucial to the rhythmic effect. Phrasing is also of vital importance. McCabe is scrupulous about all his markings on the score and feels strongly that players should adhere strictly to his phrase indications. The wind works often have clear breath marks in addition to phrasing. These are frequently written to indicate the phrasing in a place where a rest would result in the previous note being too clipped and should be observed even when there is no physical necessity to take a breath. McCabe looks for 'commitment' in the performance of his music, describing the most important quality as being 'dramatic atmosphere'. This is partly created by employing a wide dynamic range, and by the precise execution of all the indicated dynamics. Another factor is the use of silence and pauses. He intends the interpretation of a pause over a note or a rest to be literal: quite prolonged and not just a short gap between phrases. Any performance must, of course, have ease and the technical difficulty must not disrupt the musical flow. However, McCabe believes that a fast, technically demanding passage can often sound exciting at a slightly slower speed – 'held' rather than frantic – and that as long as the 'spirit' is right the music will come across. The precise tempo at which the music is played is not of vital importance to the composer as long as it puts across a view of the piece which is convincing. For example, the *Bossa Nova* of the Three Pieces was conceived as being 'slightly laid back' but it is often played, with equal success, at a faster tempo.

There must be room for the element of spontaneity on the concert platform; detailed preparation leaves the performer with the freedom to respond to this inspiration. However, McCabe himself does not believe that analysing the music is of an advantage to a performer. He disagrees with what he describes as 'the prevalent attitude that music is there for the purposes of analysis'. Instead he feels that analysis is something that should come after the music and the performer's response to it: 'music is such an instinctive thing'. McCabe never analyses the music he is playing, placing greater emphasis on instinctive interpretation, and believes that if a performer is really in sympathy with the work he should know what is happening in the music: 'It doesn't matter how much you know about a piece, if you're not in sympathy with it … the performance may be very good technically … but it might not convince an audience, as a performance which is committed – that is sympathetic – will do, because that essential thing is not there.'

In a *Musical Times* article written in 1965, Peter Dickinson accurately predicted that McCabe would develop 'closer to the mainstream of 20th Century music than to what would be for him the arid reaches of the avant-garde'.[2] In summing up McCabe's wind chamber music works it must be concluded that he is a traditionalist, and that he is also a composer whose music is always highly imaginative and eminently practicable. It is hoped that this chapter will have inspired the reader to further exploration of the wealth of McCabe's wind music, as the only way in which any music can truly be fully appreciated must be through performance or listening. After all, the composer himself has expressed his view that he hopes 'the music speaks for itself. If it doesn't then no matter of analytical data will help it do so to any greater extent'.[3] There can be little doubt that he would equally endorse the words of Benjamin Britten:

> What is important … is *not* the scientific part, the analysable part of music, but the something which emerges from it but transcends it, which cannot be analysed because it is not *in* it, but *of* it … it is something to do with personality, with gift, with spirit. I quite simply call it – magic.[4]

2 Peter Dickinson, 'John McCabe', *Musical Times* (August 1965), p. 598.

3 Peter Dickinson (ed.), *Twenty British Composers* (London: Chester, 1975), p. 44.

4 Benjamin Britten, *On Receiving the First Aspen Award* (London: Faber Music Ltd, 1964), pp. 17–18.

5

Chamber music for strings

Guy Rickards

Although his reputation as a composer rests primarily on his orchestral output – his ballets and concertos, particularly – chamber and instrumental genres have been of consistently high importance to John McCabe throughout his career. Leaving aside his sizeable corpus of piano music (covered separately in this volume by Tamami Honma), there are some 40 chamber compositions – defined here as being for between two and ten players – spread fairly evenly between wind and stringed instruments, plus a half-dozen unaccompanied pieces for cello, guitar, violin, recorder, clarinet and viola.

The single chamber combination McCabe has employed most often is the string quartet, with five numbered quartets beginning with the *Partita* of 1959–60 (which only acquired its number retrospectively when he composed the Second a dozen years later) and culminating at present with the Fifth in 1989, along with the unnumbered single-span *Caravan* (1988). McCabe has also written three piano quintets, two – *Nocturnal* (1966) and *The Woman by the Sea* (2001) – for the standard formation of piano and string quartet, plus *Sam Variations* (1989), where a double bass replaces the second violin as in Schubert's *Trout* Quintet. In addition to an Oboe Quartet (1968), his other string-ensemble works include a student String Quintet (1962, apparently lost) as well as the sextet *Pilgrim* (1996) and three pieces using larger, chamber-orchestral bodies: Two Dances from the ballet *Mary, Queen of Scots* arranged in 1977 for harp and strings; Concertante Variations on a theme of Nicholas Maw for eleven solo strings (1987, an arrangement of the orchestral original of 1970); and *Rainforest II* (1987), a chamber concerto for trumpet and eleven strings.

Just as his first acknowledged orchestral composition is a concerto (the First Violin Concerto of 1959), the large-scale form that he has cultivated

Opposite: Les Martinets noirs, *opening.*

93

par excellence, so in the field of chamber music he opened his account with a string quartet, the chamber medium to which he has returned most often. The five-movement *Partita* for string quartet was written while McCabe was still a student at Manchester University and while it now doubles as his official First Quartet, it was originally conceived as a single-span *Lamento*, in which four contrasting sections, *Lento – Adagio ma con movimento – Allegro – Adagio*, are compressed into a strong, concise movement lasting around seven minutes. The name and atmosphere may reflect the impact on the young composer of the music of Karl Amadeus Hartmann, whose *Concerto funèbre* McCabe encountered around this time (*Lamento* being one of the rejected titles of the work now known as Hartmann's First Symphony), but the tonal language has rather keener resonances of Shostakovich.

The year after completing *Lamento*, McCabe added four further movements, each decreasing in duration (*Fantasia*, *Arioso*, *Capriccio* and *Epilogue*, the last three played without pause), for a student quartet group. Each of these later movements takes its thematic material from the *Lamento*, particularly the first violin's *lamentoso e ben espressivo* theme, with its flattened falling octave (A flat to A), accelerating repeated-note motif with semitonal skip, rising sixth and sinuous second section. In a way each is a species of free variation of the first movement. And just as *Lamento* used retrograde and inverted forms of the theme, so do the later movements, although always within a tonal framework. The textures in the ever-increasing tempi of the *Fantasia* (concluding in a deft *Presto*) are at times reminiscent of Robert Simpson's quartets. The lyrical, central *Arioso* is more unified in mood than its precursors and gives way to the most immediately appealing movement, a lively *Capriccio* marked *Vivo e articulato*. Its *Adagio [recitative]* coda paves the way for the muted *Lento con movimento Epilogue*, which recapitulates *Lamento*'s main theme before the quiet series of piled-up bare fifths brings this impressive debut piece to a close.

It was the trio as a form, however, rather than the quartet that became something of a preoccupation of McCabe's in the short term, five being produced in fairly quick succession between 1964 and 1969, all with varying formats and instrumental arrays. Two of these – *Movements* (1964, rev. 1966) and the Sonata (1969) – feature the clarinet and with that for horn (*Dance-Movements*, 1967) are covered in Chapter 4 of this volume, although all three feature at least one stringed instrument. *Musica Notturna* (1964) is one of the earliest, written for Martin Milner, who had premiered McCabe's First Violin Concerto a few years before, and scored for the unusual combination of piano, violin and viola. Despite the slow, restrained opening

94

section (containing the exposition of the trio's bitonal material), *Musica Notturna* is a closely worked albeit atmospheric depiction of a busy, urban nightscape. No sleepy moonlit vista here, the three main sections, fast – slow – fast, play continuously through which the developing themes are treated, according to the composer, 'very much as a theme in a set of variations'. Variation forms are another recurrent feature in McCabe's music all through his career (his excellent Piano Variations had been written only the year before) and *Musica Notturna* is a fine example of the composer's multi-faceted approach, where variational procedures govern the motivic developments; however, the central *Andante molto* is one of the standard forms, an initially glacial passacaglia. In a letter to violinist Peter Sheppard Skærved in December 2000, McCabe posited that he had been

> strongly influenced … by Rawsthorne's delight in exploring to the utmost a small group of motifs (or even just one), drawing on a small reservoir of material for a composition (variation or metamorphosis technique, which fascinates me; this becomes one of the main features of the development). I also like his refusal to repeat anything exactly (*vide* also Busoni) and the sense of a tonal centre, which works very nicely in serial music as well.

Another feature of the musical language is its strong resonance of middle-period Shostakovich (for instance of the Piano Quintet or Second Trio), whose mighty passacaglias in the Eighth Symphony and First Violin Concerto may have suggested the deployment of the form in this trio. While recognisably McCabe in every bar and never losing its British identity, there is nonetheless a cosmopolitan feel to the work as a whole. In 1981, the composer made an alternative arrangement for the Australian Piano Trio, whose line-up had changed when their violist left and was replaced by a cellist.

The String Trio (1965) is the third of McCabe's seven trios to date and perhaps his finest chamber work of the 1960s. Indeed, although the composer has moved on stylistically, all the familiar fingerprints are present and it remains one of his most impressive chamber music utterances, running to 23 incident-packed minutes. The opening is one of his most memorable, a pregnant alternation of slow descending intervals and sharp, rhythmic thrust the implications of which play out across the opening *Allegro con fuoco*. This movement has an edgy, serious demeanour and although the lyrical second subject brings some respite the dominant characteristic is energy: the music seems constantly to burst and sprout prolifically, yet always

McCabe and Peter Sheppard Skærved playing at David Matthews' wedding.

in one set direction. By the close, the rhythmic element clearly has the upper hand, maximising contrast with the central *Mesto*, another set of variations. If the *Allegro con fuoco* was structurally free, with only vestigial traces of sonata form – not least in being wholly developmental – the second is unorthodox in having no real theme. Or rather, the theme evolves during the first variation out of its initial phrases. The succeeding variations, which accelerate in tempo to the climactic *Vivo* before returning to the opening mood, treat this first rather as a small thematic reservoir, a process McCabe has used in other works, not least the ballet *Edward II*. The finale is vigorous but opens cautiously; its main event is the return of the first movement's opening, functioning partly like a delayed sonata recapitulation, although it is sufficiently varied to amount to a second development, or the aftermath of one. If nothing else, its powerful close is convincing proof of McCabe's stature as a thinker in large-scale designs.

In the wake of the String Trio, the only one of the seven to date to stay within a single instrumental family, 1966 saw the creation of a Partita for solo cello and his first piano quintet, *Nocturnal*. The Partita, like the *Canto* for guitar that followed two years later, must be one of the least-known of McCabe's instrumental works. In C major and slightly built, its six movements last some twelve minutes or so and are best regarded as a variation set on the opening span – entitled *Theme* – the subject of which has its own *Reprise* between the *Aria* second movement and the spirited *Jig*. The first movement proper, a *Marcia giocosa*, is balanced by the penultimate *Marcia funèbre*; indeed there is a move from the light to the sombre as the work progresses, the second march being framed by the closely worked *Canons* and the rondo-like Finale. The final chord exhibits, in McCabe's own words 'a rare abdication from the composer's responsibilities' in that the cellist is now permitted to decide whether to include an E (the original note) or F sharp (to remind that the tritone plays a prominent role).

96

Despite its common title with Britten's great meditation on Dowland for guitar, McCabe's quintet *Nocturnal* was inspired by John Donne's *A Nocturnal upon St Lucie's Day*. It was commissioned by the Park Lane Group and premiered by the Lancaster University Ensemble in 1966. The structure is more complex than in previous works, the seven sections forming a not-quite-continuous tripartite design. (The score is marked 'to be played without long breaks between the movements'.) The first part comprises a brief, exposition-like *Andante* Introduction, requiring just two pages of score, and *Nocturne 1*, marked *Allegro vivo*, which takes up half the printed volume. This is succeeded by a tiny central triptych of a four-bar Interlude – reprising a key motif from the Introduction – framed by two *liberamente* Cadenzas (the first, 'Quasi improvisazione', spotlighting the string quartet). Over and done with in around a minute (though expressively of far greater importance), this leads to the final part, *Nocturne 2* (marked *Andante molto*) rounded off by a quiet *Epilogue*. In some respects this design is the precursor of the Third String Quartet's layout, where two large variation-movements flank a passacaglia framed by a pair of scherzos.

The atmosphere of Donne's poem, considered by many to be one of his greatest, finds eloquent expression in the music. The very opening, with its crucial motif oscillating A and B flat, is the embodiment of the lines 'For his art did express / A quintessence even from nothingness' and the Introduction's general mood reflects the 'lean emptiness'. A key element, though, is the evolution of a descending three-note motif based on the tri-tone, and a ten-note theme encapsulating it and the opening semitonal shift. *Nocturne I*, by contrast, is forceful and rhythmic, with a dynamic harmonic thrust suggestive perhaps of 'yet all these seem to laugh / Compared to me, who am their epitaph. / … you who shall lovers be / At the next world, that is, at the next spring'. The short *Cadenza I* is a rare example of aleatoric techniques in McCabe's music, but of the sort also used by Lutosławski where pitch is absolutely controlled but rhythm left to the string players to improvise. The piano frames this with a *liberamente* ascent from the depths, musing obsessively on rising sixths and thirds (C–A at first). After the Interlude's three statements of the opening oscillation, transposed to D–E flat, *Cadenza II* picks up on *Cadenza I*'s C–A motif to spin a brief ethereal web, ending on a high D–D flat trill. Is this perhaps the 'absence, darkness, death: things which are not' from which *Nocturne II* is 're-begot'? Central to it is the cello's theme, growing inexorably out of the semitonal alternation from C to B, then C sharp to A sharp. As the theme extends, components spin off to assume a life of their own in various embellishments and the music reaches a splendid climax on the C–B interval, after which the Epilogue tidies up the threads. The second *Nocturne* is one of the finest passages in early McCabe and *Nocturnal* as a whole a truly marvellous piece whose neglect is unaccountable, except perhaps by virtue of its brevity – around 14 minutes in performance.

McCabe next produced his only solo piece for guitar (although he would use it again five years later in the song set *Das letzte Gerichte*, and its electric cousin tellingly in the ballet *Edward II*), the *Canto* commissioned by the Cardiff Festival of Twentieth Century Music in 1968. There are three main sections: two outer *Allegro*s framing a central *Serenade*, marked *Lento*, in which (according to the composer's programme notes) 'snatches of a serenade and a lament are heard, as if wafted to the listener on an evening breeze'. The whole is contained within an Introduction – which acts as a basic exposition of the main material – and a coda that recalls 'as if in confused memory, events from the previous movements', the entire work lasting a mere seven minutes. Similar traits of compression and alternating, contrasting tempi can be found in the Oboe Quartet, the Sonata for Clarinet, Cello and Piano, and the Concerto for Piano and Wind Quintet (covered in Chapter 4 of this book), which provide the bridge between the String Trio and *Nocturnal* on the one hand and the Second String Quartet on the other.

After the eventually fairly expansive dimensions of the String Quartet *Partita* (which plays for over twenty minutes) and String Trio, the Second Quartet is far more concise and concentrated. It was commissioned for the 1972 Macclesfield Festival by local textile manufacturers Ernest Scragg & Sons, Ltd, and again uses variation as a vital vehicle for the development of its two main motifs. Unlike its predecessor, however, the Second Quartet is in a single, unbroken span which superficially shows traces of traditional four-movement sonata design. By this time, McCabe had also composed several large-scale orchestral works including his first two symphonies (1965, 1971), the Concertante Variations on a Theme of Nicholas Maw (1970) and the marvellous surrogate-concerto for soprano and orchestra, *Notturni ed Alba* (1971). Since McCabe had successfully mastered larger forms, it might seem surprising, then, that the Second Quartet should run out to well under a quarter-hour in performance. Yet the cogency of McCabe's writing, more focussed than before, is immediately apparent from the initial treatment of the two motifs unveiled at the start of the opening *Flessibile* section: a descending figure in the first violin and the viola's and cello's chordal response. This initial sub-movement is lyrical but never quite relaxed, the closeness of the thematic argument ensuring that musical, rather than purely melodic, flow is paramount. The ensuing

Opposite: String Quartet No. 2, opening.

98

scherzo section, *Vivo*, is volatile and restless (as if magnifying the undertow of the opening), the music darting back and forth like prey eluding a predator but always with its goal in plain view. That goal is the grave and passionate *Largo*, the heart of the whole work, containing – in the composer's own description – several 'vehement solo cadenzas'. The *Deciso* (a favourite marking of the composer's) finale is lively and forceful, though undeniably under the emotional sway of the *Largo*.

For all its brevity, the Second Quartet is an unsettling work, traversing some uncomfortable expressive terrain. It was only after completing it that McCabe recognised the 1960 *Partita* as his official 'First', as if realising that this was a medium he would return to again. Number three was several years away yet and he had a request from violinist Michael Davis to consider first, for an unaccompanied violin piece. The result was the coruscating *Maze Dances*, completed in 1973 and premiered by Davis the following year at the Wigmore Hall. The work is built in five sections (with the usual prefatory introduction) from two basic ideas, labelled by the composer the 'Maze idea … a scurrying, circling theme which seems to be running around in a maze', with which the work begins, and the idea of the dance – not as a separate motif but as a concept that infects and transforms the Maze idea through a series of different dance styles in the main sections. One could view the work as another species of variation-form, but as much on the concept of the dance as a specific theme. Played without a break, the sections fall into an arch shape with rustic-sounding outer parts (possessing at times a Bartókian twang) encompassing more choreographed slower sections, with a brief, bright scherzo at its heart. Interestingly, Peter Sheppard Skærved – who has recorded both this piece and McCabe's best-known solo string work, *Star-Preludes* – views *Maze Dances* as an expression of a zigeuner-style technical aesthetic in modern violin playing, more improvisatory in spirit than that demanded by much later twentieth-century works for the instrument. *Maze Dances* certainly evinces a feeling of expressive extemporisation, but against a rigorously controlled backdrop.

After producing the delightful string-orchestral Sonata on a Motet (1976, deriving from early sixteenth-century composer Thomas Tallis' great 40-part motet *Spem in alium*) and Two Dances for Harp and Strings, extracted from his ballet *Mary, Queen of Scots* (1977), *Star-Preludes* (1977–78) proved to be his next string instrumental piece. Another work 'possessed of huge structural and formal rigour', according to Sheppard, *Star-Preludes* and *Maze Dances* sit across a major divide in McCabe's music, that of his abandonment of serialism during the writing of the Stabat Mater in 1976.

McCabe may never have been a slavish dodecaphonist and would continue to use serial methods as part of his compositional armoury from time to time, but there is no denying the sense of freedom that relying wholly on his own wits now gave to his music. There are passages in *Star-Preludes*, not least the ecstatic central span (subtitled 'White Dwarf'), where that freedom becomes almost tangible, yet it works so well expressively because of the rigour behind the notes. As a result the music sounds more modern in feel than in many of his earlier pieces.

The work plays continuously for a touch under a quarter of an hour and has its origins in the movements of the stars, although the section titles were only added after the work was finished. The opening *Lento* is subtitled 'Pleiades…' after the delicate group known also as the Seven Sisters, and is the pool from which all the themes derive. Those of the succeeding *Andantino* ('Andromeda…'), *Vivo* ('Sirius…') and *Andante lirico* ('White Dwarf…') show a family resemblance to each other rather than being out-and-out variants or developments of the opening material, though the concluding *Vivo* ('…suiriS') and *Lento, come prima* ('…sedaielP') are curtailed reprises in retrograde of the first and third sections, an inventive and in performance telling variant on the composer's habit of returning to his opening material at the conclusion of a work. (Indeed, the two 'Sirius' movements with the central 'White Dwarf' form a mini-composition within a composition, like the binary star formation that inspired them.) McCabe composed *Star-Preludes* for Erich Gruenberg, with whom he enjoyed many years as a duo partner, and they premiered the work in Los Angeles in April 1978.

The Third String Quartet followed on relatively quickly, commissioned by the Fishguard Festival and unveiled there in 1979 by the Gabrieli Quartet, to whom it is dedicated. It is cast in five movements, arranged symmetrically in three parts like an arch, the weightier outer ones enclosing a central group of three brief intermezzi consisting of two scherzi (with the instruments muted throughout) around an innermost *Romanza*. Thematic inter-connections abound between the movements: the opening *Variants* (named from one of the finest works by Alun Hoddinott, whose fiftieth birthday fell that year) provides, with its predominant thirds and sixths, the basic material for the whole work and is quoted in the second and third movements, while the closing *Passacaglia* functions like a commentary on the first.

The first movement alternates slow and fast tempi in typical McCabe fashion – though here with unusual potency, the initial stark *Moderato* built from little more than a D minor–major chord for the quartet, a sequence for the viola and a nervy, chromatic motif in contrary motion for second

MODERATO (♩=60)

violin and cello. The first violin counters with a *dolce* second subject, and these two motivic groups extend and intertwine leading to a slightly Simpsonic *Vivo*, making impressive use of a simple C major scale with added C sharp at its apex. The ensuing *Lento* is a synthesis of the two main ideas, the cello spotlit as principal melodist, and the tempo then returns to *Vivo* with opposing pulses of 9/8 and 3/4 producing a galloping development or variation on the first *Vivo*'s material. This gives way to another *Lento* and the movement's climax, a dynamic *Allegro deciso*. A spectral slow coda rounds out the Quartet's first part in a quiet D minor.

The first of the two muted scherzos was inspired by Beethoven's *Rasumovsky* Quartet Op. 59 No. 3, with its rapid scale runs passed between the instruments with the barest harmonic support. The *Variants*' opening motif is recalled briefly at the centre and again in the ensuing *Romanza*, which is dominated by a nervy viola solo. The second, *Presto possible*, scherzo is athematic (although the interval of the third is prominent throughout), essentially a crescendo and diminuendo from a unison F to a bar where all twelve notes of the chromatic scale are sounded. The final *Passacaglia* 'derives its overall shape and flow from the concept of a Lakeland stream, descending from a quiet mountain tarn through various transformations and an increase in boisterousness as it tumbles down towards the lake, in whose placidity it finds rest'. McCabe has added that the landscape around Patterdale and Ullswater is specifically associated with his conception. The ground bass is in two parts, the first a shifting, gently dissonant opening sequence built from repeated notes, thirds and semitonal clashes, the second a partial development of it with a tritone sting in its tail. As the movement progresses, this sting gets drawn, first as a fourth, then a third as the polyphonic textures increase in complexity as the music heads towards the lake, reaching an *Allegro agitato* where material from *Variants* is recalled. The music finally closes in a meditative *Lento*, the opening bars recalled now in tranquillity.

The Third Quartet's scale – at over 27 minutes in length it is one of McCabe's largest chamber works – is as much an indication of its importance in his output as the scope of its compositional processes. In every respect it was a summation of his new-found compositional freedom at the close of the 1970s, yet its inspiration in the countryside of the Cumbrian lakes and mountains also signalled a new expressive direction that would come to dominate his music for the next decade. The theme of this new direction was ecology, featuring in two series of works inspired by deserts and rainforests. One of the first products was the piano trio *Desert III: Landscape* (1982), first performed by the New England Ensemble (who had

Opposite: String Quartet No. 3, opening.

commissioned it) at the University of New England, Armidale, New South Wales. McCabe has long fostered a relationship with Australia, where he has been a frequent performer, and there is something of the stark interior of that continent in the trio's expressive profile. However, as the composer has himself commented, the inspiration 'stems as much from the strength and complexity of the Australian desert fringe landscape as it does from the sense of a vast emptiness which is the impulse behind the beginning of the work'. That beginning is desolate, undeniably representative of the 'vast emptiness', but there is more to this opening movement, in the composer's favourite slow *Lento* pulse. Slowly, ideas seem to emerge from the static void though it is only in the scherzo-like *Vivo* that follows that they achieve anything more than cursory form. The *Lento*, then, is a form of Introduction-cum-exposition, with the *Vivo* a varied exposition repeat and initial development in which the motifs scurry and scuttle (to paraphrase the composer's own description) just as life teems in apparently empty wastes. If this is suggestive of lizards (the subject, incidentally of the wind-and-percussion *Desert I*) and salamanders (treated in a much later brass band work, in 1994) darting back and forth, then the central, intense *Lento* may represent the scorching heat of the desert at noontide. The differing textural combinations and metres betoken other forms of life culminating in what the composer has termed 'cicada music', which eventually expires in a high string harmonic. The finale (the movements are played without pause) is a compound-form structure, starting with a highly rhythmic *Deciso* that appears out of nowhere. Although the music is a further development of the principal idea, a series of semitones that infests all the movements, the rhythms were 'influenced by Aboriginal didjeridu music' according to the composer and in wave after wave these intensify to *Allegro vivace*. At its height, a *Maestoso* epilogue steals in, heralded by a breathless pause, to usher the listener back to the opening of the work, signifying the expanse of the desert, now not quite so empty as it once seemed.

Hard on the heels of the trio came the single-movement Fourth String Quartet, written as a double celebration, of the Delmé Quartet's 20th birthday as well as the 250th anniversary of Haydn's birth – indeed one of a number of pieces (including the magisterial Haydn Variations the following year) in honour of the quartet composer par excellence. When premiered by the Delmé in October 1982 the Quartet bore the subtitle *Un piccolo divertimento* but the full score shows this as crossed through, as if the composer realised that this remarkably unified and cogent work was neither *piccolo* nor a *divertimento*, even allowing for Haydnesque understatement. Its principal formal idea was derived from the great Austrian master, that of alternating variation. Usually this implies two themes varied in turn, but here McCabe reversed the concept in a series of nine extended variations on an *Adagio* unison melody heard at the outset. This highly chromatic tune, containing eleven notes out of the possible twelve, contains sub-motifs which through the course of the Quartet achieve a measure of autonomy, generating distinct developments in their own right. Were this an orchestral score, 'Symphonic Variations' would be a most apt title.

The theme shows from the outset a tendency to move out of phase with itself, the cello sliding up a semitone to start a restatement on B – the one note not previously included. The first variation proper, *Vigoroso* ('brusque and rhythmical' according to the composer), initiates a fundamental principle for the work's structure in that it is rather a movement in miniature containing a number of variants of the main melody and its sub-motifs. As the theme fragments, a wealth of organic developments ensues in increasing contrapuntal complexity. The succeeding *Andante*, by contrast, spotlights the viola which meditates on a different set of derivations from the main theme than hitherto, surrounded by violin arabesques. Its mood is blown away by a brief *Vivo*, where *con sordini* violins, *pianissimo*, alternate with heavier interjections from the viola and cello. The *Andante* fourth variation centres on a *dolce* violin line which is a prime example of McCabe's motivic processing, based on the principal melody's opening three-note phrase and which is later combined with a *cantabile* cello counter-variation. The keystone, as it were, of McCabe's structure is a Haydnesque pause, after which another hectic scherzo breaks out, full of frenetic activity and sudden pauses. As much a variant on the preceding *Vivo* as of the main theme, the ensuing *Lento* also seems to relate back to the *Andante* fourth variation, though with the second violin assuming centre stage front.

McCabe described the seventh, *Moderato*, section as a 'double variation gaining speed' that flows into a fleet *Allegro deciso* with swift-moving violin *tremolandi* and a pregnant cello ground bass. The concluding *Lento* is the work's summation, the cello bearing the main thematic interest with a haunting solo slowly unwinding onto a repeated G, while the upper strings expire finally on a unison C sharp, the quartet's initial note.

The Fourth remains McCabe's finest quartet to date, indeed arguably his finest chamber composition. Six years were to pass before he essayed the form again, and then only in the miniature *Caravan*, although the mercurial Fifth Quartet followed on a year later. In the meantime, however, came *Pueblo*, a seven-minute study for double bass (1986–87) with its inspiration relating to McCabe's *Desert* series. The score bears a superscription from Reyner Banham's *Scenes in America Deserta*, extracts from which the composer had set memorably in a commission for The King's Singers the year before:

> Clouds, high and flat, were now building up in the sky, the wind was settling to silent calm, the weather was very cold, and the stream through the center of the pueblo was almost frozen across, the Indians chipping out ice to melt down for water.

McCabe has commented that the 'aim in writing the piece was to express in musical terms a response to the vivid picture of a scene relating to life in the American desert conveyed by Reyner Banham's text' and its various episodes, played continuously, are extended variants on the 'high circling motif' played at the outset and reprised in harmonics at the close. In 1999, a new version of the work was edited with the composer's blessing by Richard Dubugnon and premiered by him in June 2000 at London's Conway Hall. *Caravan* (1987–88) also has connections to the *Desert* series, as it was inspired by the image of a desert caravan approaching the listener from the distance and coming ever gradually – across its eight-minute dura-tion – into focus. The work, constructed as a gradual crescendo, also deals with the notion of the perception of pace (as would the Fourth Symphony, *Of Time and the River*, a few years later) in that as the caravan gets nearer it appears to be moving faster. From a cautious start, with all four instruments muted, the piece gathers momentum to end apparently quickly, 'aggressively' almost, yet the tempo (*Allegro*, crotchet = 138) is unchanged throughout.

McCabe followed this with his second work for piano quintet, *Sam Variations* (1989). The piece was written at the request of the Schubert Ensemble and designed to be played with the *Trout Quintet*, being scored for the same combination of instruments. (The layout of piano, violin, viola, cello and double bass was not Schubert's idea but followed the example of Hummel's Opus 87.) The

John McCabe. Photo: Peter Thompson.

Sam Variations play continuously for a touch under a quarter of an hour and may be considered either as a single-movement work or a succession of seven short, predominantly quick, pieces all derived from the theme McCabe wrote in 1975 for the TV series *Sam*. The theme itself is never heard in full, but alluded to only, most closely in the quiet *Lento* coda.

McCabe's use of this pleasant little tune was itself an act of homage to Schubert in that it mirrors the Viennese composer's use of an earlier melody – from his song 'Die Forelle' – in the slow movement of his Quintet. McCabe's seven sections have the nature of variations or character-studies although the composer has himself pointed out that the format is quite unlike a conventional set. Rather, they share a common point of origin in the unheard original theme, bound together by the ritornello-like string passage that opens the work and which returns in highly varied forms at key points, almost like a set of variations within a set of variations. The first three sections are all quick, the initial *Deciso* followed by a bright *Vivo* and an *Allegro marcato* before giving way to the compound fourth section, which McCabe has himself described as 'three variations in one', when a *Quasi recitativo* passage for the double bass melds with a dancing *Vivo* for violin and viola, offset by a cello-and-piano arioso (*Lento*). Two further swift sections ensue, *Vivace* and *Allegro moderato e marcatissimo*, before the slow coda, which evolves into a chorale over a quietly throbbing bass.

From this relaxed, almost occasional piece – which yet deserves to be played far more often in its own right – McCabe returned (for the last time at time of writing) to the string quartet for a second commission from the Fishguard Festival that same year. After the Haydn-oriented compositional rigour of the Fourth, the Fifth emerged as an entirely different type of work, a series of related but contrasted sections (fourteen, this time) played continuously and not unlike the construction of *Sam Variations* but on a much larger scale and mimicking a three-movement design, broadly slow – very fast – fast. Unlike any of its predecessors, however, the Fifth has a very specific extra-musical inspiration, the series of fourteen aquatints entitled *The Bees* by Graham Sutherland, which McCabe saw at an exhibition in Picton Castle in south-west Wales. His intention was not to write a modern-day chamber *Pictures at an Exhibition* (or even revisit the experience of *The Chagall Windows*), however, as that type of illustrative composition holds little interest for him. Rather, the pictures suggested a musical response in the same way that the Lakeland stream gambolling down the valley side suggested the structure for the finale of the Third Quartet. The subject matter of Sutherland's aquatints is reflected in McCabe's music only in the general atmosphere of each section, though the sections are arranged in quasi-narrative sequence from egg, larvae and pupae through to a ferocious battle in the hive between workers and drones.

The first five sections collectively form an extended slow movement, each one maintaining a *Lento, flessibile* tempo. In the opening *Metamorphosis: Egg. Larvae. Pupae* the initial building blocks of the whole quartet are presented, the intervals of the seventh, the second and semitone being particularly prominent, most notably in a sinuous chromatic line that acts as a species of second theme. Also heard is a sequence of descending fifths – this last interval comes to assume increasing significance as the work progresses. The second section, *Hatching I*, emerges out of a series of overlapping variants of the sinuous theme, which provides the ground bass for the melodic developments that follow. *Hatching II* is a development on the preceding section, with a marked increase in polyphony. In *Nuptial Flight*, the hitherto long lines heard are truncated and compressed as the various motifs are combined in the most forceful music thus far. *The Court* brings the opening group of sections to a close, opening with a declamatory development of the sequence of fifths, succeeded by a *cantabile* cello solo, and duos for the viola and cello and the two violins.

A brief rest signals the onset of what might be termed the 'middle' movement, a series of three related scherzos with a lyrical trio. The composer himself has described this sequence as a 'double scherzo, interlude (a slow movement acting as a kind of trio) [and] another scherzo'. The first two sections are both dynamic and rhythmically forceful. *Figure of Eight Dances: Orientation to Sources of Nectar and Pollen* opens *Allegro leggiero* with a new motif that is essentially the chord of E major with the alien A sharp added. Light and airy, it is followed by the driving *Round Dance: Orientation to Sources of Nectar and Pollen*, marked *Allegro vivo*. The trio is formed by the eighth section, *Bee and Flower*, a relaxed meditation with hints of Britten and Tippett on a *dolce* subject, the roots of which lie in the quartet's very opening. The 'other' scherzo comprises three sections: the vigorous, driving *Wild Nest*, the roots of which also derive from the opening bars, which is developed further in *Primitive Hive I*; *Primitive Hive II* acts as a kind of recapitulation to close this central span of the quartet.

The final 'movement' is the shortest and comprises just three sections, which together run for a touch over five minutes. *Bee Keeper* is a fast-flowing (*Allegro deciso*) transformation of one of the work's initial motifs (with the semitone prominent) and acts as an upbeat to *Expulsion and Killing of an Enemy*, most aptly marked *Allegro nervoso*. Here, the main motivic strands of the work are brought together into the most aggressive passage heard thus far, which clashes with an angry variant of the sequence of fifths (sounding utterly unlike its original form). But having expelled the enemy, an even more combative section, *Fight between Workers and Drones*, breaks out setting the previously fused motifs in opposition. At length, the concluding passage from *The Court* returns, *Lento pesante*, to quieten things down, the cello brusquely finishing the work with a G minor chord rooted on C.

McCabe's next string work could hardly have been more different: the February Sonatina for solo viola (1991) – the previous month having been allotted to clarinet in 1990. In a three-movements-in-one design, with a duration of some seven minutes, it was commissioned as a test piece for the 1991 Lionel Tertis International Viola Competition and Workshop. The vigorous opening section is based on a theme dominated by perfect and diminished fifths and the seventh and repeated notes. The slow central section gives prominence to the seventh and some gentle two-note oscillations; it was inspired 'both by the strength of tone of the viola and by the pounding of waves breaking on a rocky sea-shore, and the dispersal of their energy among the rocks'. Since then, McCabe's output of chamber music for strings has slowed, with just four works in the following fifteen years. However, each of these has been a major utterance, of substantial dimensions and scale, all four using combinations not previously seen in his output. First to appear was *Pilgrim*, for string sextet in the standard layout with pairs of violins, violas and cellos (1996; two years later he made a version for double string orchestra). It was commissioned by the Luton Music Club for the Raphael Ensemble and premiered by them in St George's Theatre, Luton, in February 1997, with follow-up performances later that week in Bedford and Leighton Buzzard.

The title suggests a connection with Bunyan's *The Pilgrim's Progress* and it was reading this great fable of personal self-discovery and perseverance that, as with seeing the Sutherland aquatints for the Fifth Quartet, prompted a musical response. 'It made a great impression', the composer has commented, 'not least because of its theme of a journey of self-discovery, and a rediscovery or renewal of faith. These are ideas which have a strong interest for me, not in religious terms but in their application to every aspect of human life (including great journeys), and this piece reflects my response in musical terms to this concern.' Once again, the music of this eighteen-minute single-span fantasia is in no way pictorial or illustrative of Bunyan's story; nor, in this instance, is any element of the work's construction related to any of its episodes. Nor is there any connection, musical or otherwise, with Vaughan Williams's wonderful operatic treatment, long though McCabe has been familiar with it (and despite his avowed reverence for its composer).

I
188
Vln I
Vln II
Vla
Vc
Db
ff
unis
div
brillante
198
203
pizz
mf
poco a poco cresc

Pilgrim is cast as a large slow movement with two contrasting faster episodes that, in the composer's words, function 'somewhat like the trio sections of a classical scherzo, save that the tempo relationships are inverted (the classical trios would have been slower, not quicker)'. The opening *Grave* presents the work's basic material, formed from repeated notes and intervals of the second and third, alternating between vertical chords with linear elaborations of them. As the tempo moves to *Andante*, first the violins, then violas and finally the cellos combine in gentle polyphony *con sordini*, gradually releasing the mutes as the textures become more impassioned. The first of the fast trio-sections, *Allegro deciso*, bursts in like a sudden shaft of light into a darkened room with a bounding dance-like momentum (not unlike early Copland) that is irresistible. The initial statements, marked at first *marcato e ritmico* and later *danzato*, are divided between two trios each comprising a violin, viola and cello, after which the sextet textures speed along in a constant state of flux. McCabe has commented how much of the thematic developments have an upward-striving motion and this is particularly noticeable in this section. The initial *Grave* tempo returns for the extended central section, which combines elements of the opening slow section's various components. It, too, contains upward-moving themes and is tangibly lighter in mood than the initial part of the sextet, although mid-way there are some decidedly *Verklärte Nacht*-like pizzicati. (If these represent a homage to Schoenberg it is not acknowledged by the composer.) The more relaxed second trio, *Allegro non troppo (un poco moderato)*, builds on these trends with themes comprised of wider leaps and intervals, with thirds, sevenths and (later) fourths prominent, culminating in an exquisitely dissonant web of overlaying quavers, triplets, semiquavers, quintuplets and sextuplets. The initial tempo returns to cap this main climax of the work and gradually resolve the various strands into a single luminous whole.

Three years after *Pilgrim*, McCabe produced a Sonata for cello and piano for the 1999 Presteigne Festival and the duo of Alice Neary and Gretel Dowdeswell. While concertos, string quartets and symphonies loom large in his output, McCabe has studiously avoided writing sonatas. This is only the third work of his to bear the title, although it is the closest of them to a late twentieth-century sonata-style composition. Its creation was, according to the composer, 'the fulfilment of a long-held ambition', and the resulting two-movement work is a fine example of his late style. It is also one of several satellite works from the ballet *Edward II*, in which the cello (to quote the composer) 'becomes the "voice" of Edward' in a couple of key moments. Although much of the Sonata's thematic material is drawn from *Opposite: Pilgrim, extract.*

111

the larger work, the main idea for the sonata pre-dates the stage work and actually gave rise to several motifs for the ballet, not all of them connected to the King. In any case, the motifs are reworked in ways so utterly unalike as to make any kinship between the two compositions masked to all but the keenest ears. (This makes the Sonata quite unlike the Fifth Symphony and *Fauvel's Rondeaux*, which make a virtue of recapturing elements of the ballet's special sound-worlds.)

The Cello Sonata plays continuously for a little less than fourteen minutes, with each of its two movements bearing a brief exposition-like introduction. Its compact form and cogent musical argument give it the weight of a work much larger than its apparently modest dimensions. The grim, grinding opening with its serpentine counterpoint unveils the basic intervals and motifs of the sonata which, as the music edges into the long opening slow movement, coalesce into distinct themes. The atmosphere becomes more lyrical by the half-way mark (about four minutes in to the whole); this is the heart of the work, the writing at its closest expressively to the music for Edward himself. However, at the sonata's mid-point the tempo increases with the rise of an urgent, insistent motif and rhythm (derived from the opening pages, nonetheless) and the second movement, a species of scherzo-finale, begins albeit that the introduction sports a more serious demeanour to what follows. After about a minute, a more vivacious, but not entirely untroubled, dance-like episode rattles in and continues to expand and develop. Its climax is the coda which resumes the first movement's initial statement and pulse; this quietens things down, leading to the final declamatory gesture, a harsh and varied recall of the opening bars.

McCabe's next chamber piece for strings was his third for piano quintet, but of an entirely different nature to either of its predecessors or, indeed, works such as *Pilgrim* and the Cello Sonata that immediately preceded it. As with the Fifth Quartet and *Pilgrim*, the inspiration for which lay partly in extra-musical sources, *The Woman by the Sea* (2001) was prompted by a visual stimulus, this time Kenji Mizoguchi's film *Sansho Dayu* (1954), a tragic story of a mother's two young children (a boy and girl) who are kidnapped and sold into slavery. A partial redemption occurs at the climax when the now adult son escapes and is reunited with his now blind and crippled mother. This is not the first time that cinema has so inspired the composer – the Second Symphony famously arose in part from Peckinpah's *The Wild Bunch* – but he has commented that

> [the] final scene with the image of the old, lonely woman outside her shack occasioned the mood and form of this work – there is

otherwise no attempt to portray the events or characters of the film. There is, however, a relationship with the sound of the woman's vain calling out of her children's names over the ocean, the sound of her calls transformed into two similar rising phrases heard soon after the opening in the violins (while the viola and cello repeat a semitonal figure derived from the violin fragments).

The Woman by the Sea is cast as a single, extended *Adagio molto*, with a contrasting central *Allegro molto* scherzo, which itself contains a lively trio. The opening sounds like loneliness made tangible in sound, the keening, upwardly striving string lines offset by the dull thud of a three-note cluster in the piano's bass. Harmonics and snapped, Bartókian pizzicati add to the starkness of the music as it alternates between tortured polyphony and ethereal calm in a claustrophobic tonal landscape defined by seemingly impotent tension. Repeated-note figures break in to try to force a harmonic solution, giving way to a piano cadenza after which the scherzo-like central section breaks out, *pianissimo*, like a breath of fresh air. The contrasting trio section seems more regular in pulse but in fact alternates metres of 6/16, 5/16 and 9/16; its stream of semiquavers, however, increase the sense of light and hope breaking in on the tragic world of the opening. Eventually, however, the headlong progress runs into a wall, perhaps suggestive of the huge amount of time lost by the mother and her children due to their separation (the daughter, in fact, is dead). The return of the opening *Adagio molto* tempo in a spectral coda functions more as a development of the opening than a reprise, as if the slow movement had continued unheard behind the scherzo while the latter occupied centre stage front. *The Woman by the Sea* was commissioned by Peter Mallet of Art SPACE (the Society for the Promotion of Arts and Culture Euro-Japan).

The textural language of *The Woman by the Sea* is markedly different from much of McCabe's previous output and his most recent piece is different again: the fifteen-minute violin duo *Spielend* (2003). The title is German and translates as 'playing', and there was undoubtedly a sense of fun and sport behind its conception. Playing here refers not just to performing but to engaging in a race – the two players often 'seem to be having a contest to see who can finish the themes first, or who can divert the other's attention to a new texture or rhythm', as the composer has put it. And there may also be an element of self-portrait in the slow central movement, which 'plays around' with elements from Poulenc's Violin Sonata mirroring the way McCabe himself explores music, culminating in an eight-part fugue. A 'kind of extended musical pun', to quote the composer again, *Spielend* is in three sections, playing continuously and with a surprise ending which 'may catch the unwary listener by surprise'.

McCabe has plans for further chamber works but, not being one to compose for his bottom drawer, will wait for commissions to realise these ideas onto paper. These include at least two further string quartets the formats of which are already taking shape in his mind, and it is high time he returned to the medium at which he has excelled. His chamber catalogue may already contain many works of profound beauty and great technical resource but, at 67, the composer may yet have his best work to come.

6

Composing processes

An interview with John McCabe

George Odam

John McCabe is almost alone amongst his peers as an active composer in regular receipt of commissions, and as a piano recitalist playing a wide range of the classical canon plus much contemporary work, with a large and growing catalogue of recordings, as can be seen later in this book. He also works as a writer, scholar and critic and spends much time and energy organising and promoting live performance of classical music in his home area of Kent. The model of the musician that he presents is one that is resonant of much of the current thinking about the training and professional life of musicians, who now need to be diverse enough in their skills to be able to navigate through the rocky waters of commercialism of the arts. As such, he provides a guiding light for young musicians in professional training.

But the satisfaction that he gains from a depth of experience as both creator and performer, and the deep and rich insights this provides, reaches back to before the obsession with specialism that began to emerge at the time of the western European industrial revolution. This more diverse and better integrated model of the professional musician would easily have been recognised by Mozart, Beethoven and generations of composers before them, for whom performing and composing naturally interacted and nourished each other. McCabe has never followed fashionable composition schools nor sought to establish a niche for himself personally by retreating from society into technological, scientific or religious mysticism, or hermetic solitude, but has remained a working musician who is a firm and vigorous champion of his fellow musicians and, perhaps somewhat influenced by his grandfather's example, engages actively and willingly in promoting his chosen art widely within the society in which he lives and acts as a tireless champion of British music through his own playing, recording and writing.

I have been privileged to know John McCabe for the whole of his professional life both as a composer and pianist. In both roles some of the hallmarks of his work have been a consistency of purpose, amazing technical skill and attention to detail plus an engaging modesty and willingness to communicate. As a pianist he has always been adventurous in choice of repertoire, which a glance at his solo discography on p. 227 will reveal. Many popular features of the nineteenth-century classic/romantic canon are noticeably absent, but British composers are well represented along with a good smattering of those from America. Mozart is there, Beethoven is absent, but the outstanding entry is under Haydn. His recital programmes, of course, explore a much wider territory, including Beethoven, Schubert, Rachmaninov, Ravel and Liszt, Schoenberg and Webern, and Elizabethan keyboard music. In the discography, alongside Haydn, the names of Rawsthorne, Nielsen and Satie also figure strongly. One obvious thing connecting this otherwise somewhat diverse collection of composers is the obvious and delightful sense of humour conveyed through their music, ranging from quirky and eccentric to the most generous and playful of human communication. McCabe's playing brings out these qualities superbly through his incisive clarity of tone and instinctive understanding of the structural, dynamic and harmonic frameworks, and his command of the necessary technical resources to accentuate them.

It has always been of interest to me that humour, this instinctive fundamental in human communication, is far less to the fore in his compositions than contact with the man might suggest. During a recent interview with him, on which the largest part of this article is based, I asked him directly whether his sense of humour appears in his compositions. With an amused chuckle he immediately retorted, 'No!' Over the past 40 years, a keen sense of humour has characterised our correspondence and conversation and this produces for me a very interesting paradox when writing an article in which I am trying to investigate some of the sources of his composing style and to convey, using as many of his own words as I can, how he goes about composing. Later in the interview he stated:

A sense of humour, which has been a strong element in English composers that have influenced me, like Rawsthorne, Vaughan Williams and Walton, doesn't really appear much in my music. Perhaps the most light-hearted piece I have written was *The Shadow of Light*, which is in homage to the music of William Boyce on his tercentenary. It's a bit like *Chagall Windows* in that it has groups of movements. There are three sports and I worked out a collection of topics that would be roughly relevant to William Boyce's time, like certain kinds of sports, aspects of life of the time. I saw the whole thing as a dream of his time and I looked through a lot of his scores and used several of his tunes. It ends with a fugue that brings back a lot of the earlier bits. Throughout the piece there are episodes of dream music that return at the end as the piece fades away. Interestingly, that piece has drawn such sharply contrasting critical comment, both for and against, that I wondered whether they had been listening to the same piece!

Consistency of purpose remains a distinguishing feature of his compositions. A few bars of a newly composed piece immediately establish a personality that has been unchanging and is easily recognisable. Few mature modern composers have displayed more indifference to changing fashions during an age of exceptional change than John McCabe. Although his music of the 1970s and 1980s did progress through a period where the influence of Second Viennese composers and their acolytes became more discernible, serialism had been an interest of McCabe's as a university student or even before. As a fellow university student in the 1950s, I was most grateful for his tuition in this strange new area, mention of which was suppressed throughout our three-year course, although the Alban Berg Violin Concerto did appear on the final year curriculum taught by one of the more progressive younger members of staff. Fashion in both classical music and popular culture has affected McCabe little, although he has always been and remains keenly aware of new trends in the arts.

Over the years his palette of musical colours has remained consistent and his choice of musical marks have become distinguishing features. In all, this makes for music that is highly accessible, and has allowed this composer to work across many genres and media including television and film. McCabe is always aware of the needs of the musicians who perform his music and never challenges either performers or listeners just for the sake of it. The story of his entry into the highly traditional world of the brass band is spelt out in Paul Hindmarsh's chapter. Despite a perceived challenge to both performers and audience, both have eventually found his music highly accessible and his work has become standard repertoire. His aim has always been to provide something that will stretch and enlarge musical experience without challenging either so seriously that either players and listeners are lost. His music in all other areas continues to display the same quality, and part of his success – as witness the continuing stream of commissions, performances and recordings – lies in this ability always to be himself.

During the interview we touched on many aspects of his work, the first of which was structure. McCabe declared that:

> … on the whole I do take a somewhat schematic approach to composition. For instance, in the composition of *Rainforest I* the opening of the piece is like a declaration of a huge chord which is built downwards note by note at the start of the piece and in fact is released note by note upwards at the end.
>
> This is how the first section is constructed, until the entry of the string quartet group which is very spectacular because they haven't played for the first five minutes but then suddenly come in very loudly. Up to that point the chord has been built downwards and each instrument has their own note and plays around it and then moves on to a second note. This is then taken over by a second instrument and the first one moves back to its original note and the whole chord is built up like that. All those little melismas in the piece, sometimes with a narrow compass and sometimes with a wider compass, all centre around the note that each instrument in particular is dealing with at that time. This continues until we've worked downwards to the bottom of the chord and then there's a crescendo and finally the string quartet comes in and it moves on. I regard this as a very schematic way of doing things and this is a very typical way for me to create.
>
> I do think naturally in terms of schemes and I like to work them through. The central idea of *Rainforest I* was that rainforest chord which I remember writing down first. I thought about it for a while. That scheme and the way that I handled it came to me afterwards, so a scheme is not always the first thing that I think about. But then sometimes it is!
>
> In *Time and the River* it was the idea of tempo change and a gradual slowing down and gradual speeding up that did occur to me really as the first idea. The other idea was the tonal thing going from D to G sharp and then back again.

Early in his career as he was beginning to establish his harmonic palette, it was often his custom to use the working out of chordal structures as one of the devices to get himself going. The Second Piano Concerto, for instance, stems from three chords. But McCabe does not rely solely on the harmonic approach and feels that it all depends on how he wants to express the initial idea, in terms of roughly writing something down. Sometimes he

Opposite: Rainforest I,
opening.

118

To Charles Wadsworth and the Chamber Music Society of Lincoln Center.

RAINFOREST I

John McCabe
1984

* Written in C (i.e. as sounding)
© Novello & Company 1984

will start with a series of chords and sometimes it's just a verbal description. Sometimes it's a tune or perhaps just a rhythm.

He certainly doesn't like to repeat the same sort of structure each time. But there are things that do recur, and he points out that almost every one of his major works is continuous, and that he finds it very difficult to have gaps between movements. McCabe states that this is why he next wants to write a symphony in four movements just because he has never done it. Cycles also interest him – as, for instance, in *Chagall Windows* – and he sees cyclical form as a very human thing. McCabe philosophises that humanity always does the same things and repeatedly makes the same mistakes, evidence of which we see all over the world again and again. He complains that politicians continue to make the same mistakes and to kill people as a result and that we never seem to learn from the past. Conversely we draw a lot of inspiration from the past, and this is a very curious two-edged process that fascinates him.

> In *Chagall Windows*, windows one and twelve are next-door to each other and form a natural circle in the synagogue where they are located, so that is a given formal process. As I looked around I straight away decided that the music had to be continuous, although it might actually be in groups of sections rather like symphonic movements, rather than appearing as series of twelve character pieces. The end reflected the beginning. So there is an implied symphonic structure in the work which is similar to the form of *Notturni ed Alba*.

The fascination for cyclic structures had been there for a long time, and McCabe has recently reminded me of a letter I wrote to him after the premiere of *Notturni ed Alba* in which I reminded him of a walk we had taken together beside a Manchester canal as students when we discussed a piece that he wished to write based on a dusk-to-dawn sequence. *Notturni ed Alba* is such a dusk-to-dawn piece, which emphasises renewal. It has a scherzo that begins with percussion only, and it has a big central slow movement and a first movement that is moderately slow. But it also has a quick section in the middle so its symphonic form is not clear-cut, although there are four sections with a big finale.

We touched on the vexed old subject of symphonic structure. His sixth symphony – Symphony on a Pavane – was given its premiere in early 2007, and at least two others are planned, so he must have ideas about what constitutes symphonic form. However, he said:

I don't think there is such a thing as an ideal symphonic structure. I think Mahler's Second Symphony is a wonderful symphony and so is the Sixth, but I'm not so happy about some of the others. Berlioz's *Symphonie fantastique* is a marvellous symphony, but then so is Debussy's *La Mer*, which is, of course, not called a symphony at all, but is in my view one of the greatest of symphonies. How he builds a complete symphony on two notes without anybody noticing is quite remarkable! I agree with Robert Simpson's definition of the symphony and that is that it must travel. I agree with this basic premise which is that if something must travel it must go somewhere. You can't really have a formal definition of symphonic structure. How can you say that Sibelius Seventh Symphony is more of a symphony than Berlioz's *Fantastique* or Mahler's Sixth or even Webern's Symphony?

This led to the related subject of the symphonic poem:

Fire at Durilgai is a symphonic poem and it is very much like Sibelius' *Pohjola's Daughter*, although it doesn't sound like it! *Notturni* is also a concerto for solo soprano and orchestra. There isn't a cadenza – or actually there is a kind of unaccompanied cadenza. Some critics in the past have suggested that *Pohjola's Daughter* is in fact a symphony, although I don't agree with that. The connection with symphonic style lies in the size and scope of the ideas within them, but there is no actual generic symphonic structure, otherwise how would you cope with Sibelius 7th?

McCabe had recently been writing an article on Carl Nielsen's piano music that required a good deal of analysis. He realised that something that specially appealed to him about Nielsen's music is that Nielsen's process is very frequently quite irrational, but that the strange thing is that you can see exactly why this is so. McCabe sees this as most curious because the irrational shouldn't reveal itself rationally! But in his view, Nielsen manages to do both. McCabe sees this as the subconscious element in composition coming out. However organised a piece is, and much of Nielsen's music is very closely organised, the irrational is the spontaneity that scientists still find such a great difficulty in building into robots.

Vaughan Williams had a very pragmatic approach to composition when he said that he didn't sit down and think it out first and relied instead on the inner process, on instinct. That is very much my way of working. I like to have some scheme in mind, quite often rigorously applied but not always, but what goes on between the bricks so to speak, is entirely dependent on instinct, and I have material in my mind that I constantly rearrange, but I will find myself doing something completely unrelated that merely seemed a good idea at the time.

McCabe likens the composing process to the more common and everyday experience of getting on a bus, where all we need to have is a very clear idea of where we're going, although we really do need to know that we are getting on the right one! So a composer needs to know where he or she is going, and McCabe solves this musically by writing the beginning and the ending of the piece quite early in the process, just so that he knows where he is going, and this helps him to know that the whole piece lies somewhere between them. After that writing it down is simply a process of getting it out of the brain. Some days are bad days and only a bar and a half may be written, and on other days the writing flows. Following this procedure allows him to construct small and often separate sections, building pieces

Examples of sketch materials used by John McCabe in the composing process.

of a compositional patchwork, and then gradually assembling them into a whole. For McCabe this has been by far the best way of working because it allows him to work quickly. If one section proves to be a problem he always knows that there is another section that he can move to, returning later to finish the problem section, and allowing the other problems to sort themselves out without him thinking directly about them.

I never really remember how I constructed a piece some years after the event. When it's been performed and checked through, and maybe corrected, that's the end of it, and it's out of my hands and no longer belongs to me, as it were.

Variations have figured strongly as a chosen structural matrix in John McCabe's music, from the early Hartmann Variations onwards.

I have always loved variation form, since back in childhood with the Brahms St Anthony and also the Tchaikovsky Theme and Variations from the Suite No. 3, which I still think is a magnificent work, and one

of the first recordings that I had was of the Liverpool Philharmonic playing it. And then, of course, the Rawsthorne Symphonic Studies were a very early influence. Playing piano recitals I have done programmes that are entirely built on variations of different kinds: chaconne, passacaglia and so forth. It's such a wonderful form because you can do anything you like with it. I did, however, manage to annoy an American musicologist by claiming that my Concerto for Orchestra was an extension of the passacaglia. Variation form is very much playing with notes, almost like a sport. I suppose this is another connection with Englishness, since we are known as a sporting nation, even if not a very good one some of the time, and variations figure largely in the output of English composers. But that doesn't explain why variations figure so largely in the work of German composers. Some of Max Reger's best pieces are variations, and the Telemann variations and the Mozart variations are wonderful pieces. Partly, I guess, it has to do with containment, because the theme actually directs the progress of the piece. Britten's *The Turn of the Screw* is a wonderful piece of variation form, and it is the only piece I can think of where an A major chord is genuinely tragic, whereas normally A major has more of a springtime feel.

Examples of sketch materials used by John McCabe in the composing process

We talked about stimulus and inspiration. As an internationally respected composer and performer, McCabe has travelled widely in the USA and Australia, and the Near East as a resident academic or to give concert recitals. He has often taken these opportunities to experience a variety of landscapes at first hand. The title of this book, *Landscapes of the Mind*, was suggested by McCabe himself, and helps the listener to understand that links with the natural world are very important to him as a composer. He stated:

> The stimulus can be a literary one and I'm certainly very much inspired by landscapes, actual, described in books and imagined. Visits to rainforests, deserts and canyons have all been creatively stimulating. *Fire at Durilgai* is inspired by two books but also, of course, it also draws me back to my burns in childhood. I fell in the fire at the age of three and I was very badly burned and couldn't even be moved to hospital. The odd thing is that I absolutely adore fires! And you would really think that I would be terrified of them and have an aversion for fires. But I really love them, and I'm very sorry that we are not now allowed to have bonfires in our garden because I was very good at making them – although I'm not a pyromaniac! I love the way that fires develop and I'm fascinated by the way that the current of fire moves from one place to another, and the sheer natural force of this great element of fire. In *Fire at Durilgai* there are two literary fire sources. One is *Desperate Remedies* by Thomas Hardy, his first extant book, the other is *The Tree of Man* by Patrick White. They both have descriptions of monumental fires, as indeed, so does Hardy's *Far from the Madding Crowd*. Durilgai is a fictional estate in New South Wales in Australia and the big house is burnt down. There is a fantastic description of the side of this house finally collapsing as a result of this fire; and the fire itself is immensely important in the lives of the characters themselves. I found this a really very moving description and it describes very nearly my own experience and feelings about fire, as does the Hardy. That's why I decided that I needed to write a fire piece, and the Patrick White description of the beginning and development of the fire is so evocative and that's really where my starting point came from.

Opposite: Fire at Durilgai, *extract.*

The reference above to the period of childhood and early adolescence is a recurring theme in his work, and McCabe's impressively encyclopaedic knowledge of literature stems from this period very early on in his life,

124

when reading was the main window into the outside world to a child much confined to his house, laid low by illness and lacking the regular stimulation of school friends and teachers. The landscapes created in his imagination at that time, and the liberating sense of freedom provided by recuperation in the real and superlative hills and lakes of Cumbria at the age of nine, lie at the core of his experience and are constantly recreated in his music.

> I have always been fascinated by Australia ever since I was a child reading about the Burke and Wills expedition, which was a great mess but a heroic effort. When I was about 10 years old I was lent a lavishly illustrated copy of the diaries of that expedition and it was full of detailed descriptions of the desert that gave me a binding interest in desert landscapes of all kinds. Going to Australia to perform rekindled my strong interest from childhood. I have also been fascinated by the American landscape not only of deserts, but also of the great canyons of the south west. I also loved visiting the deserts in Kuwait and Saudi Arabia. That was the first time that I had been out into the desert proper, and it was really fascinating even though it was only for day trips. Landscapes can be a trigger for composition for me and provide an atmosphere and sometimes even specific sounds. The opening of *Horizon*, for instance, was triggered by shifting grains of sand and a chord patterns change and build-up with repeated patterns on a chord and then a new chord that comes underneath – a cluster effect – with the sort of dominant seventh coming in underneath it. And that all came from the idea of grains of sand shifting. But on the whole there's nothing very specific, it's just atmosphere. It probably linked in with my predilection for quiet endings because of the vastness of desert landscapes, disappearing into the distance.

One of the comments that recurs regularly in reviews and commentaries of McCabe's work is the quality of Englishness. The most recent works have yet again given rise to such comments. At the time of writing, the issues of what constitutes Britishness and within that what are the identifying attributes of Englishness have become part of current political dialogue. The devolution of powers to Scotland and Wales since the mid-1990s has led to a heightened awareness in the English of their culture and values, brought into sharp focus by rapidly expanding immigration and the demand for induction into the host culture and how this should be defined. Although McCabe denies that there is such an identifiable quality as 'Englishness', he concedes that perhaps quiet endings may be a clue.

126

It is also quite an English thing. I really can't think of another nation that has produced a lot of great music which so often depends on an epilogue. Even with such a positive composer as Vaughan Williams, so many of his symphonies either end quietly or have an epilogue which ends quietly. The Sixth Symphony doesn't have an epilogue but it ends quietly. Everyone has their theory about which key Vaughan Williams Sixth Symphony finishes in and most think it is E minor, but I often think that it is E flat major.

One of the dominant features of English history is that it has constantly been invaded. I suppose my devotion to English music, English literature and English culture in general is possibly a way of affirming my Englishness since I am only part English, having had a German mother. I do play a lot of the music of Alun Hoddinott, who is definitely not English, and, as it happens, Welsh is the one thing I am not. But we must never forget the Angles and the Saxons and the Irish colonising of North Wales, the Normans and the official language being French for quite a long time. This probably does lead to a feeling of insecurity about identity. But Englishness as a quality is intangible. It is tangible when it's folk song, but we're not talking about that. That's something I've hardly ever done except for folk-song settings. There is a nostalgic sense of loss that is prevalent in a great deal of English music. Sometimes it can be enormously depressing as in Peter Warlock's *The Curlew*, but I do enjoy Constant Lambert's Piano Sonata, and I think that *Summer's Last Will and Testament* is a wonderful piece.

The conversation finally turned towards audience reaction and accessibility. Although McCabe uses tonal harmony and relies on layering and ostinati as points of aural focus, he uses an added note dissonance that is highly distinctive and personal, giving all his music a colour bias that is attractive and engages the ear.

The dissonance that I like to use has evolved over the years and is a sort of bitonality. What is significant is that the composers whose music affects me harmonically are people like Alan Rawsthorne and William Schuman, Hartmann in his earlier symphonies and, possibly, Hindemith. I love certain jazz and I particularly like certain jazz artists such as Stan Getz, Gil Evans, Miles Davis and Stan Tracey. I very much enjoy West Coast jazz from the 1950s which everybody says is very bland and I suppose it is. Harmonically, I have certainly been influenced by those jazz musicians' added note structures. But I still like that because of the ease of the patterns and the lightness of the music, but I am not a fan of Traditional jazz.

Quite early on I became interested in classical Indian music through the influence of Messiaen, and later, when we moved to live in Southall, London, which is a big Indian community, my interest was reawakened. Our first neighbours were a young Indian couple, who played the sitar and the tabla. They invited us one evening for a recital and an Indian meal, which I much enjoyed because I had already become interested in Indian music and had several long-playing records. I must say that I get very depressed by the whole Bollywood thing, where it seems to me that you get the worst of both worlds, of Indian music and western pop music. The pop-music industry in our country has bought up all the space in the media and put an enormous amount of money into it. I have found some of the linking through into popular music by some composers too self-conscious, but if your mind is open all the time to new experiences you will find things that will renew you. It was drumming in the popular music of the 60s which did influence me strongly, groups like The Four Seasons, but it wasn't the harmonic or melodic content and was just the drumming. Nowadays you can't avoid hearing pop music which is one of the reasons why I don't listen to it! If something is very fashionable I automatically react against it!

McCabe has always considered that his music would be fairly accessible to a wider public, but more recently he has noticed that people have begun to find works such as *Notturni* and *Chagall Windows* more difficult. He believes that this reflects the times we live in, and the amount of extremely easy music that is programmed and supported through the media at the moment, for which he has very little respect.

Over the last century, dissonance has always been a central issue between composers and audiences and there has been a certain amount of amelioration of dissonance in my music in more recent years, but this has had nothing to do with audiences and changes in fashion. People have always liked light music, but these days you can get symphonies which are really light music pieces. They call them symphonies, but they are actually light music and often not very good light music at that. There are very few people around of the calibre of composers like Eric Coates who were able to write with immense imagination and not fall into the trap of four bars at a time. I happen to like symmetry, but it is very dangerous because it is so predictable. What you have to do is to steer a course between being symmetrical and asymmetrical. But knowing exactly when to surprise the audience and when not to do it is the art, and Vaughan Williams knew exactly how to do it and Walton too. Even if he uses four-bar periods, right at the end of it he will have a modulating chord and not just a sit-down chord, and his tunes go on forever! I always tell students to look at the trio from Walton's *Richard III*, the big *nobilmente* march tune, because at the end of every phrase there is something that links you on again and it's not just a device, it's a real positive force. The element of surprise is important to human beings.

McCabe commented on the way that he feels that critics and promoters today push forward young composers into the limelight for very brief periods and that, under this pressure, all of them sound the same. Over the twentieth century the recording industry and concert promoters have strengthened the cult of virtuosity for its own sake. The insistence on performance difficulty has been an element that has helped to increase the gap between composers and audiences. McCabe has always felt that is very important to write bearing the players in mind and that this is an essential part of the craft of orchestration.

They must not feel that the music is written by someone who hates the instrument. I have played music in the past by people who seem to hate the piano, and it's really not a lot of fun. In composers like Beethoven or possibly Tippett, the ideas are so strong that that is how they have to be, and an awkwardness sometimes results. But I'm not interested in difficulty for its own sake. The orchestra is my instrument, just as the piano is, and I regard the piano as an orchestra. I have always loved percussion and even as a child I was very impressed by it. I remember hearing the performance of *Gayaneh* on the radio in a Music for Schools broadcast and I got a score of that very early on. I have always loved percussion and adored the sound of it. So has always been natural for me to regard the percussion department as a normal part of the orchestra like strings. When I sketch things the percussion music has an equal prominence in the sketch.

In the more experimental music of the second half of the twentieth century fragmentation of line and structure, that were prevalent in the last century, simply have not really interested McCabe, although he made one piano piece, *Gaudí*, that explores a similar area.

> I was very much interested in one of Stockhausen's *Klavierstücke* and I had in mind writing a big rondo with lots of different episodes. So I took a piece of card and I wrote a tune on it and pasted it up in the way that Stockhausen did, and then I decided to improvise the piece. Normally I don't improvise but I did improvise that piece. I labelled them a, b, c, etc. and when it seemed to me that I had a satisfactory sequence I would just write down a, b, c, etc. and then I would move on to the rest of the piece. But it took longer than writing normally does. But I like the piece and I think it's quite a successful piece because hopefully some of that spontaneity comes through.

Concluding this discussion of derivations and processes we returned to the subject of landscapes and their equivalence in the visual arts.

> I don't really think about music in terms of colour and I have no synaesthetic experience. There are some composers, such as Frank Martin, whose work I enjoy enormously, who sound monochrome to me and that in turn affects my understanding of their emotional world. With a composer like Roussel, who is not flamboyant at all, but a wonderful orchestrator (for instance, the mystical symphonies and *Evocations*, which is a wonderful early work for chorus and orchestra) there is a colouristic world in there that I respond to very much. But it is not a very obvious one. Although the Pop Art movement has been fun, and the paintings are nice to look at, I much prefer the work of someone like Mark Rothko, and I find myself really drawn into his painting. Walk into any art gallery anywhere in the world and the first thing you will see is an imitation of Mark Rothko or possibly a blank canvas! Graham Sutherland is one of my favourite painters. Someone like Damien Hirst, who is a very good businessman, is finding a different way of painting figuratively. The exaggerated expressionism of somebody like Francis Bacon doesn't really appeal to me either in painting or in music.
>
> There is a loose kind of comparison between figurative landscape painting using a central vanishing point and tonal music, and even in the earlier serially based compositions of mine, you can always detect a tonal centre at any given point. But I didn't organise tonality very strongly except in certain given works. It has returned more strongly

130

in later works, for instance *Of Time and the River* and *Edward II*, indeed all the ballets, are very tonal in terms of organisation. No matter what the harmony is like, the tonal centres are still very strong and pretty much organised.

The most recent works, the richly coloured Symphony on a Pavane and the romantic and spacious Horn Concerto (*Rainforest IV*) with its prelude and epilogue, strongly continue the above themes and demonstrate well McCabe's continuing and developing vision skill and inspiration.

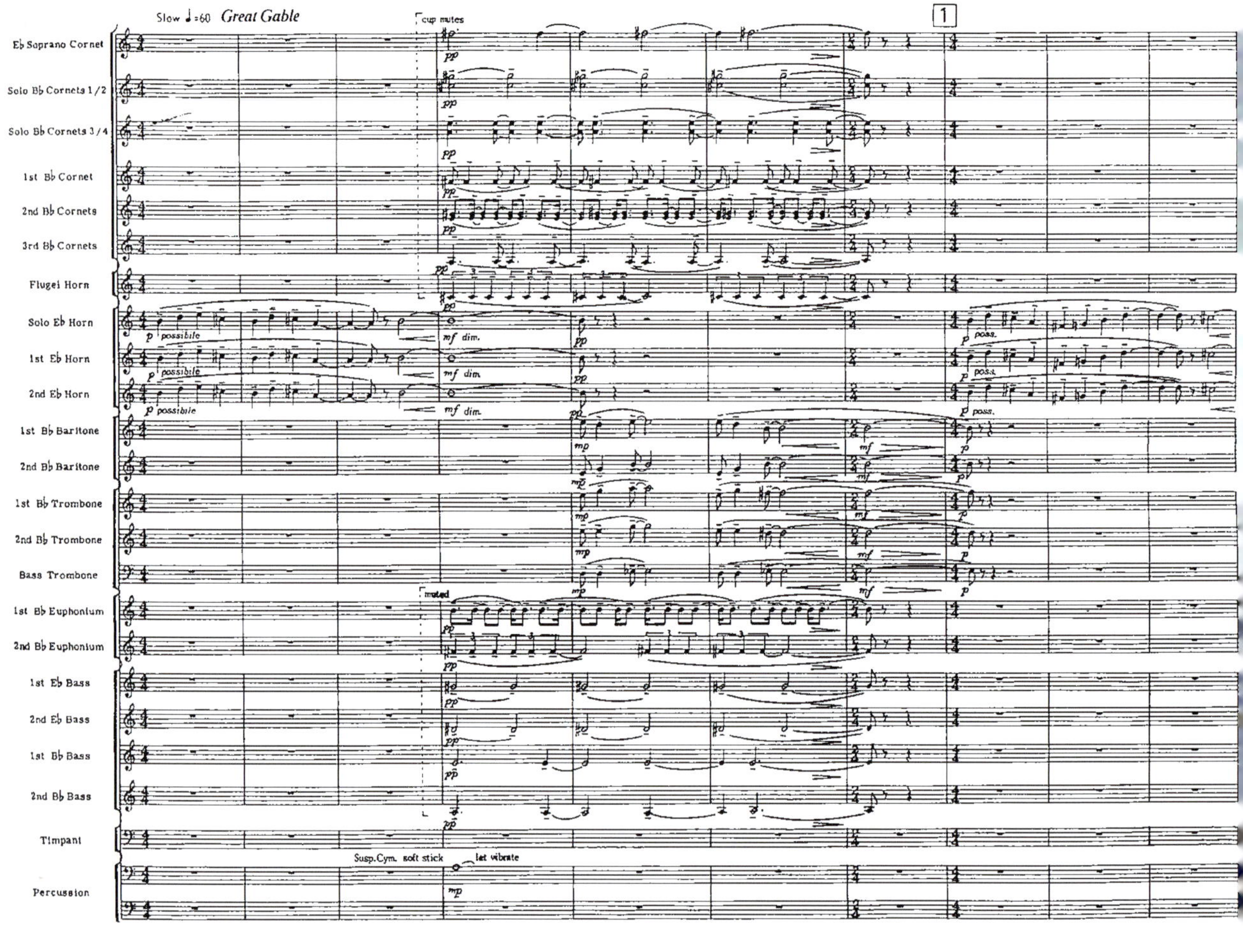

Cloudcatcher Fells *for Brass Band* (Great Gable), *opening.*

7

The music for brass and wind

Paul Hindmarsh

Although John McCabe has found the sound worlds of wind and brass 'endlessly fascinating', he has written for bands and ensembles only when he has felt he had something fresh to say: 'There's no point in writing something that you're not interested in.'[1] There are just ten major works for brass and wind band, constituting a comparatively small but significant contribution to the repertoire. McCabe's standing within the brass band community is particularly high. He is considered to be an innovator in his approach to sound and structure – with a reputation that exceeds many of the more prolific brass band specialists. This is due in large measure to the continued success of *Cloudcatcher Fells* (1985). It remains a much cherished work in the brass repertoire of the late twentieth century and is arguably one of his most often performed works, given the number of times it is used as a test piece in brass band competitions. The five wind band works (including the wind version of *Images*) are spread over almost 30 years, from the tightly organised Symphony for Ten Wind Instruments (1964) and the elegant simplicity of Canzona for Wind and Percussion (1971) to the more expansive canvasses of *Canyons* (1991) and *Rainforest III – Dandenongs* (1991). The six brass band works (including the expansion of the ensemble piece *Desert II – Horizon*) are spread over almost 25 years, from the illusive abstractions of *Images* (1978) via the evocative musical landscapes of *Cloudcatcher Fells* to the impressive solemnity of *The Maunsell Forts* (2002).

Images is a pivotal work standing between the handful of purely abstract early works and those later ones revealing McCabe's response to landscape. Common to them all, however, is his unorthodox approach to texture and timbre, brought about by the blurring of conventional distinctions between orchestral and chamber 'voicing'. All the larger band works contain

1 John McCabe, 'Portraits in Brass', BBC Radio 3, 1992, produced by Paul Hindmarsh.

extensive passages of chamber-like interplay. The wind orchestra offers a more extensive and subtler palette that the brass band, but McCabe exploits to the full the colour contrasts between all the instrumental families – low brass versus high woodwind or cornets, double reeds versus 'blown' instruments, as in the early Symphony or many passages in the brass band works. Elsewhere he blends instrumental timbres in unexpected, ear-catching ways, as in the melodic heterophony or shadowing in *Rainforest III* and the blend of high euphonium and muted cornet in 'Grisdale Tarn', the third section of *Cloudcatcher Fells*. In this respect McCabe could be described as a rather 'painterly' composer, searching out subtle details and tones that are layered over a firm, but constantly shifting, background. Each work is very different in concept, colour and construction, but there are a number of governing principles of form and argument common to them all.

Themes and melodies tend to revolve around pivotal or repeating phrases, fashioned from small intervals: tones, semitones, major and minor thirds and – most characteristically of all, perhaps – the augmented fourth or tritone. In this context, the impact of ideas that range more widely or take on a more angular aspect is decisive, as in parts of *Rounds* or *The Maunsell Forts*. The broader musical processes are tightly organised, with seemingly contrasting material appearing out of and sharing the same musical 'DNA', and governing both melodic and harmonic characteristics. They unfold through repetition, overlapping textures, and temporal and textural layering, including a range of contrapuntal, especially canonic, and mirror devices. These are elements that the Polish master Witold Lutosławski might have written down in his unbarred boxes. Indeed, there are three instances in the wind and brass music when McCabe uses the 'Lutosławski' boxes for atmospheric effect – the start and close of *Desert II* and *Canyons* and a brief passage for the cornets in *Images* – but he prefers to maintain control of momentum, proportion and formal balance through the convention of bar lines. The effect of the layered textures and metres is frequently intensified by the superimposition of independent chord formations and progressions, blurring the underlying sense of key with polytonal colour. The opening bars of *Images* and the broad cantabile section in 'Angle Tarn' (*Cloudcatcher Fells*) are clear examples.

McCabe writes his music down rather in the same way that Elgar did, not necessarily taking 'route one' from kick-off to goal, but in a more circuitous way: 'Once I'm ready to go, I want to get as much on paper as possible. I can't do what some composers do and write from A to Z in a straight line – I'm more inclined to write in a mosaic fashion, as if it were all the blue bits this week, all the red bits next and so on.'[2] For example,

2 Quoted in Christopher Thomas, 'The 4barsrest Interview', 2005, available online at www.4barsrest.com.

134

'Angle Tarn' was the first part of *Cloudcatcher Fells* to be written down. This piecemeal approach goes hand-in-hand with the multi-layered and mosaic-like structures that he devised for each of the big wind works. Sir Michael Tippett developed a rigorous mosaic process in the late 1950s and early 60s; his second Piano Sonata and Concerto for Orchestra are the two seminal works. McCabe's approach – inspired to some extent by Tippett's example, perhaps – is less formulaic. McCabe's formal outlines are also multi-faceted, with arch-like, single movements enclosing, in various ways, the range of expression and activity of a multi-movement work. The early Symphony for Ten Wind Instruments follows a tightly controlled scheme of six short interrelated movements, which flow seamlessly into each other. Two of them are further subdivided into three shorter episodes. This framework ingeniously provides contrasts of ensemble and soloistic interest, plus an element of exposition and symmetrical reprise.

Symphony for Ten Wind Instruments
Commissioned by the Portia Wind Ensemble; first performance December 1964, Wigmore Hall, London.
2 flutes; 2 oboes; 2 clarinets; 2 bassoons; 2 horns

TUTTI 1 – Allegro: [A B A form] This is a short, energetic 'primary subject', juxtaposing running melodic figuration, formed from characteristic out-of-sequential and repeated semitones and thirds with a bolder, syncopated ostinato chord sequence.

SOLO 1 – Lento: This dialogue between flute and clarinet, built out of elegantly conceived melismas and triadic arabesques, could be thought of as a 'second subject'. It is supported by slow and stately chordal accompaniment from the other instruments.

TUTTI 2 – Vivo: A rapid scherzo in 5, built on a 3+2 repeating pulse, is gradually overlain by a more sustained melody high on oboe and flute and based on the same intervals as Tutti 1 [A]. As the ostinato disintegrates the melody begins to assert its quiet dominance throughout the ensemble in little canonic trios.

LENTO: A tri-partite slow movement. In GROUPS, the soloistic interest – based on a rhetorical 'scotch snap' – gradually opens out from mid-range horns and oboes into a 'call and response' dialogue between the double reeds [oboes and bassoons] and the non-reeds [flutes and horns]. This gathers momentum into TUTTI 3, the very brief but highly dramatic central climax of the whole work, which then subsides into TRIOS – four short canonic paragraphs reviewing the principal musical ideas heard so far. Flutes and one oboe ruminate on the opening flute theme [B], clarinets and one bassoon reflect calmly on the Tutti 3 music, the horns and other bassoon take a fresh look at the scherzo melody, and finally flute, oboe and cor anglais reprise the lento theme.

TUTTI 4 – Vivo: The return journey begins with another three-part movement, beginning with a ferocious scherzo derived in part from the ostinato pattern heard at the start [Tutti 1, B]. The energy gradually dissipates into CONTRASTS – a short transition where triplet and arpeggiated fragments from Tutti 4 are heard high on piccolo and low down on bass clarinet. TUTTI 5 is an altered and forceful reprise of Tutti 1.

LENTO: This extended coda begins with SOLO 2 – a new version of the 'second subject' given to horn and bassoon – and the symphonic arch is brought to a poignant close with a reminiscence of music from the heart of the work – Groups and Trios.

The following year, 1965, McCabe was invited by his publishers to contribute to a series of publications for amateur instrumentalists – *Music for Today*. His offering was a little Fantasy Op. 35, for a quartet of two trumpets, french horn and tenor trombone. In keeping with the brief, it is a modest score. The individual parts lie comfortably within their mid-range, and the four-part ensemble texture persists unrelieved throughout in treble, alto, tenor and baritone 'voices', with no overlapping and few rests. The notes would even lie easily under the fingers of a young pianist wanting something other than Bartók's *Mikrokosmos* to play. Within these constraints, however, the four miniature movements are clearly differentiated in tempo and character, and as a simple example illustrating how McCabe builds his musical fabric this could not be clearer. A brief *Introduction*, beginning on open fifths, sets out a simple linear phrase, which is passed down the ensemble like a relay or round. This becomes the theme for a lilting 9/8 *Pastorale*. The energy and bite of the dances in *Mikrokosmos* springs to mind in the *Capriccio*, with its awkward but persistent 11/8 gait and its obstinate chordal 'trio'. At the close of the short *Corale*, all four players get the chance to play the first phrase in canon as a tailpiece, just as in 'Trios' of the Wind Symphony. The Fantasy ends with a short fughetta, which revolves round a theme built from oscillating tones and semitones and a typically insistent syncopated ostinato.

'One thing I have particularly enjoyed', McCabe has said, 'is combining harmonies with melodies that go from one instrument to another, sometimes rather a challenge for the players.'[3] In his next piece of brass chamber music, this idea of a kind of musical relay greatly enhances the range colour and texture that a quintet of two trumpets, horn, trombone and tuba offers. *Rounds* was commissioned by the Hallé Brass Consort, who gave the first performance in February 1968 at Salford University. The horn takes the baton in the concise opening fanfare, presenting a strident fourth-based theme with a pivotal augmented fourth (tritone) providing an unexpected intensity. Heraldic fanfares in triplets from the trumpets gradually fuse into a repeating chordal accompaniment that overlays the tuba's expressive cantabile expansion of the horn theme in the second section. The musical relay veers between the playful and alarming in the central scherzo, twice breaking down into 'hocketing' major sevenths, as melodic outline passes round the ensemble at breakneck speed. Order is restored in the Lento section, where the opening horn theme is passed up and down the ensemble and then used to support a new, rather eerie 'distant' fanfare dialogue between the trumpets. The final Allegro provides both the climax and reprise, with leaping major sevenths replacing the more controlled major fourth in a final dramatic thematic transformation and extending the compass of the 'relay' theme to almost two octaves.

In the next wind work, *Canzona*, range and colour is provided by the mix of wind, brass and percussion, rather than through extremes of register or melodic 'relays'. Commissioned for the 1971 Farnham Festival, in Surrey, it was premiered by young musicians from Frensham Heights School and scored for flute, oboe, two clarinets and bassoon; two trumpets, horn and trombone; percussion and piano. A simple mosaic construction highlights the contrasts of instrumental characters. Forward momentum is provided by dancing syncopated chord patterns, repeating against an insistent drum beat. Among the melodic elements is an upward flourish, beginning on flute and reminiscent of the gestures that open Monteverdi's *Orfeo* and 1610 Vespers with such élan. The long pedal points on the piano reinforce this musical parallel. McCabe, though, compromises the tonal perspective throughout, by making the augmented fourth (tritone) the primary interval rather than the open, diatonic fifth.

Writing for the more homogenous brass band is generally regarded as rather specialised, with its prescribed instrumentation of ten cornets, flu-

3 Quoted in Thomas, 'The 4barsrest Interview', 2005.

gel horn, three tenor horns (alto instruments not to be confused with the French horn), two baritone horns, which are tenor instruments at the same pitch as the three trombones and two euphoniums, plus four tubas and percussion. With the predominance of lower brass, it can be an unwieldy medium to write for and composers not steeped in the culture, or with little experience of its idiosyncrasies, have resisted it. Despite being born, raised and educated in the brass band heartland of Lancashire, McCabe was 'singularly unaware of the band heritage' and did not get involved until the 1960s.[4] He was introduced to the unique sound of a British brass band by the distinguished horn player Ifor James (1931–2004) in the 1960s. They worked together as a horn and piano duo a great deal throughout this period, and it was while they were in Ifor James's northern home town of Carlisle that they went to hear a rehearsal of the local St Stephen's Band. Ifor James and his father both had connections with this once famous band. In 1927, Carlisle St Stephen's had been the first band from the county of Cumbria to become National Champions, and among its list of distinguished guests had been the English composer Gustav Holst, who conducted a concert with them in 1933. Through Ifor James, McCabe became fascinated by the sound of brass band instruments and their creative potential.

4 Thomas, 'The 4barsrest Interview', 2005.

Between 1972 and 1978, James was the Musical Director of the Besses o' th' Barn Band, bringing to this famous North Manchester ensemble his professional acumen and experience. Besses was not a 'crack' contesting band during this time, but Ifor James used his connections with leading conductors and composers to broaden the concert life of the band and thus its repertoire. André Previn visited the band at its Whitefield band room; tuba virtuoso John Fletcher gave the premiere of a concerto commissioned from McCabe's contemporary Edward Gregson in 1976. John McCabe's debut with Besses was as soloist in Mendelssohn's *Capriccio Brillant*, which they also recorded. McCabe found the band's playing 'staggeringly good … with an enormous wealth of technique and abundant natural musicianship'.[5] With such a skilled resource at his disposal, he pulled out all the creative stops for his ambitious Besses commission – *Images* (1978) – premiered by Ifor James and the band on 30 March 1978 at Goldsmiths Hall, London.

5 Quoted in Thomas, 'The 4barsrest Interview', 2005.

Five years later the skills of all 96 bands in the elite division of the National Championships were tested by the work, when *Images* was set as the test piece for the Regional Qualifying rounds in 1983. Never in the 150-year history of brass band contesting had a choice of test piece been met with such universal opprobrium by conductors, players and audiences alike.

According to the brass band press, McCabe's music was full of 'outrageous modernism', clearly a step too far for the brass band contesting movement of the early 1980s. Playing in the National Finals at the Royal Albert Hall is every band's greatest aim. The 28 amateur musicians in each ensemble live and breathe the qualifying work sometimes for weeks of painstaking preparation. So, if a test piece presents baffling musical and stylistic challenges, as *Images* did, rather than the customary technical hurdles to be surmounted within a conventional tonal framework, reactions are bound to be intense and unequivocal. There were similar, though not quite so universal, storms of protest when the uncompromising work *Prague* – by McCabe's contemporary, composer Judith Bingham – was set for the same competition in 2002. In the brass band culture, the value or quality of a work is judged, in the main, by how hard it is to play or how successful the contest – by anecdote rather than rigorous musical 'critique'. John McCabe found the controversy rather amusing. 'Having been regarded by the concert classical world as a bit reactionary (unfairly I think!), it was very entertaining to be cast into the role of the revolutionary criminal'.[6]

Without the burden of tradition or expectation behind him, McCabe approached the medium in his own terms: 'I think of the band rather as I think of the orchestra, i.e. several instrumental choirs, and use them in that way – and of course, since I love the sound of any one of the orchestral groupings, I tend to use the band in that way also.'[7] *Images* was genuinely revolutionary in the way McCabe separated out the colours and voices of the individual sections. For the first time in a contest work, each instrument, down to the four basses, had its own part. There was no place to hide. Using the four solo cornets as a *concertante* group diminished the traditional role of the principal cornet as the main soloist. Instead, McCabe favoured the tonal brilliance of the highest instrument in the band, the soprano cornet, and the more mellow timbre of the flugel horn. McCabe's orchestral and wind band palette seeks out extremes of range – low sustained basses supporting more active flutes and piccolo. Enhancing the role of the soprano cornet in particular, as well as extending the range of muting effects, was an attempt to replicate that: 'You might lose the highest register, but the band has a tremendous variety of tone colours, with or without mutes.'[8] The way McCabe maximises the colouristic potential of both individual players and instrumental families within the band in this and later works, especially *Cloudcatcher Fells*, has been hugely influential. The depth and subtlety of tone in *Images* is perhaps heard to fullest effect in the version that the composer made for symphonic wind band, premiered on 14 May 1978 at the University of Redlands, California.

6 Quoted in Thomas, 'The 4barsrest Interview', 2005.

7 McCabe, 'Portraits in Brass', 1992.

8 McCabe, 'Portraits in Brass', 1992.

139

a firmer nod in the direction of traditionally functioning tonality.

However, this apparent simplification of language was not so much a response to the occasion – composed as some kind of compensation for *Images*, or through a desire to please – as a direct and personal response to a much loved area of the Lake District. As in all McCabe's landscape pieces, the image, or more accurately the composer's view of it – whether desert, rainforest or mountain – goes right to the core of the musical inspiration, directly influencing the way themes and harmonies behave – their form and character – as well as broader brush-strokes of texture and atmosphere. For example, the opening theme of *Cloudcatcher Fells*, with its undulating construction, could be viewed as a musical paradigm of a mountain landscape – as viewed from a distance perhaps or underneath a huge sky. Its modality also conditions the evocative, open-sounding harmonic frame and perhaps also its warm, expressive quality.

By contrast, *Desert II – Horizon*, composed in 1981 between *Images* and *Cloudcatcher*, begins not with an epic vista, but with the smallest of details. A desert of sand might appear to be a static, blank, empty canvas, but as McCabe observed in a 1992 BBC Radio 3 interview, 'A desert is never still. Grains of sand constantly shift in the wind, building sand dunes. It's that sense of vast space built out of tiny grains of shifting sand that I wanted to start and end the piece with … I have one instrument after another coming in with a very quiet repeated pattern, building up an [evocative] tex-

10 McCabe, 'Portraits in Brass', 1992.

ture in the upper register.'[10] The tiny unbarred fragments, built out of layers of shifting semitones in the upper brass, begin randomly but gradually to accumulate and coalesce into dense, resonant polychords. This is painting with sound in one sense but, more significantly, the fabric of the work has been carefully derived from the behaviour of the physical landscape, with the full effect gained from the longer perspective that the sequence of massive chords brings. *Desert II – Horizon* was inspired by Middle Eastern desert landscape and was written in 1981 for the Philip Jones Brass Ensemble. Six years later, McCabe opened out the sound-scape from ten-piece symphonic brass to full brass band with percussion at the suggestion of the conductor Howard Snell, a former member of the ensemble.

The work is more simply structured than the other wind and brass pieces, with three substantial episodes – marked Lively, Slow and Decisive – enclosed within the 'fade-in' opening and 'fade-out' close. The lively music is clear and crisp. The sequences of open fifths in the bass present perhaps a clichéd image of the progress of a camel train across the horizon. However, in the vast arid and monochrome expanses of sand, any object or activity will appear to dominate the horizon, to lead the eye. So here, the exaggerated, not

142

to say desiccated, quality of the repeating phrases provides an unmistakeable musical character. The image gradually fades into a shimmering mirage of wispy scales on the upper brass. McCabe also says that images of refreshment in a desert oasis may also come to mind in the central slow section, where there is a more liquid, almost hypnotic quality to the invention. Melodic outlines in the foreground are blurred through characteristic close canons and cascading effects on the cornets/trumpets, techniques that were explored in *Images* and that will sustain *Rainforest III* a decade on. The harmonic background is slower and more sustained. In the final decisive section, fresh perspectives are brought to earlier music – fast and slow – and, after a dynamic climax, the flurries of sand once again dominate the skyline. In the final bars the music disintegrates back into its elemental, fragmentary state.

The lakes and fells of Cumbria have been a part of John McCabe's life since boyhood, when he spent three months in the Patterdale area of the Lake District for health reasons. The inspiration for his next brass band work *Cloudcatcher Fells* (1985) therefore comes from deep within. He has spent a lot of time there since, both for work and relaxation. The first Violin Concerto (1959) was sketched in the 'Lakes' and the last movement of String Quartet No. 3 also has 'Lakeland' associations. The title comes from the poem *Cockermouth* by David Wright (1920–1994), the fourth verse of which reads 'And Derwent shuffles by it, over stones. / And if you look up the valley toward Isel / With Blindcrake to the north, cloudcatcher fells, / Whose waters track past here to Workington.'

Cloudcatcher Fells is the only one of McCabe's musical landscapes in which each episode is given a specific location. However, the piece should not be thought of a simply a personal travelogue, a memoir or a series of musical scene paintings. The richness of the work lies in its multi-faceted symphonic variation design and in the way McCabe's responses to the nine locations influence directly the detail and dynamic of the musical argument.

Cloudcatcher Fells for brass band
Commissioned for the finals of the 1985 National Brass Band Championships, Royal Albert Hall, London

The nine sections are grouped into a sequence of four larger sequences – slow (1–3); fast (4, 5); slow (6); fast (7–9).

1. *Great Gable* – This is the highest point of an imposing massif, part of the Wasdale Fell formation to the north of Scarfell Pike and the west of Patterdale. The horns present a nine-note motto theme in unison. Simply constructed in the dorian mode (the D minor

Cloudcatcher Fells *for
Brass Band* (Grasmoor),
extract.

'white-note' scale on the keyboard) from minor thirds and tones, its undulating contour is shaped like a series of mountain peaks viewed, as it were, in relief, from a distance or against a very large and perhaps cloudy sky – as represented by the miraculous shimmering chords on muted cornets that punctuate the three statements of the theme. The tune changes slightly on each appearance, reflecting perhaps how the play of clouds and the changing light alter the view. Beneath the cloudy sky, as it were, the trombones and lower brass present a gently syncopated thematic variant that will generate much of the rhythmic drive in the faster sections to come.

2. *Grasmoor* – Considered to be one of the most beautiful areas of the national park, the Grasmoor Fells lie to the north-west of Great Gable, on the other side of Buttermere. Grasmoor itself stands a little further to the west in splendid isolation and this aspect is hauntingly captured in the music through the layering of the sustained syncopated theme in the low brass, against a broader series of peaks and troughs, this

144

time sweeping through the entire cornet section from lowly third cornet to the quartet of solo cornets and back again. The sense of space is so skilfully engineered as activity increases. The five primary notes of the motto bounce between individual cornet parts and are set against a slowly unfolding bass line, which draws our ears inexorably to the first full chord.

3. *Grisedale Tarn* – This is the large oval shaped body of water standing at the head of Grisdale, the valley that extends south-west of Patterdale. Here the motto theme is transformed into lilting siciliana. There is a balletic poise about the solo line, which is passed from euphonium to cornets and back, and its gently syncopated accompaniment. As the music unfolds, the elegant surface is disturbed by more threatening undercurrents from deep below the surface on the basses and by arabesque-like detail high up on the solo cornets.

4. *Haystacks* – This is one of the most popular fells for walkers. Located between Buttermere and Great Gable, its name derives from its jagged tops. Musically, *Haystacks* is the first part of a scherzando. The impetus of the music stems from the way McCabe uses the syncopated chords heard beneath the 'clouds' in *Great Gable* to generate jagged bursts of activity around the band. The soprano cornet has a particularly precarious time in the little trio section. There is almost a jazzy feel to the way that the percussion binds the elements together here and then leads the way into the next section.

5. *Catchedicam* or *Catstye Cam* – This is a steep-sided conical peak, lying just to the north-east of the great Helvellyn chain, five kilometres due west of Patterdale. This second scherzando episode, marked *Giocoso*, is as near to a jazz riff as McCabe gets, with the chord formations now set in irregular metre patters – 4/4, 5/8, 7/8 – and after a moment of respite on the trombones, a searing first climax, where McCabe's layering of texture, metre and melody comes into its own.

6. *Angle Tarn* – There are two angle tarns in the Cumbrian Fells (a tarn is an upland pool or small lake). This one nestles between the summits of three of the lower fells to the east of Patterdale, and it was regarded as one of the most scenic of the summits tarns by the great fell walker Alfred Wainwright. John McCabe describes it as his 'most favourite place in the whole world'.[11] The music of *Angle Tarn* is some of the

11 Quoted in Thomas, 'The 4barsrest Interview', 2005.

Angle Tarn.

most warm-hearted and affectionate that he has composed. The structure of the opening mirrors the very start of the work, but additional rhythmic impulses and overlapping cornet and baritone/euphonium arabesques create a glistening, brighter surface. At the heart of this substantial slow movement is a broad and generous melody. Contrasting tonal and textural layers above and below also engage the ear: above, a trio of cornets blur the image, as though through a reflection or heat haze; below the surface, the bass's longer lines remind us perhaps of the massive landscape that surrounds the tarn.

7–9. *Grisedale Brow – Striding Edge – Helvellyn* – These form the eastern spur of the great Helvellyn chain and feature in the final portion of one of the Lake District's most challenging and imposing fell walks from Patterdale to the majestic peak itself. The sheer physical

146

effort demanded by the fell walker seems to be captured in the way the music grows in textural activity and momentum through the first of the two faster sections. *Grisedale Brow* begins lightly, almost nonchalantly, but gradually the exertion begins to take its toll. Scherzando textures, not unlike those already heard in *Haystacks*, become fractured. Textures become fragmented and tortuous. A soprano cornet solo sounds deliberately effortful and short-winded. The long ridge of *Striding Edge* is an one of the most imposing sights in the Helvellyn range, and also one of the most precarious to traverse. There is an easy path, but McCabe's impetuous and at time faltering mosaic of duets and trios reveal, in musical terms, something of its dangers. As the momentum gathers towards its climax, the sound is suddenly obscured. Only the muffled sounds of muted horns and baritones are left. The motto theme (that is, the view) is hardly audible (in other words, visible). But as quickly as the mist came down it lifts to reveal the peak of *Helvellyn* in all its glory. Here, as the final summit is reached, the main theme, heard in the distance at the start of the work, is now revealed close-up as a series of emphatic triadic chords, ending this masterly work in with the triumphant sound of burnished brass, treble *forte*.

The variation form has been fertile ground for so many of the important brass band scores since Vaughan Williams's Variations of 1957. *Cloudcatcher Fells*, with its synthesis of musical logic, technical challenge, evocative content and, crucially, its personal association is one of the finest examples. Such is the significance of the piece within the brass band canon that it has become a seminal study work among students of the repertoire and has been the subject of research projects, none more interesting than the work of Ruth E. DeDarsno. Her PhD dissertation in the 1990s involved transcribing British brass band works for American symphonic wind bands as a means of providing a musical bridge between the two genres. Her impressive transcription of *Cloudcatcher Fells* is available as part of John McCabe's published work.

After the success of *Cloudcatcher* at the 1985 National Championships, there followed the inevitable requests for *Cloudcatcher* mark 2. McCabe does not go in for sequels. As is evident from this commentary, he embarked on a new work for wind or brass only when there was an appropriate idea, strong enough to bring fresh inspiration. So there was a gap of some six years before he added to his band catalogue. The wait was well worth it, however, as four substantial pieces were produced in quick succession.

Canyons was the first, a commission from the Guildhall School of Music & Drama in London and McCabe's only work to date for the large symphonic wind orchestra. The first performance took place in the Barbican, London on 9 July 1991. Three months later, on 11 October, *Rainforest III (Dandenongs)* for thirteen winds was premiered by London Winds at the Norfolk and Norwich Triennial Festival. The following February *Harbour with Ships (Five Impressions)* was performed by the Phoenix Brass Quintet at Peel Hall, Salford University, and a few months after that *Northern Lights*, a joint commission from the Britannia Building Society (now Fodens) Band and the Royal Northern College of Music (RNCM), was premiered at the RNCM just down the road in Manchester. What is remarkable about these pieces is their very different characters and sound worlds.

After the relatively restricted range of the brass band, McCabe clearly relished the more varied palette and wider compass that the wind orchestra afforded. For large stretches of *Canyons*, for example, the high woodwinds are supported by a bass line sometimes three octaves lower. Inspiration came from the imposing landscapes of the American south-west, where desert meets mountain in some of the most awe-inspiring vistas on the planet. Once again, McCabe was insistent that *Canyons* was not simply scene painting: as he says, it

> is not an attempt to match in music the grandeur of this landscape, nor is it an attempt to describe in music the indescribable, but simply an exploration of musical ideas which in themselves derive from my response to this area – it is bursting with inner energy as well as obvious massiveness, and there is a sense of distance which is important too.[12]

12 From the composer's programme note, Novello & Co.

Distance and the immensity of the horizon is what the opening and closing bars seem to be about: a fade-in of spacious, echoing trumpet calls on open fifths, followed by a gradual accumulation of unmeasured repeating thematic fragments, which coalesce into a series of massive chords. *Desert II – Horizon* begins in a similar way, but the sound here is altogether richer and more intense. The chordal 'massifs' are supported by heavy pounding percussion, answered by more strident fanfares and followed by a brief more sinuous fugato paragraph. A fleet-footed scherzo reworks some of the thematic snippets into an impressive and gradually expanding collage. The central *lento* offers a brief respite, before a return of the chordal ideas, beginning on trombones, heralds a final moto-perpetuo dance. At the fierce climax of the piece, a sequence of heavy chords is set against quick-fire retorts on drums (as it were, a concentration, or intensification into a few seconds of the first main section) and the music arch is closed with the thematic fragments re-emerging on trumpet and piccolo in the fade-out ending.

Where *Canyons* is all about vivid colours, bold gestures and clear contrasts of tempo and texture, *Rainforest III (Dandenongs)* is about subtle shadings, blurred images, and fluid lines and structures. The inspiration, like the other two rainforest pieces and one of the desert works, is Australia – more especially its unique sub-tropical forests and sun-burnt bush. Creatively and personally, Australia could be described as McCabe's second home. His many concert and lecturing tours there have afforded opportunity for gathering potent landscape inspiration. It was some time spent in the Dandenong National Park 44 kilometres east of Melbourne in March 1991 that released the creative juices for this hypnotic work. The Dandenong range is a popular stop on the tourist route, with its many cultivated gardens and forests: a beautifully manicured English Garden reminds the traveller of home; the William Ricketts Sanctuary, with its collection of ancient ferns, is altogether more exotic. Dominating the skyline is the peak of Mt Dandenong itself, standing at 633 metres high. This is not especially high when one considers the wild and rugged topography of the Cumbria or Nevada. It is, however, almost entirely covered in dense sub-tropical woodland. Even on a bright sun-lit day, the canopy diffuses light. The play of shadows distorts the image. The trees themselves enclose the visitor in a world of foreshortened views and subtle muted colours. Only at the various man-made clearings, the look-out posts or the observatory, does the canopy break to reveal the broad flood plain in which the range is set, with the skyscrapers of Melbourne dominating the horizon.

The music sets out to reflect 'the massive, intricate solemnity of the rainforest. The extraordinary sense of vast echoing, almost cathedral-like spaces had a strong influence on the material and its development.'[13] So, this is not a rugged work, painted in broad brush strokes like *Canyons* or the fast music in *Cloudcatcher Fells*. It is a work of ritual, of subtle shades, of a fluid mosaic of texture coming in and out of focus, of musical shadows and echoing melodies. Glimmers of brilliance, like the sound of the bell-bird, emerge out of the musical canopy from time to time. For all its apparent stillness, the forest is never really still or quiet.

13 Programme note, Novello & Co.

Rainforest III – Dandenongs

Dandenongs is a fifteen-minute slow movement, designed as a complementary work to Mozart's *Grand Partita* and also sharing the same instrumentation and free-flowing approach to form as the two late and great wind sonatinas of Richard Strauss. Just as in the early Wind Symphony, the ensemble is divided into instrumental families: the upper woodwind (two oboes and two clarinets); the four horns; the two bassoons and contra-bassoon (or double bass). The lugubrious tones of the two basset horns provide the fulcrum between the upper and lower winds, as they do in the Strauss works. However, the combinations are less prescriptive than in the earlier work. The music flows seamlessly through a series of related episodes to form a now-familiar McCabe single-movement arch. Andante moderato is the only tempo marking.

[A] Gentle heterophony on oboes and clarinets – symbolic of the interweaving of creepers or hanging bark. The configuration of the scales becomes the mode from which the whole work stems. It is answered more forcefully by a chordal motif on the bassoons, deriving from alternate notes of the scale. A little fanfare by the two basset horns provides a transition into the second episode.

[B] The four horns present the work's principal melody: a broad 'second subject' in canon. Its outline of gently repeating fourths and thirds is obscured by its presentation as an unsynchronised round. A raised Lydian fourth (the Lydian mode is the white-note F–F scale on the keyboard) adds a touch of piquant intensity.

[Ai] The horns fall silent as the upper and lower woodwind intensify their dialogue towards the first climax.

[C] Oboe and clarinet take up the horn theme, but not in canon this time. While the oboe colourfully embellishes the tune, the clarinet shadows the outline, providing the impetus for a long chirruping oboe solo, shadowed by clarinet and set against slow, statuesque chords on bassoons and basset horns, inspired by the eerie acres of tall ghost gum trees.

[D] Three repeating elements form a slow ritualistic dance; screeching scales on oboes and clarinets are answered by a distorted version of the bassoon motif, with trudging quavers on the horns binding the material together.

[E] In this quieter central episode, textures are less dense and more fragmentary, as a series of delicate but ornate duets featuring oboes, clarinets, bassoon 1 and basset horn 1 unfold against a backdrop of low chords and horn interjections.

[Di] The musical arch begins its return journey with a more forceful version of the ritual dance.

[Ci] The shadowing is now inverted and then extended into the most beautiful and haunting passage of the work. The solo begins on clarinet in its husky chalumeau register, shadowed by bassoon and with the 'ghost gum' chords transferred to the treble ranges. A solo oboe responds with a more wide-ranging repeating figure. Four instruments provide shadowing variants – delicate canonic arabesques on second oboe and second clarinet and hocketing fragments on horns. At the climax the downward rushing scales of [A] plunge dramatically into a new and more active episode.

[F] In place of a reprise, McCabe offers dynamic new closing material of scurrying chromatic scales and fanfare-like figures. Its final culmination is one of the most inspired moments in all the wind and brass works.

[Bi] As if the wooded canopy suddenly disappears at the summit, or a clearing, the broad cantabile heard first on the horns, and which generates much of the other material, is now heard unadorned and in full voice over three octaves. As the music thins out, first bassoons and then horns and clarinets fall away until just the two oboes remain.

[Aii] In the briefest of codas, the downward unsynchronised scales of the very opening are replaced by rising filigree scales in unison, over a low sustained 'tonic' G low down on the contra-bassoon.

Harbour with Ships is McCabe's most extended chamber music work for brass. Subtitled 'Five Impressions for Brass Quintet', its most striking feature is the morse-code-like chattering of the two trumpeters at the start. As in the earlier quintet *Rounds*, solos and duets form a significant part of the structure. The slow second movement features extended cadenzas for the French horn, for example. The scherzo comes next and its playful mood continues to some extent into the Andante, where the composer has great fun with a hocketing texture even more perilous in layout (for the players at least) than the fragmentary relays in *Rounds*.

Northern Lights is the least known and the 'lightest' of the brass and wind works. McCabe describes the musical language as being perhaps similar to that of *Cloudcatcher Fells*. Textures are transparent, the themes are based on consonant intervals – major and minor thirds, perfect fourths and fifths, which combine into arpeggiated figures. Its structure, however, is much more straightforward and one dimensional than the earlier work. Enclosed within a typical arch-like episodic frame is a prelude and fugue. The music opens boldly, almost prosaically with a bracing 'ump-ah' chord sequence – like a call to attention. Out of this flows an extrovert fanfare, characteristically built from patterns and chords based on layered thirds. The second episode is a flowing Andantino. The sound of four muted tubas and glockenspiel sets an extended soprano cornet solo in stark relief. McCabe's other favourite brass soloists – the flugel horn and euphonium – are given test-piece-like cadenzas based on the fanfare figures, and a brief reprise of the full fanfare material leads to the fugue. McCabe dug deep into his old sketch books for the theme, which dates from 1959 or 1960 during his own student days at Manchester University. There is a nice connection here and McCabe 'was delighted to find, at long last, this opportunity of using it – slightly modified'.[14] The title *Northern Lights* has nothing to do with the *aurora borealis* that illuminates the night sky of the Arctic; the connections are personal. McCabe is a Northerner himself, and the piece was commissioned by the Royal Northern College of Music for two bands from the north-west of England. The piece is also dedicated to the memory of one of the great luminaries of the brass band of the twentieth century – Harry Mortimer CBE. *Northern Lights* is an engaging and enjoyable work, but it has never really 'taken off' in the brass band world. This may have something to do with its comparatively modest technical demands, compared with his other brass band works. It is perhaps not quite as effectively 'voiced' as its earlier companions, yet there are five levels or divisions within the brass band structure and *Northern Lights* would greatly enrich the repertoire choices for those selecting test pieces for the section immediately below the elite Championship division.

McCabe followed *Northern Lights* with *Salamander*. Commissioned by Michael Webber for English Heritage to celebrate the tenth birthday of the Historic Buildings and Monuments Commission for England, it was designed to be used as the accompaniment to a firework display. The spectacular premiere took place in June 1994 outdoors in the music dome by the lakeside at Kenwood, on the northerly fringes of Hampstead Heath in London. It was played on that occasion by the massed ranks of Grimethorpe Colliery band and the DUT Yorkshire Imperial Band (Leeds), conducted by Geoffrey Band. The composer remembers being mightily impressed with the way the array of fireworks was co-ordinated to fit the more demonstrative passages of the music. Of course, the choice of the mythical salamander as the subject could not have been more appropriate. In ancient times the salamander was, according to *Brewer's Dictionary of Phrase & Fable*, 'a mythical lizard-like monster that was supposed to be able to live in fire, which, however, it quenches by the chill of its body. [The name] was adopted by Paracelsus as the name of the elemental being inhabiting fire.' It was this definition that was the inspiration for this piece.

Salamander is by far the most homogenously scored of the brass band works. The outdoor setting and the need to be heard above the bangs and crackles of fireworks may have been in the composer's mind. There is far more octave doubling than in any of the other wind and brass works. Voices are blended in what might be described as more traditional brass

152

band manner. That is not to deny the work's colourful, not to say flamboyant, character. Its orchestral, rather than chamber-like, quality may also have something to do with the fact that he was putting the final touches to his ballet *Edward II* when the commission came; the two works are closely connected. The haunting central lyrical section of *Salamander* is a reworking of one of the most beautiful moments in the entire *Edward* ballet – the plangent cantabile and shimmering, almost impressionistic textures of the *pas de deux* for Edward and Gaveston from Act I, Scene ii.

Salamander is a wonderfully affirmative score, reflecting something of the character of the ballet music in its melodic range and direct mode of utterance. McCabe describes the pieces as 'a passacaglia (variations on a ground bass), quite tricky and tightly organised. The bass tune is there all the time in one shape or another'.[15] It takes the form of a pattern of interlocking triads, perhaps taking their cue from the limpid falling triads that give the *pas de deux* its expressive quality. At the start we hear a version of the tune rising, salamander-like, out of the bass pedal G and then through the band until it resounds in its downward configuration – a series of brilliant tutti chords, with the notes of the tune at the top. Flickering and crackling over the top if this rising gesture is a quick-fire figuration of interlocking semi-quavers, which when heard against the long pedal point sound distinctly Brahmsian, and that is no coincidence. One of McCabe's favourite works from the nineteenth century is Brahms's Fourth Symphony, which ends with a masterly passacaglia and opens with a theme based on a series of interlocking thirds and sixths. *Salamander* builds to a terrific climax, via a breathless fugue – built out of some of the elements of the ground bass – to a final blazing statement of the original chordal version.

Salamander has been used as a competition piece on two occasions: the first for the British Open Brass Band Championship at Symphony Hall, Birmingham in September 1994 and the second, more recently, at the European Brass Band Championships in 1997. Its lack of extended opportunities for the band soloists may be a reason why it has not been used more often, because in every other respect it contains all the ingredients of a successful contest and concert work – fast and loud passage work, a forthright opening and an exciting ending, with extended moments of elegant and expressive lyricism as a contrast.

John McCabe has never felt the need deliberately to over burden his so-called 'test pieces' with technical traps and tricks. In fact, during the 1990s he became rather disillusioned with the brass band world. He began to sense that the desire for ever more brilliant virtuosity for its own sake was getting in the way of genuine musical expression and understanding:

15 Programme note, Novello & Co.

153

For the most part I've managed to write exactly what I wanted, such as *Salamander* and *Cloudcatcher*. I ran into trouble, as I fully anticipated, with *The Maunsell Forts*. I had decided not to write any more band pieces and then got the idea for this piece – an idea that I felt I had to fulfill. I warned everyone that (a) it would begin and end quietly and slowly and (b) as a result the band would hate it. It was a piece that I had to write and I'm not somebody who wants to churn out yet another loud, fast collection of thousands of notes.[16]

16 Quoted in Thomas, 'The 4barsrest Interview', 2005.

Well, it was not a popular choice to mark the 150th Open Championships, either with the players or the audiences, as the expectation was for something more celebratory. The reaction was not as fierce as that which greeted *Images* in 1983: *The Maunsell Forts* was admired for its musical qualities, but it simply did not chime with the occasion and has therefore been overlooked ever since.

The Maunsell Forts came to be written after many years of gentle probing and prodding from the organisers of the British Open and from the present writer, who eventually persuaded BBC Radio 3 to commission it for the 2002 Open Championships. It is McCabe's own personal favourite among his brass band compositions,

154

because like *Cloudcatcher* it has an added element. The earlier piece derived from deep love of one particular corner of the Lake District around Patterdale, which I've known since 1947. *Maunsell* derives from the second world war anti-aircraft defensive forts, rather H.G. Wells-like tetrapods in the Thames Estuary and the reflections which seeing them conjured up for me. And they are only just off-shore where I now live, so it's a more personal thing for me than writing about, say, a war memorial in some other country.[17]

17 Quoted in Thomas, 'The 4barsrest Interview', 2005.

There were six sea forts erected to protect the shipping lanes of the Mersey and the Thames. They were designed by Guy Maunsell and constructed in 1942. The four that remain, in various degrees of salt- and wind-induced decay, act as a bleak reminder of the war years, like something out of *The War of the Worlds*. McCabe visited three of them by boat on a calm summer's day in 2001. Shivering Sands and Red Sands are collections of single buildings on stilts used variously for living and keeping watch for enemy aircraft. They were connected by precarious rope walkways, open to the elements. The other fort, on the Essex side of the Thames Estuary, is Knock John – a large single platform supported above the water by two huge concrete pillars and topped out by a single multi-purpose building.

McCabe found the collections of tetrapods particularly fascinating and it is their mysterious shapes looming large out of the estuary that form both the underlying mood and also the structure of the music. The subtitle 'Nocturne for brass band' refers, as McCabe has said, 'to the fact that it would have been at night that the greatest danger came'.[18] It is a substantial score – at 16–17 minutes, almost as long as *Cloudcatcher* – but in terms of its material much more economic. It is also full of enormous contrasts. There are two substantial episodes of fast music: one based on a powerful descending theme, which goes round and round the band, obsessively driving the music forward; the other a passacaglia, framed by wave-like surges of texture and including sharp retorts as vivid as night-time anti-aircraft with tracer bullets. These two sections stand proud of the musical 'seascape' around them – a structural analogy in music for the forts themselves, perhaps. The three connecting ritornelli – with their bell-like resonating chords, fanfares and restless, axial phrases – are as uneasy in sound as the rope walkways must have been to negotiate. This rondo-like form is then framed by the atmospheric opening and the long elegiac coda. There are some fascinating technical correspondences between the start here and the opening bars of *Cloudcatcher*. Here the music wells up from the depths in an overlapping upward formation to reveal the work's main theme, gently

18 Programme note, Novello & Co.

Opposite: Maunsell Forts for Brass Band, opening bars 7–11.

swaying on the horns and baritones. The cornets answer with a glistening array of repeated notes forming a high, dissonant polychord. Where the clouds had obscured the expanse of *Great Gable* in the earlier piece, here in *Maunsell* the moonlight perhaps casts ominous, threatening shadows. The harmonic frame could not be further removed from the nostalgic added sixths and open fifths of its predecessor. It is the ambiguity of the augmented fourth, the tritone, that is the overwhelming presence here, no more so than in the fanfare figures and in the rushing wave formations.

The long coda forms an eloquent and moving elegy. The writing for the band is some of the subtlest and most sophisticated that the composer has achieved, with treble and bass 'choirs' fanning out to enable the middle of the band to add a rich resonance. Towards the end, just before the nocturnal seascape returns to end the piece as it began, the soprano cornet, doubled three octaves below by a single bass tuba, leads the cornets and trombones in a brief and poignant chorale. A phrase of it had been heard earlier in the introduction almost hidden on euphoniums and baritones, but here, for those that know J.S. Bach's St Matthew Passion, the reference to the chorale melody 'O Sacred Head once wounded' ('O Haupt voll Blut und Wunden') is unmistakeable:

It would have seemed less [than] honourable to write a work finishing with a loud and triumphant conclusion, in view of the subject matter. The Thames forts still stand, as a memorial as well as intriguing and remarkably affecting artifacts, an unexpected page of recent but not yet forgotten human history.[19]

19 Quoted in Thomas, 'The 4barsrest Interview', 2005.

For many, including the composer himself, *Cloudcatcher Fells* and *The Maunsell Forts* are his most personal achievements for wind and brass, enshrining a deep personal experience from childhood and adulthood – one reflecting a much-loved region and the other an act of remembrance. The haunting rituals and symbols of *Dandenongs* and the sheer richness in invention of *Images* might also be added to this list. John McCabe, like his much admired contemporary fellow English composer Robert Simpson, came to the brass band medium fascinated by the sound, but blissfully unaware of the conventions, not to say idiosyncrasies, of what remains a somewhat insular and narrow musical world. That ignorance was a blessing, because he has enriched the medium in his own terms, by taking his unique approach to orchestral sound and structure and applying it to the wind ensemble and the brass band. The results, particularly for the brass band musician, have been hugely influential. His liberation of the instrumental families – separating out the colour palette, providing individual parts for the whole assembly – his love of mosaic construction, the elegance of his formal designs and the economy of his thematic working have all been influential on other, younger and more specialist brass composers. How sad then that in recent years he has become less enthusiastic about writing for brass band. Perhaps there may be more to come for mixed symphonic winds, but it seems that the *The Maunsell Forts* may be John McCabe's last work for brass band.

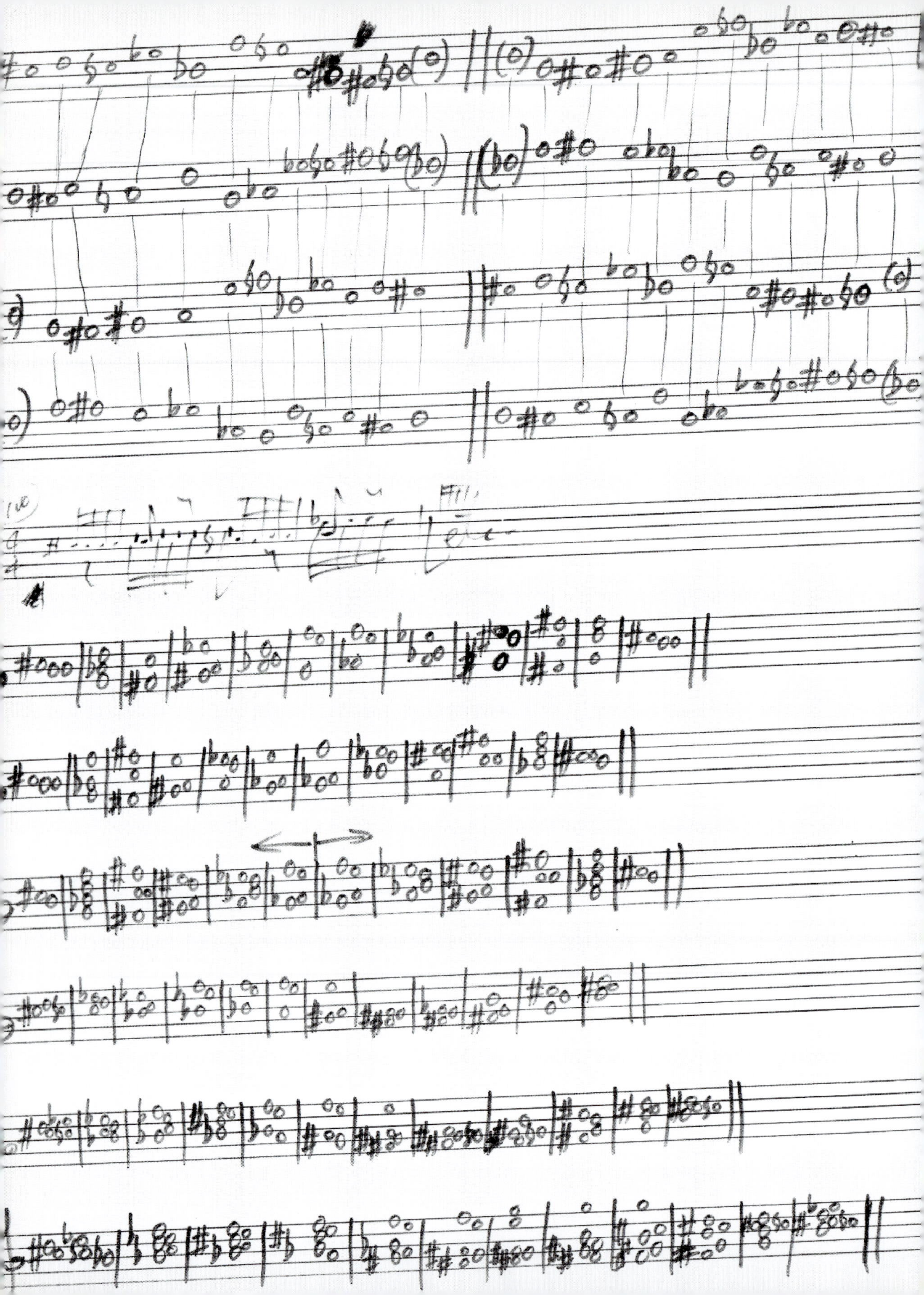

8
The piano music

Tamami Honma

Introduction

Well known for his wide-ranging recordings of several centuries of the piano repertoire, as a composer–pianist, John McCabe does not subscribe to the neo-classicist doctrine in which the performer is regarded not as an interpreter but rather as an executor of the composition. On the other hand, McCabe has a close respect both for the written score and the more traditional role of the performer as interpreter, striking an informed balance between the two extremes of the grand Romantic interpreter of which Stravinsky and others so disapproved and the neo-classical response that discouraged the performer's freedom.

This orientation between the two poles of the performing tradition is connected with McCabe the composer's ability to accommodate and absorb vastly different styles in his compositions. McCabe demonstrates equal affinity in his own performing towards the music of, for example, Haydn (whose complete piano sonatas were recorded by McCabe in one of his landmark recordings) and late Liszt. One should certainly also draw attention to his vast performing and recording repertoire of twentieth-century piano music, within which his life-long promotion of the full spectrum of British music and generous championing of his colleagues is probably unparalleled. It is therefore not surprising that many influences inform his approach to his own piano compositions and colour individual works deeply and in different ways. For example, the piano music of both Haydn and Liszt forms the background to McCabe's two most substantial piano works to date, the Haydn Variations and *Tenebrae* respectively. But, as these essays aim to show, a more complicated web of influences and relationships exists, so that his piano composi- *Opposite: Early pre-* tions, taken as a whole, form a wide-ranging history of his own considerable *composition sketches,* exploration of music, life and art, belonging to both past and present eras. *c. 1968.*

161

Due to the multi-faceted nature of his substantial oeuvre for the instrument, any exploration of McCabe's piano music is likely to produce a different result each time, since endless possibilities seem to be invited and encouraged. Rather than being closed or self-contained works of art, McCabe's piano compositions reach out into the world, beckoning towards other times and places, commenting and, above all, demanding the pianist's, and the listener's, deep involvement as an essential part of the process of interpreting signs and creating meanings. When I work with this composer on my performance of his piano music, his aim does not appear to be to shape or direct the interpretation with authorial infallibility. Rather, his approach is more to enrich my own path with his suggestions. In a sense, his works are half-finished, full of further unrealised potential, and the other half is left up to the pianist and then the listener. One could say that, after the creation of a work such as *Tenebrae* is complete, it then begins a journey on which any given performance is only one staging post, not a final destination. It is therefore the aim of the following series of sketches to open the door on some of these possibilities, starting with the most complex and multivalent work of all.

Opposite: Tenebrae, *opening.*

162

Andante (♩ = 48)

Piano

Tenebrae (1992–93)

Tenebrae (1992–93), while of comparable length to his earlier Haydn Variations, is at once McCabe's magnum opus for the piano, a monument of twentieth-century piano literature and yet his most personal narrative. One important key to understanding the significance of this work lies in its single named source of literary inspiration, Hermann Broch's *The Death of Virgil* (published in 1945), and in the parallels between the three worlds that could be said to cast their shadows on this essentially philosophical composition. These three worlds – the ancient world of Virgil and his Aeneid, the early twentieth-century world of Broch leading up to the writing of his novel and, thirdly, the personal circumstances of McCabe in the early 1990s – are implicated in the genesis of *Tenebrae*. Furthermore, the inspiration behind the work seeps out and infects the notes on the page to the extent that a reading of *Tenebrae* as absolute music would deny it an essential element of its meaning.

The first of these three worlds is intimated by the Latin title itself, *Tenebrae*, which means 'darkness', 'shadows' (and, by metonymy, the spirits or shades themselves) and is a word frequently used of Virgil's underworld in Book VI of his *Aeneid*. Broch's epic narrative, *The Death of Virgil*, was written towards the end of the Second World War but set in the Virgilian world and focuses on a key debate of disillusionment that he writes into it. He casts his story as a description of the dying Virgil ('with death's signet graved upon his brow') arriving by sea at the port of Brundisium in an escort of imperial ships. (McCabe particularly emphasises this gargantuan opening section of the novel as being an impulse for *Tenebrae*.) Surrounded by gluttony, greed and vice of every kind in the imperial court, Virgil is disillusioned about the role of his poem, and of art in general, in a world so devoid of moral virtue, and Broch's narrative thus becomes a symbol of the problems in relationship between art and ethics. Virgil agonises over what to do with the manuscript of the *Aeneid*. At length, Broch's Virgil receives a command from within himself to burn the manuscript in keeping with his belief that the aesthetic has no moral value in this world. What use is art, when art can do no more than create a pause in suffering without ever having the power to remove it? Underlying Broch's dilemma, and forming the background to the composition of *Tenebrae*, is the topical Nietzschean antithesis between, on the one hand, the amoral Dionysian ideal of aesthetic value and, on the other, the moral Socratic ideal of ethical value, the latter being anti-music and art-destroying.

Broch saw art as, at best, oblivious to human suffering and, at worst, transfiguring suffering into a spectacle, and he himself, like Virgil, considered burning his own manuscript. His publisher had pleaded with him that Dante had done far more for civilisation with his poetry than Broch had done by drafting League of Nations resolutions. In the end, Broch, like Virgil, decided not to destroy his manuscript on the grounds that it might after all be of some service to humanity. The conclusion to be made is that Broch's ideal of art is essentially philosophical – transcending art – and one could suggest the same is true of *Tenebrae*, a deeply ethical work in which Broch's world in turn prefigures McCabe's.

The three worlds of Virgil, Broch and McCabe live one inside the other like Russian Matroyshka dolls. But, just as the world of Virgil is refracted through Broch's narrative, so Broch's concerns are reinterpreted (one might use Harold Bloom's term, 'misread') by McCabe, who had his own agenda at the time of the composition of *Tenebrae*. McCabe states that he was influenced in this composition by the personal loss of three of his much-loved and admired musical friends during 1992, the conductor Sir Charles Groves and the composers William Mathias and Stephen Oliver. In *Tenebrae*, McCabe brings us a vision of this personal underworld, reaching into the dark areas of the mind in search of a redeeming light – elusive, in the end, for McCabe as it was for Broch.

McCabe with Sir Charles Groves.

In this way, the themes of the confrontation with mortality and the

conflict of the ethical and the aesthetic form the background to *Tenebrae*. More than a mere catalyst, these narratives transform the musical material, investing it with an inner life and significance. The extraordinary language evolved in *Tenebrae* – the textures, timbres, phrase elaboration, dynamic contrasts, transformations, and rhythmic and contrapuntal complexities – is a language that extends the bounds of the composer's other piano works to date, just as Broch's language goes to expressive extremes. While McCabe's other works by comparison play within their musical rules, the fabric of *Tenebrae* has rips and tears through which the raw creativity flows, as if dispensing with the intermediate aesthetic garment in order to express directly the ethical core. In this sense, *Tenebrae* is a work of philosophy all too rare in a post-Beethovenian age when art for art's sake is the norm. It strives to be an ethical discourse in the form of a musical composition.

Tenebrae is based on a number of musical motifs – rhythmic, harmonic, melodic and textural – evolved freely in an episodically structured fantasy resembling a narrative stream of consciousness. A main theme announced early on in the bass unfolds expansively and is developed in successive episodes with right-hand accompaniments. After a gradual intensification of pace, a *vivo* section builds terrifyingly to an extended and violent climax, Promethean in its force. This reaches a bravura quasi-cadenza which lays bare some of the raw musical motifs and dissolves them in the crucible of their creation. The immense build-up of energy is dispersed through a repetition of the descending and decelerating opening gesture of the piece. A key moment of sublime revelation is reached as this yields to the return of the main theme, now serene and in the treble, with an ethereal countermelody emerging out of the fluid accompaniment figure. McCabe's Orpheus, however – like Broch's – cannot dispel the beasts but can only make them pause, as the melody is thereafter reprised in the bass with a disquieted filigree accompaniment high up at the top of the piano. The final disintegration of the musical fabric into fragmented, disjointed echoes of earlier agitated episodes leads into an uneasy silence that preserves the ambiguity of the work and denies a resolution of its musical or philosophical questions.

The first of three specific musical impulses cited by the composer is the nature and form of Chopin's Barcarolle in F Sharp Major (itself a late work crossing the bounds of the musical conventions of the time). Parallels include the introductory gesture, the left-hand main melodic figure and the lilting semiquaver rhythms in 6/8, the filigree figurations of the closing section and, more pervasively, the gradually unfolding nature of the melodic invention. Beethoven's technique of using widely spaced *Opposite: Tenebrae,* hands to exploit the extremes of the keyboard is acknowledged as another *extract.*

167

borrowing, noticeable in the violent climactic parts and also in the ending's filigree writing. The keyboard writing challenges the limits of the piano as did Beethoven's *Hammerklavier*. The mood of the piece is much more aligned with the third musical source named by the composer, Liszt's two late pieces entitled *La Lugubre Gondola*, written at a time when he was experimenting with a new language and preoccupied with thoughts of death. This third musical borrowing hints most closely at the essential ethical significance of this work.

Variations (1963)

In contrast to *Tenebrae*, McCabe's early Variations of 1963, his first large canvas for piano solo, is much more classically constructed. The eighteen short and clearly delineated variations follow an ordered succession, adhering to groups, with the penultimate variation ending with a short cadenza leading into the final grand statement of the theme. The variation technique used is essentially one that preserves the melody and alters the rhythm and harmony. The work started life as a set of studies that turned into a set of variations, and the circling theme on which it is based keeps coming back to the note or chord with which it began.

There are two basic elements of importance in the theme of the Variations. The first is the main motif (with its syncopated rhythm itself a source of variation), which is stated three times, each statement an extension of the previous one. John Ogdon, in his introduction to the published edition, says: 'The quasi-hypnotic repetition of the opening motif recalls more the effect of an Indian Raga than that of most Western music'.

The second basic element is the intervening measured tremolo. In variations four and five, the first element is varied and extended in the absence of the second. In variation six, the second element of the theme provides the material for the hammered left-hand ostinato accompaniment, while the right hand declaims chords based on the first element, so presenting the two elements simultaneously. Lisztian textures abound in the sets of virtuoso variations immediately before and after variations ten, eleven and twelve, which for their part form the contemplative heart of the work. The principle of variation, albeit presented here more formally than in other works, has always been retained as a favoured compositional technique by McCabe in his subsequent works.

Shorter works from the 1960s

Crystalline and brief, the set of Intermezzi, written in 1968, has much more in common with the tradition of the Beethovenian bagatelle and

Bartók's *Mikrokosmos* (the latter not least in its didactic intent) than with the Brahmsian romantic character piece that its title might suggest. Leading directly from one to another, the five pieces combine expressive wit with extreme clarity of texture. The main thematic material of all the pieces is economically derived from the intervals of the opening fanfare, close variants of which return and are combined at several points during the composition. The character of each piece is sharply drawn, from the gently undulating chords of the first piece to the effervescent toccata of the last. The typically episodical structure of McCabe's compositional method, with variation and contrast as the key agents, is nowhere more succinctly demonstrated than in this masterful set of miniatures.

The Three Impromptus, written for John Ogdon and published in 1963, five years earlier than the Intermezzi, may from the title alone suggest Chopin, but as with the Intermezzi any inferences should be made with caution. The McCabe Impromptus are much shorter works than the impromptus we are used to from Chopin or Fauré, or their forebears Tomášek and Voříšek. Each of the McCabe Impromptus is based on a simple pianistic idea and much more akin to one of the shorter preludes of Chopin, a musical album leaf. The first, for example, is a lively piece based on a triplet motif that could easily be a modern-day prelude. The second sounds a note of nostalgia with its Sicilian rhythm and suggestive title *Lento malincolico*, the brevity and nostalgia evoking something of the atmosphere of a *Vision Fugitive* by Prokofiev. The final impromptu passes by in a flash, a dramatic fragment of less than a minute's duration.

The set of Five Bagatelles for piano was composed in 1964, shortly after the Impromptus, but in a different, far less romantic style. By nodding towards Beethoven, they suggest the brevity and precise compositional construction that is their being. But the closer model would be the *Sechs Kleine Klavierstücke* of Schoenberg, from whom McCabe borrows a simple serial technique as well as the broader characteristics of extreme fragmentation and leanness of texture.

These Bagatelles are arranged more in the manner of a miniature dance suite and, while the Italianate five movements (entitled *Capriccio*, *Aria*, *Elegia*, *Toccata* and *Notturno*) are not usual for a Baroque suite, they nevertheless have a balletic quality. This further suggests the path of Schoenberg, who was regarded as using old forms to clothe his new works at one stage of his career and who himself composed a longer suite for the piano.

McCabe's eclecticism of the 1960s (and beyond) was sometimes backed by a didactic intent, and he has written to explain the genesis of the Bagatelles: 'These short pieces were written in response to a commission from the late Robert Elkin, who wanted a work to give to students an opportunity of learning some serial music and getting to know something about serial technique, yet which would not be very difficult to play'.

For example, the second half of the *Capriccio* is the first half backwards, with intervals upside down, and the rhythmic schema of alternating 5/8 and 7/8 bars is as simple as the pianistic texture. The opening melody of the lilting *Aria* is a twelve-note row that is then transposed into a duet in canon. The extremes of the tiny *Elegia* take it from *fortissimo* to extremes of *pianissimo* in an uneasy close. The brutal *Toccata* clashes sharply with the preceding movement, and the final *Notturno* is the merest fragment of a whisper, ending *ppp a niente* in a distinct gesture towards the ending of the sixth of Schoenberg's pieces.

Fantasy on a Theme of Liszt (1967)

The Fantasy on a Theme of Liszt, composed in 1967, was for a long time McCabe's largest piano piece and remains a favourite among pianists and audiences. Although it does not have a longer duration than the two longest studies (*Gaudí* and *Mosaic*), it is far more dramatic because of its through-composed narrative structure (in contrast to the studies' static tableaux), and also because it is McCabe's most creative foray into the virtuoso piano world of Liszt. While Liszt is an important influence on most of McCabe's piano compositions, including the early Variations, the Haydn Variations, *Tenebrae* and several of the studies, the Fantasy on a Theme of Liszt is the most single-minded homage to the romantic period in which Liszt occupied a significant place.

On the page, the Fantasy on a Theme of Liszt looks like a Liszt piano work and much of the musical material is derived from the opening theme of Liszt's *Faust* Symphony. However, this fantasy never spells out the theme in its original form. Rather, it is 'used', in the words of the composer, 'as a thematic reservoir from which all the piano figurations are derived, as are many of the chords'.

The piece opens with an imposing symphonic breadth, evoking a Mahlerian expanse with hushed pedal As reaching up from the very bottom of the piano, out of which the other sounds gradually emerge like an awakening Titan. The thematic content of the opening is heavily laden with invocations of the sequences of augmented triads that distinguish the *Faust* Symphony, but which are now disintegrated and scattered across the registers like ruins of another time.

Out of this dual effect of the symphonic Alpine cloud and the romantic ruins bursts the opening Allegro with a fury not unlike the main allegro after

170

the opening of the Liszt B minor Sonata. The initial presentation of the material in an opening *Allegro moderato*, before the *Allegro vivo* proper, employs a device characteristic of the composer of a highly self-referential work, namely a summary of the compositional material, the equivalent of a musical commentary left in the score itself by the composer. This self-commentary manifests itself in the form of a sequence of isolated augmented triads laid out in a couple of abbreviated phrases in a prominent position at the head of the work. The augmented triads that had been mere scattered fragments in the very opening cloud are here collected into distinct melodic motifs and given rhythmic impetus and shape. Repetition, commas, dynamic jolts and a rhythmic slow-down are all used to draw this brief passage up above and outside the work. With attention having been directed to the material in this way, the *Allegro vivo* that ensues after a brief pause then elongates and develops this in the manner of a romantic fantasy.

These different modes of presentation – the opening shapeless fragments, followed by the gathering of the material into distinct and isolated *McCabe at Fujisawa* motifs, then the onslaught of the *Allegro vivo* itself – create the impression *Castle, Japan.* of multiple musical voices or layers, resulting in a strong sense of musical narration. This creates a more fundamental connection with the romantic fantasies of Liszt, Schumann and Chopin than the mere borrowing of notes. Schumann is noted for his extreme examples of laying out the musical material in the form of secret ciphers that the performer can read (and there is much debate about whether these should be played, for example the opening ciphers of *Carnival*, or just winked at by the pianist). In McCabe's case, like Liszt's, they are clearly part of the essential musical fabric and definitely to be played, creating the sense of a narrator's voice rising above the music and speaking about it.

The composer draws particular attention to the connection with Chopin in one of his own notes (not just Schumann and Liszt), mentioning his Ballades in general, and the First Ballade in particular. The dichotomy between the virtuoso episodes and the lyrical passages caught in between is the key to this modelling. Apart from the more obvious parallels such as the quiet opening, alternation of fast and slow episodes, and the virtuoso ending,

it is the narrative quality of the McCabe and its source that is of greater significance. In addition to the creation of the different voices in this work, Fantasy on a Theme of Liszt exhibits a discontinuity between the episodes that strongly parallels the form of the Ballades by Chopin and, one could say, romantic forms in general. The opening *Allegro vivo* not only bursts onto the scene, but also fades into the faraway *Andantino* lament in a manner which is less of a transition and more of a dissolution. Like a revelation, the shackles of reality seem to melt away and we find ourselves in a dream passage that seems to be occupying a different level of reality from the previous narrative. It is ironic that this visionary and fantastical *Andantino* draws from the same thematic well, and quotes the same motif that opened the *Allegro*, spinning it into a gossamer thread, for the dramatic impact is of irreconcilable opposites co-existing, like the *ego* and *id*, or Florestan and Eusebius. In those terms, McCabe's work evokes the romantic fantasy more closely than at first might meet the eye.

Studies (1969 to present day)

McCabe's ongoing cycle of studies for the piano is a series of strikingly individual stand-alone works, some very substantial in length, which were composed variously throughout his career. They share with the sets by Chopin, Debussy and Ligeti their narrow scrutiny of a small set of pianistic or compositional problems. The first four date from 1969 to 1970, and form an initial appraisal of the genre, the first two more purely musical and the third and fourth broadening out with extra-musical associations.

The first study, *Capriccio*, dating from 1969, exploits repeated notes, developed against a background of chordal sonorities and harmonics. The toccata-like repeated note motifs spill over into decorative *fioriture* and cadenza figurations. A huge range of dynamics from subtle pastels to the most intense strokes, the use of both extremes of the keyboard, stratification of sound, the importance of sonority and silence, a Beethovenian economy and exploitation of motifs, a clear unfolding of events, and a musical order set out the ingredients for McCabe's reassembly of the genre.

Study No. 2, *Sostenuto* (also of 1969), is a study in layered sonorities. In its lineage, it is a reappraisal of elements in several of the studies by Debussy, particularly what one might call its 'sister' piece *Pour les sonorités opposées*, but also *leggiero* passages from *Pour les huits doigts* (or *Pour les cinqs doigts*) and harmonic aspects of *Pour les Sixtes*. The models are significantly altered, creating an altogether new path in the tradition.

In these opening two studies, however, the subject matter is purely musical, whereas in the third study in the series, composed in 1970, we have

172

the first substantial non-musical impulse that McCabe appears to have recognised in his piano output up until that time. It is a significant turning because the idea of a non-musical source is then behind every one of his later piano compositions (except notably Haydn Variations and *Scrunch*), culminating in the narrative structure of *Tenebrae*, as we have seen.

Gaudí, the third study, dating from 1970, is nearly as much a painting as it is a musical composition. The visual appearance of the score lends it the semblance of an architectural drawing constructed out of discrete visual motifs, or blocks. This effect is enhanced when one notices that there are no barlines (except for faint dotted barlines that are there more to aid the pianist's learning process than to parse the musical paragraphs). In the absence of any periodic structuring or framework provided by barlines, all sense of rhythmic paragraphing is delineated by the phrasing of the music itself – its texture, register, harmony, rhythm and dynamics.

The piece is constructed from a series of blocks, and each individual block is homogenous and unified within itself. Each one is imaginatively defined with its own distinct set of musical components. For example, one block may be a handful of several loud chords, lightly decorated, and with a simple rhythmic and harmonic progression. Another may be a brief arpeggiated flourish, or a delicately written-out trill, or a broken octave-like progression of bells, and so on. Sometimes there is a distinction between right hand and left hand creating a more complex interaction of stasis and movement, but mostly the homogeneity is across the hands and the interactions are between blocks rather than within them. The study is predicated on these miniature blocks, each one a tiny pianistic study in itself.

The way that the blocks are put together is what gives the piece its whimsical and sometimes brutal character. Their juxtaposition creates all manner of contrasts and surprises within the overall framework of a rondo with slightly varied recapitulations of sequences of these blocks. The overall impression is of a highly fantastical and ornately bizarre development of a neo-Baroque edifice. The initially two-dimensional appearance of the score is conjured up into an illusion of three, with a sense of both solidity and mass.

The repetition of visual motifs in the score, the construction out of boldly idiosyncratic blocks of music without barlines, the unconventional juxtapositions and recapitulations, all these elements hint at the inspiration of the piece, the architectural wonders of Antonio Gaudí particularly as represented in Barcelona today. In the composer's initial notes for this piece, he emphasised certain aspects of Gaudí's art that he wanted to express, namely: 'bells / deep gong sounds; contrast of decoration with

173

static sculptural forms; intricate, ornate ornamentation; variety of planes, textures, and materials; juxtaposition of the ferocious and the idyllic'.

With this third study, although composed very close to the time of the second, we have departed more from the concision of the Chopin or Debussy model; this considerably longer study weighs in at around fifteen minutes. There are several musical impulses in this fantasia, not least the intensity of the Spanish light and dark as interpreted through Debussy, and the reinterpretation of Liszt's piano writing through Bartók. While the composer has indicated that 'the strongest influence on *Gaudí* was Stockhausen', the emotional intensity combined with the use of contrast, repetition and the piano writing itself all suggest another musical model, Messiaen's *Vingt regards sur l'enfant Jésus*, in which many of the same key characteristics abide as the composer noted in Gaudí's elemental architecture.

The moments of stillness just before dawn are captured in *Aubade*, the fourth study (composed 1970), whose fragments of melody evoke a mood of recollection and form a contemplative close to the first four studies. It takes as its primary model the decorative grace notes (appoggiaturas, acciaccaturas, arpeggiations and further elaborations) of Debussy's study *Pour les agréments*. Again, the transformation of the material of the earlier composer is complete, and the voice of the later composer rejects the tradition – ironically – in the very act of homage. Fluid and picturesque, there is also a nocturnal feel about *Aubade*, reminiscent of Bartók's night music. Ornaments act as veils (shadows) over more concrete underlying shapes. *Aubade* has the sort of markings one might find in atmospheric orchestral writing, such as a *pppp* marked also *lontano*. As a study, it is first a nocturne exploring a particular chord and second an exercise in degrees of variation within dynamic ranges, especially the softest.

Nearly a decade later, McCabe continued his series of studies with two more, the Paraphrase on *Mary, Queen of Scots* and *Mosaic*, bringing the total to six. At this point in the cycle it is becoming clear that the composer's series of studies are emerging into a series of study-portraits, a tradition represented in the *études-tableaux* of Rachmaninov. While Rachmaninov and McCabe had different sources for their works and dissimilar musical aesthetics, they both bring to the genre of the study an additional scope, scale and extra-musical impulse. However, while with Rachmaninov's secret narratives we are allowed only an occasional and unintended insight into the specific paintings and sources that may be behind his musical portraits, with McCabe the act of homage is an explicit act, meant to be discovered, gaining a lot of its potency from the Bloomian

174

act of misreading the source so as to create something new. We are meant to observe things, and they are there to be discovered and interpreted.

The Paraphrase on *Mary, Queen of Scots* (Study No. 5), composed 1979, is a homage to the nineteenth-century operatic paraphrase for solo piano, exemplified by Liszt, Thalberg and others. In this case, the paraphrase is based not on someone else's opera but on the composer's own ballet, for McCabe had written the full-length theatrical ballet *Mary Queen of Scots* in 1974–75. The key word 'paraphrase' in the title draws our attention to the Lisztian process of creating a solo piano fantasy out of a variety of the melodic and harmonic material of a stage work. In the Lisztian model, the elements are forged anew into a dramatic unfolding usually towards a per-oration and combination of themes at the end.

The irony here is that this piece is in the form of a prelude and fugue. What is humorous about this is that a fugue is the ultimate musical form for combining themes and therefore, in an odd sort of way, it is satisfying and appropriate that a Lisztian operatic paraphrase should end with a fugue. It is also not unamusing to note that a prelude and fugue is traditionally a rather rudimentary and highly academic musical form, a somewhat unlikely calling card for a Lisztian paraphrase (one thinks of Strauss' ironic uses of academic forms in his tone poems). This serious form of musical laughter chimes in with a theme in McCabe's piano works, a classical delight in the manipulation of the musical materials at his disposal in the name of invention, operating here on the level of form and genre. In addition, the somewhat academic- and objective-sounding nature of this work, in the context of a nineteenth-century paraphrase, draws further attention to the work and creates distance from the model.

These musical ironies aside, the two parts of this paraphrase illustrate two aspects of Mary Stuart from the ballet: the first her private self, the second her public aspect. The former is represented by the prelude, which is partly a simple transcription taken from an interlude depicting Mary Stuart in her domestic circle, which, in the ballet, precedes a scene including a *pas de deux* for Mary and Darnley. The improvisatory feel of the opening befits the genre of the prelude, as does the build-up to four staves at the climax of the prelude in a gesture to Rachmaninov.

The more public aspect of Mary Stuart is illustrated by the battle of wills and clash of interests between herself and Queen Elizabeth I. A double *pas de trois* lends material to the fugue, an *allegro deciso* with an academic dryness and precision that subverts the tokens of the nineteenth-century pianistic paraphrase. Soon we begin to hear the virtuoso elements creep into the gradually disintegrating fugue, such as alternating double octaves, use of four staves, right-hand runs, double thirds and chords, repeated note passages and so on in a lexicon of nineteenth-century display up until the closing flourishes, but always with a self-consciousness that distances the listener from the source and rules out an innocent reading of this fascinating work.

The 1980 sixth study, *Mosaic*, dedicated to Welsh composer–pianist William Mathias, is another large-scale tableau, similar in length to *Gaudí*. This glassy and *pointilliste* study again takes as its inspiration the visual arts, but this time it is constructed not out of the adamantine blocks of the Sagrada Família cathedral in Barcelona, but rather the tiny pieces of an intricate mosaic from one of the mosques in Damascus, where the composer had been on a concert tour the year before. In this eastern religious art form, elaborate design rather than pictorial representation underpins the creative process.

As if to provide a musical parallel for this non-representative aesthetic, the thematic material for the piece is an eleven-note row. The piece starts with only the first five notes of the row (C sharp – D sharp – D – E – C), which are conspicuously built up note by note into the eleven-note whole and then, at the end of the piece, the material is methodically reduced to just the first note. The notes themselves are continuously varied, reiterated, built into chords, energetic coruscations and sparkling figurations throughout the piece in a series of shifting tiny variations on a microcosmic scale, which suggests a mosaic pattern. The repetitions of tiny, disjunct fragments culminating in a glassy cadenza resembles the elaborate recurring designs in a mosaic.

The sustaining pedal is used as a distancing device during a three-stave section in which there is a long unfolding of double fourths and seconds over bass octave pedals. By indicating for the pedal to be held down continuously over these two pages of music, the composer imitates the elusiveness of the mosaic, whose ancient and fragmented design shimmers as the eye constructs a whole out of the tiny shards. This contrasts with other passages where dry, *staccatissimo* points of light are used to create the mosaic effect.

It may have seemed for a while that six was going to be the sum total number of studies, a 'book' in Debussy's language. However, after a hiatus of just over two decades, the composer began producing more studies at the beginning of the twenty-first century. There are already five such new ones completed at the time of writing (April 2007), bringing the total to eleven, but there is every hint that the composer would not wish to stop at twelve. The recently composed studies, numbered seven to eleven, are all explicitly subtitled as homages, mostly to modern French composers, but there is one to Scarlatti, who had an important influence in the history of French music, and one to Mussorgsky. Furthermore, it would be wrong to assume that the homage in each case is a simple one-to-one relationship, as there are always other influences lurking and complexity is never far away.

As a compositional approach, the homage has a history that can be traced through the nineteenth-century revival of Baroque music, until it came into its own in the twentieth century. The homage gets to the very heart of McCabe's inspiration and musical aesthetic. His relationship to the traditional canon of classical works reaches far into his own compositions and is a central part of any attempt to understand them. The borrowings themselves, ranging from quotation of specific works to the influence of styles and genres, give his recompositions a belatedness and a darker hue than their forerunners. McCabe's borrowings are also more confrontational – they challenge and overturn their models just as importantly as they pay tribute. The five specific homages under discussion are thus far less reminiscent of the tender evocations by Ravel, Borodin or Chabrier – rather they betray more haunted and anxious relationships. They also return to a tauter and more compact form of study than some of the earlier more expansive tableaux that we have seen; indeed they could be seen as distillations of his compositional style.

A piece I regard as one of the miracles of modern piano literature, the seventh study, *Evening Harmonies* (Study No. 7 – *Hommage à Dukas*), was composed in 2001 as a test piece for the Scottish International Piano Competition of that year. The main title is immediately suggestive of Liszt's transcendental study *Harmonies du soir*. The main borrowings are the gesture of the opening bar (but recomposed with dark leanings towards *Funérailles*) and the keyboard textures of the section marked – like the Liszt passage to which it refers – *Più lento con intimo sentimento*. A layered soundscape evokes at the start the darkness of the evening, pregnant with beautiful colours from sundown onwards until the dead of night. Unsettled, full of potential and with frightening elements, the feeling of the unknown presides and a terrifically effective fear and tension is created in the *Allegro* section, which melts away into a mysterious *murmurando*. The composer acknowledges Dukas, citing 'his beautiful *Prélude élégiaque* for piano, his *Poème dansé* for orchestra, *La Péri*, perhaps above all his masterly opera *Ariane et Barbebleu*' as being a constant source of inspiration to him.

I was delighted and honoured that, amongst such a fine collection of studies, *Scrunch* (Study No. 8 – *Omaggio a Domenico Scarlatti*) and, a short while later, *Snowfall in Winter* (Study No. 9 – *Hommage à Debussy*), were

177

written for me. I adore the quirkiness of *Scrunch*, its humour not unreminiscent of Haydn, along with stylistic elements derived from one of the other great keyboard composers, Scarlatti, in particular his Sonatas in A Minor (L 429) and D Major (L 206). Composed in 2000–01 and described by the composer as essentially a *jeu d'esprit*, *Scrunch* is a dizzying toccata with jazzy rhythmic interplay. Its middle section contains a succession of oddly fanciful episodes, amounting to a great experience and thrill for the performer and listener alike. I gave the premiere of this piece in Weill Recital Hall at Carnegie Hall in June 2002.

Looking back at his studies in 2002, the composer wrote 'They are beginning to represent a personal history of my music-making', and the next two refer to two colossal figures in that history: Debussy and Ravel.

Snowfall in Winter is, to begin with, a musical postcard of a visit to Lithuania in May 2003, the circumstances of whose conception are unusual. It was the occasion of the composer's first tour of Lithuania, an extensive and important musical exchange with a community of vibrant composers and one which included the performance and recording of his Second Piano Concerto (with me as soloist), among several orchestral works, which took place in Vilnius with the St Christopher Chamber Orchestra. We were having dinner at a spirited Russian restaurant in Vilnius, in the company of the cultural attaché of the Japanese embassy, Madoka Saji (to whom this work is dedicated). One of the desserts was entitled 'Snowfall in Winter' – a beautifully presented concoction. Centred on the white porcelain plate was a sizeable, freshly baked and warm meringue 'snowball' with perfectly shaped and slightly browned spikes all round it. On the circumference of the plate were the effects of silhouetted 'footprints' on the snow created by subtle sprinklings of cocoa powder over a stencil. Whilst we were admiring this, I suggested to the composer that it might be a good title for a piece and the rest is history. I premiered this piece at St John's Smith Square, London, in November 2003.

In McCabe's homage, the title alludes to Debussy's enigmatic prelude *Des pas sur la neige* ('Footsteps in the Snow') and the piece forms a meditation on the quiet scene left abandoned by Debussy. The entrancing rhythmic accompaniment of the Debussy model remains a picturesque image of footsteps in the snow in the later composer's re-interpretation, but in a higher register creating the effect of a memory or echo. Against this pristine and icy backdrop, the first note of the melodic entry is the same as Debussy's, but the character of the later piece is more frosty and specific. The melody is built out of delicately syncopated ostinato figures, but the nuance is more akin to a still night depicted by Bartók, with its primitive

Opposite: Evening Harmonies *(Study No. 7 – Hommage à Dukas), opening bars.*

178

Andante flessibile ♩ = 60

Piano

ppp

sempre una corda

pp

Pno.

sempre legato   *p*   *pp*   *p*

Pno.

pp   *p*   *pp*   *p*

Pno.

pp   *p*   *mp*

Pno.

pp   *p*   *mp*

sound world. Harmonies built on seconds, sevenths and whole-tone structures, melismatic turns of phrase and whispy cadenza figures, fluid rhythms, half-pedals, precisely shaded dynamics and stratified textures are all reminiscent of Debussy, but the voice is unreservedly McCabe's own, with his signature twilight effects. The superimposition of two different triads in a strikingly statuesque chordal passage towards the end of the piece is a good example of this, and the harmonies traced by some of the filigree work are also very characteristic. In McCabe's scene from a pianistic *Winterreise*, the listener is enticed into a landscape where only one set of footprints is left before returning to the concert hall. A study in quiet dynamics and pale colours, *Snowfall in Winter* magically creates white shadows.

Tunstall Chimes (Study No. 10 – *Hommage à Ravel*) was composed in 2004. The title refers to Tunstall Church in Kent, whose peals inspired this study in bell-like sonorities. As with *Snowfall in Winter*, the overlapping sounds depend on very subtle gradations of pedal throughout to enable the sonorities to resonate and mingle. The composer prefaces the work with a note emphasising the need to pay great attention to the use of the sustaining pedal, adapted to the acoustic environment.

It forms a pair with *Snowfall in Winter*, for as *Snowfall* recomposes Debussy's *Des pas sur la neige*, so *Tunstall Chimes* recomposes Ravel's Sonatine, a work that the composer says has always been a staple of his pianistic repertoire. McCabe's version is a toccata in two parts. The first part bears a relation to the first movement of the Ravel, and the mixture of whole-tone and diatonic components in the sonorities he uses are based on the Ravel opening harmonies and melodic contours of the first phrase. He even lays out for us his building blocks of sound at the very start of the piece in the form of an introductory musical palette of slow, quiet chords.

The start of the piece proper, the quicker section, isolates aspects of the rhythm, harmony and melody of the end of the opening phrase of the Ravel model, and in the harshness of a more brilliant light exposes the discontinuities that make up the original and exploits the potential for a more fragmented presentation. The piece consists of these juxtaposed fragments from the past, reassembled into a whole that goes much further than the Ravel in tearing down standard eight-bar structures. Ravel's Sonatine was itself already noteworthy for its innovative style of development going back to classical and Baroque means. Its opening theme is developed by tacking on a fragment at a time, resulting in rhythmic shifts, unexpected syncopations and an improvisatory feel, a reaction against nineteenth-century normalisation of melodic phrase structure. But whereas the Ravel was essentially intended as a continuous piece, the McCabe lays bare and

Opposite: Snowfall in Winter *(Study No. 9 – Hommage à Debussy),* opening bars.

181

celebrates its seeds of discontinuity and fragmentation at the start, with pauses and commas emphasising the already visible joints.

The second half of *Tunstall Chimes* is a variation of the first half, but at the same time it is based on the third and final movement of the Ravel Sonatine, closely reviving Ravel's pianistic toccata figurations and combining them with the pealing of bells. McCabe's more energetic and syncopated rhythms, produced by the string of unexpected downbeats, again serve to break up the model, though not with the same determination as before, and the closing flourishes end on a climax of brilliance.

Study No. 11 is called *Epithalamium* (Homage to Mussorgsky), from the ancient Greek word for a song sung by young men and maidens before the bridal chamber, for which Sappho and Theocritus are remembered. Almost a contradiction in terms, on the one hand this title hints towards the intimate origin of the work as a commission by John Sell as a birthday gift for his wife, Jane. On the other hand, the homage overtly borrows from a most public occasion, the grand Coronation Scene of Mussorgsky's opera *Boris Godunov*. The composer makes the link between the private marital poem and the grand operatic scene through the use of bells. After starting with the two colossal chords that permeate the Mussorgsky scene like a giant oscillating pendulum, McCabe abruptly disintegrates them into a seven-note broken-chord pattern that provides the material for the harmonic and melodic invention of the work. But the feeling of bells is ever-present throughout the composition and gives it its fundamental character, as the gradually shifting harmonic and melodic patterns interact with the rhythmic pulse creating subtle bell-like syncopations.

The structure of the work as a series of fragmented variations juxtaposed in a highly episodic form is a characteristic of many of McCabe's piano works, essentially a through-composed variation form with a lyrical central sequence. In taking apart the model and reassembling its raw materials into a variegated montage in this way, the composer of the later work creates a series of private commentaries on a public work. This is the second time the composer has taken a primarily theatrical inspiration for one of his studies and, again, he seeks to contrast the public and private, as the elements of the piece work together to alienate us from the grandeur of the original. The very first silently depressed and held quasi-Mussorgskian cluster chord that makes the piano resonate mysteriously through the silences of the opening pages, and again near the end, is one emblem of the distance from the source at which we now stand. The objectivity of the musical dissolution of the original chords, and the pauses, silences and abrupt dream-awakening shifts of sonority, dynamics and tempo are other examples.

The beautifully hypnotic lyrical section conjures a work that bears its fruit heavily; a wonderfully intriguing new study dating from 2006.

Haydn Variations (1983)

It seems appropriate to end a discussion that began with *Tenebrae* with a look at McCabe's only comparable work in terms of sheer grandeur of ambition, his almanac of compositional fireworks, the Haydn Variations of 1983. The Haydn Variations were written for British pianist Philip Fowke, who gave the first performance in October of that year. This is a work on a far grander scale than the earlier Variations and, while it rivals *Tenebrae* in scale, its impulse and direction are more classically oriented. One could say that the composer here wrote his sonata, already ten years before *Tenebrae*.

The work is based on a deceptively simple theme, making this somewhat of a Diabelli Variations in McCabe's piano output to date. Like Beethoven's Diabelli Variations, this work, in uncovering the essence of the theme, builds up an architecture of immense complexity founded on a premise of ironic simplicity.

There is more to Haydn than one theme, however, and McCabe's work pays a much wider homage to the musical wizard, whose piano sonatas McCabe has recorded in their entirety, by the use of a variation technique that could be viewed as an extension of the manner of strictly thematic invention employed by Haydn and that is laid out in intricate detail in the mostly forgotten compositional treatises of the classical period by Riepel, Mattheson, Marpurg, Koch and others. Joseph Riepel, a particularly noteworthy proponent, said in his 1752 treatise that the techniques required for working out a minuet were no different from those required for working out a concerto, aria or symphony. In another example, Johann David Heinichen, in his 1728 treatise, talks about disturbing symmetry as an expressive means. What is interesting here is not so much the baroque doctrine of *Affekt* or the symbolism of expression, but more the basic techniques of phrase extension and thematic invention that the various scholars of the time propound.

This compositional technique is a fundamentally thematic approach, which takes a given theme or motif and develops it, or rather varies it, by disassembling it and using its elements as a source of further invention. In McCabe's case, not only the melodic but also the harmonic content of the work is derived quite rigorously from this thematic material. This no doubt relies on the wit and sheer mechanical expertise of the composer more than on the inspiration of the muse. However, in displaying this compositional

183

virtuosity, the composer of this work goes far beyond the realms of mere rhetoric and achieves the sublime, setting it firmly in the tradition of J.S. Bach's Goldberg Variations and Beethoven's Diabelli Variations, both of which also draw unlikely significance out of a few simple initial notes.

An illustration of this technique is the prosaic-sounding opening, which isolates and sequences two elements of the Haydn melody: both the initial mordent (D – E flat – D), and the subsequent stepwise five-note descending figure (G – F – E flat – D – C sharp). Everything about this opening statement – the relation of the notes to Haydn's theme, the unvarying motor rhythm, the unison and brilliant bravura octave texture and the unflagging *fortissimo* dynamic – give it the character of an analysis of a particular aspect of the Haydn theme, like an invitation to a compositional workshop. The bare thematic bones are deprived of any further context as yet, other than the most rudimentary such as a germ of the syncopated energy that will become important later on. And this, tellingly, is the way the work begins.

Immediately following the opening octaves is a *Deciso* passage whose hammered repeated notes at first seem like a treatise on what to do with the opening mordent, again depriving it of any distracting additional layer of meaning and stripping it down to its component parts, which it then coldly transforms. However, the Haydn Variations is a work that builds up into a whole that is greater than the sum of its parts. The repeated-note passage turns out to be the subject of a fugal episode, and this fugue continues on a journey towards a burgeoning complexity that goes beyond craftsmanship into the profound and the philosophical.

A token of this deeper meaning is the manner of the one and only appearance of the Haydn theme itself in the piece. The theme, quoted from Haydn's Piano Sonata in G Minor (Hob XVI, No. 44), is here marked *quasi lontano* and occurs a long way into the still, central heart of the work, midway through a *lento e sollenelle* subvariation. The pedal is marked to be held down throughout the statement of the theme and, as there are not many pedal markings in the score, this belatedly recollects the similar long pedal marking at a key moment of the first movement of Haydn's late C Major Piano Sonata. The context McCabe creates around the theme – both the ethereal counterpoint and the position in the work – cloaks its otherwise simple nature in a mystery and sublimity that is far beyond the mere compositional fireworks that underlie the classical variation technique. As a result, the theme does not come across as the mere theme. Rather, appearing as it does at this late stage and in this way, it comes across as a hushed whis- *Opposite: Haydn* per in the manner of the *sotto voce* from Beethoven's *Tempest* Sonata, the *Variations, opening bars.*

185

voice from the tomb that captured the imagination of the romantics, or the otherworldly voice of the 'poet' as Schumann would represent it. And after disintegrating into a pentatonic arpeggiated melisma – a gesture towards that other world – it ushers onto the stage an *andante, pianissimo* sequence of chords of mournful diatonicism, interspersed with delicately ornamented recitative. There is no greater moment of homage than this soft elegy.

For a broader organisational principle in the variations, McCabe nods in the direction of Haydn's use of the double variation technique in his Variations in F Minor (Hob XVII, No. 6) of 1793. This allows McCabe to interweave lyrical and more decisive episodes, though in his case there are not two themes, but rather the one theme manifested by two different variations.

The operation of this principle is most clearly demonstrated in the first run of variations. The lyrical face of the theme, marked *Pochissimo meno mosso*, makes its début when it emerges out of the *martellato* fugal variation, and an alternating juxtaposition of the two opposites becomes the dominant structural motif. They alternate in swift succession, and almost immediately begin stealing aspects of each other's identity so that the distinction between the two is brought into question. The joints between the contrasting variations are also often blurred, merging the variations into one continuous opening tableau, which is brought to a head by an energetically syncopated *Allegro*, followed by a fugue that articulates closure by smoothing out the rhythms and revealing the clearest outline so far of the theme's melodic contours.

The Janus-like nature of the work is exposed most brutally in the short interlude that follows, where the two faces are represented by two fragments whose violent opposition is exaggerated by pauses inserted in between, sudden tempo changes and every expressive contrast imaginable. However, as the two fragments alternate, they gradually adopt each other's characteristics in an overtly self-conscious fashion, a musical demonstration of thematic cross-dressing. This subversion of the traditional bridge passage into what is essentially a rupture in the musical fabric exemplifies a layer of ironic self-consciousness in the work that is never far from the surface in Haydn's own work, especially where Haydn's mannerisms wink more towards the influence of Lawrence Sterne than a purely idealised classicism. It is this sort of musical irony which lifts Haydn above the level of the treatises and which McCabe picks up on in his compositional relationship with Haydn.

The opening tableau is balanced by the complex panel of slow variations that then unfolds, exploring the lyrical and affecting material to the

186

moment of revelation of the theme and far beyond in expressive terms, ending in elaborate dissolutions of the material into *leggiero* melismatic figurations as the introspection reaches its ultimate point. One recalls that Haydn strove to be deeply expressive in his own slow movements or, as Dies – Haydn's early biographer – put it in 1810, the master's ultimate aim was to 'touch the heart in various ways'.

A virtuosic closing sequence, paying homage more to Liszt and Ravel in its piano writing especially, returns us from the depths to the public realm and in so doing balances out the grand triptych. The variations of this finale build seamlessly from the initial, almost imperceptible murmur to a bravura climax which is, however, left truncated, leaving in its wake the smallest kernel of the work, the repeated notes of the opening, here recapitulated in stuttering utterances, an unexpected return to the objectivity of the exposition, which dissolves into trills.

It is in keeping with the deeper purpose of this work that, to end it but not close it, there should follow a quiet, shadowy epilogue that returns to the opening mordent and five-note descending figure, but this time the sequences are directed upwards and the mode is lyrical. More importantly, the bare bones we started with are now cloaked in a wider context of meaning into which they finally disappear altogether, leaving behind a silence which contains the secrets of the work that the bones can only hint at. It is this final silence that is the most telling of the many silences in this eloquent composition.

I:- Fanfare piece
II:- Scherzo & Trio?
III:- Chorale with Variations
IV:- Finale (Rondo burlesca)

V:-

9

The vocal music

John Vorrasi

In the autumn of 1986, shortly after my return from performing with the William Ferris Chorale[1] at the Aldeburgh Festival, I met John McCabe and his wife Monica, who were in Chicago attending a liturgical service that the William Ferris Chorale was singing, celebrating the centenary of the founding of Our Lady of Mt Carmel Parish. That meeting was the beginning of a long and musically rewarding partnership that continues to this very day. The more I come to know the brilliant orchestral and chamber music of John McCabe, the more remarkable it seems that for a long time I knew him only as a composer of choral and vocal music.

The William Ferris Chorale has performed two all-McCabe concerts, recorded his choral works, given several American premieres and commissioned a work, *Amen/Alleluia*, for its 20th-anniversary season. For his part, John has performed his own piano and chamber works as well as Elgar's *From the Bavarian Highlands* with the ensemble. In fact, the last concert William Ferris conducted before his untimely death in 2000 was a 60th-birthday tribute for John. Sharing a performer's and listener's view of John's vocal music is an especially gratifying task.

Sweeping generalisations about musical style, especially when discussing an artist as inventive as McCabe, can be dangerous, but there are certain fundamental elements in his works that remain constant. Harmonically the music is generally quartal or quintal, with polyphony per se eschewed in favour of a homophonic clarity of the text, which, especially in the later works, is both distinctive and challenging. This, combined with the unique abilities of the ensembles for which he writes specific works, allows McCabe to adopt an almost chameleon-like character for his music. That is not to say, however, that McCabe does not always sound like McCabe, for he truly does. The pyrotechnics may be different from work to work,

1 Composer William Ferris and tenor John Vorrasi founded the William Ferris Chorale, an ensemble that specialises in twentieth-century choral music. One of the hallmarks of this ensemble is their Composer Festival Concerts, bringing composers to Chicago for week-long festivals of their music.

Opposite: Sketch for Concertante Music, 1968.

189

but the musical impulse remains the same – strong, distinctive and communicative.

Early works (1959–1971)

A setting of the well-known fifteenth-century *Coventry Carol* (1960) text is ostensibly McCabe's first choral work. Written for Noel Evans and the Choir of the Liverpool Institute High School for Boys, this beautiful work features a high and plaintive soprano solo over a generally homophonic choral accompaniment. A rhythmic depiction of Herod's raging leads to a return of the solo soprano with a *forte* and *molto espressivo* 'That woe is me, Poor child for thee!' melting to a rapid diminuendo and a return to a choral 'By, by, lully, lulay'. Honouring the traditional melody of this carol, the work turns at the end on a major chord. An optional organ accompaniment, with long pedal points and subtle doubling of the choral parts, is provided.

McCabe turned to John Donne's poem 'A Hymne to God the Father' for a 1966 commission from St Matthew's Church, Northampton, which he dedicated to Michael Nicholas and the St Matthew's Church choir. The piece is cast as an austere series of relentlessly bitonal harmonies, generally moving in blocks of parallel motion. In place of counterpoint, McCabe builds chords from the bottom up, one voice at a time, to introduce three sets of solo voice phrases. The composer has said that this use of soli should remind the listener that the text is essentially a personal plea, though cast in the form of a communal prayer.

Great Lord of Lords (1967), another setting of an anonymous sacred text, is published for organ and chorus, but the composer has also made an arrangement adding brass quintet and percussion. A strong *allegro deciso* accompaniment in 6/8 time offsets the solidly moving choral lines. These block choral sounds are peppered with seconds, sevenths and ninths in quartal harmony. Long canonic phrases at the second in both the upper and lower voices lead to a striking cluster chord which, after a brief echo of the opening *allegro deciso*, the organ embellishes with a cluster chord of its own.

For *The Morning Watch* (1968), McCabe selected a text by metaphysical poet Henry Vaughan. The work begins *andante con moto* with a series of *piano* clusters in the organ accompaniment, suddenly holding still to reveal two solo treble voices riding over the pedal point in a striking acclamation 'O joys! Infinite sweetness!' The chorus enters with phrases of contrary motion and continues to sing an agitated and highly rhythmic setting of the text. A solo quartet breaks through the texture and blends into a hushed unaccom-

panied chorus for the pivotal phrase 'O, let me climb / When I lie down'. The opening duet music returns, this time with the full choir singing long smooth phrases over a figured accompaniment. The work ends with an organ solo, repeating the moving phrase 'O, let me climb / When I lie down'.

The works discussed so far have been relatively short, no longer than ten minutes, but *Aspects of Whiteness* marks a major change, both in duration of the work and in the selection of text.

For this twenty-minute work, McCabe moves from setting poetry to prose, and from straightforward musical illustration to a far more abstract concept: capturing in sound, and without programme, the essence and nature of the colour white. To this end he chose a chapter from Herman Melville's novel *Moby Dick* titled 'The Whiteness of the Whale'. 'What fascinated me about the words', McCabe said, 'was their sound and their texture, and the moods these conjured up; it is my response to this that is contained in the music.'

Cluster chords abound in this piece, and while it is primarily homophonic, the central section is quicker and more markedly rhythmic. The work opens with an extended solo for piano introducing the main ideas, captivating the listener with its opening white-note chords. When the chorus does enter, it builds up a vocal version of the first piano chord, introducing a long, slow section that is marked by a gradual inward moving from the extremes of the first chord to a new discord. After this comes a shining *vivo* section, which in turn is followed by a *molto agitato* cadenza for piano. The musical segments then become shorter with solos breaking out of the eight-part vocal writing and culminating in sections of free choral *parlando* and strict *arpeggiando tremolo* in the piano. The final portion of the work reverts to an abbreviated reprise of the opening ideas, with the piano providing a quiet, still conclusion that fades into the nothingness of white. The work was written in 1967 for the Aeolian Singers, who gave the first performance at the Queen Elizabeth Hall that same year. It was revised in 1969.

The *Norwich Canticles* for unaccompanied choir were composed in 1970 on commission from the Norwich Triennial Festival. It is an especially beautiful work, full of economy and flowing melody.

The *Magnificat* begins with a soprano solo, underpinned by gentle choral chords. This melodic material is then repeated by the full chorus. The pace becomes more agitated at the phrase 'he has shown strength with his arm' and there is a playful imitation in the voices of somewhat angular melodies until the Doxology, when McCabe returns to the opening music. A brief canon between the trebles and the men leads to a slow series of progressions on the word Amen – ending on a unison.

The *Nunc Dimittis* opens with a wordless chorus (pedal points in the bass, slow-moving semitones in the alto and a rocking melody of semitones in the tenor) under a soprano solo. This same pattern continues throughout most of the piece, coming to a caesura at the Doxology. Here a slightly altered version of the music from the end of the *Magnificat* appears, with the same unison ending, only this time a semitone higher. The tying together of the Doxologies and the sensitive use of the soprano solo makes this a particularly affecting work. Brian Runnett, organist at Norwich Cathedral, was a friend of McCabe's and was instrumental in arranging the commission. That he died before the work was written perhaps accounts for the reflective nature of the setting.

McCabe wrote his Requiem Sequence for Soprano and Piano in 1971 to honour the memory of Alan Rawsthorne and Sir John Barbirolli, both of whom had died recently. He adapted the text from the Latin Requiem Mass, although he treated the words more as sacred poetry than liturgical text, altering, repeating and taking the phrases out of order.

The work is built round the opening limpid piano harmonies and the soprano's plaintive melodic declamations of the Introit, Offertorium and Kyrie, which is reminiscent of chant, especially in its rhythmic accentuation of the text. The vocal lines combine with the piano chords and embellishments to produce, in the composer's words, 'a serial reservoir of material which is used fairly strictly, even in the seemingly freer sections'.

The form is arch-like with the central point being a short and choppy setting of the Sanctus, which blends into the Domine Jesu Christe text with a sung-spoken invocation to St Michael that the souls of the departed not fall into the darkness. The work ends with a version of the opening Requiem aeternam, a touching plea that the deceased rest with the saints in eternal light.

John and Monica McCabe.

Later works (1972–present)

McCabe's longest choral work to date, *Voyage*, was commissioned for and premiered at the 1972 Three Choirs Festival in Worcester. The 40-minute dramatic cantata is scored for large forces: mixed chorus, boys' choir, full orchestra (triple winds) and five vocal soloists: soprano, mezzo-soprano, counter-tenor, baritone and bass. The text, by Monica Smith, recounts the pilgrimage of the fifth-century Irish saint Brendan, who with his band of followers sets sail and drifts on the wind and tide, trusting that God will keep them safe. In the legends of his voyage, Brendan encounters many exotic geographical locations: the Gates of Hell, where he meets Judas; the Isle of the Fiery Arrow; the Pillar of Crystal; the Isle of Singing Men; and, at last, the Promised Land.

Rather than retelling the legend scene for scene, Smith writes that she 'preferred to present a story which, while it follows as far as possible the main events of Brendan's voyage, and preserves as far as possible the Celtic flavour of the original story, could also be interpreted on other levels, such as a journey into the knowledge of self'. John McCabe has called it 'a sort of early Christian dream-time – after the Australian aboriginal term, and this to my mind is an excellent interpretation'.

Although slow moving in some sections, *Voyage* is a complex and demanding work, and quite 'Brittenesque' in its use of orchestral and vocal colour. The solo voices generally declaim their phrases rather than sing melismatic melodies or arias, and the dramatic use of the chorus is particularly effective.

Upon the High Midnight, McCabe's next choral work, is a Christmas triptych on anonymous fourteenth- and fifteenth-century texts. The large scale forces of *Voyage*, written just a year earlier, are forsaken in favour of the palate-cleansing sound of unaccompanied choir. The first movement *A Little Child There Is Y-Born* is a *con moto* series of 'call and response' between solo voices and choir, while the second movement, *Dormi Jesu*, is one of McCabe's most touching creations. In this lullaby, the soprano soloist floats a chant-like melody over a rich choral underpinning, full of luscious sevenths, ninths and seconds. It is especially moving in its simplicity and in its poignant tone painting of the Virgin singing to her infant child. A joyous setting of *In Bethlehem, That Fair City* follows, replete with brilliant 'Alleluias'. For this movement McCabe provides an optional and snappy organ accompaniment.

In 1976 McCabe worked with a somewhat unusual Latin text for a British composer – the very Italianate Stabat Mater. It is a complete setting of the Roman sequence, variously attributed to Pope Innocent the Third or Jacopone da Todi, in which the sorrows of the Virgin Mary at the foot of the Cross are graphically described. One of the most famous settings is for two women's voices by the eighteenth-century Italian composer Giovanni Battista Pergolesi. The opening movement of this, particularly in its use of passing-note dissonances, seems to have served as an iconic model for McCabe's setting, although in his version the dissonances are not passing and are built up note by note in each of the voices until a luminous and tortured chord is revealed. The soprano soloist, at times representing Mary and at other times the voice of the poet, soars above the orchestra and

194

chorus in angular yet limpid melodies. The soloist and chorus alternate the verses throughout the work with the chorus frequently harkening back to the secundal harmonies of the opening. When the choir intones 'Let me suffer with you at the foot of the cross' the orchestra too vents its pain in an anguished cadenza. The work ends with a quiet plea that all may share the heavenly glories with Mary and her Son.

Despite the fact that each movement was written for a different ensemble and that the set was composed over a period of five years, McCabe feels that the *Mangan Triptych*, three choruses to words by John Clarence Mangan, is his most significant choral work. On his choice of the poet, McCabe writes:

> It was during a flight back to England from Dublin, having just picked up a book of Irish poetry, that I was first attracted to the work of James Clarence Mangan, the Dublin-born poet who died in 1849 at the age of 46 after a tragic struggle against a catalogue of misfortunes, including poverty, madness and ill health. His work immediately impressed me with its characteristically Irish rhetorical power and vivid imagery, and at its best seems to me to have a powerfully visionary quality that is superbly controlled yet forcefully spontaneous.

The first of the three choruses, *Motet*, was composed in 1979 for the Chichester 904 celebrations and is dedicated to George Guest and the Choir of St John's College. It is the most accessible for listeners and is tied together by a rich eight-part ritornello 'Solomon! Where is thy throne? It is gone in the wind.' While the ritornello is marked *Maestoso*, the episodes in between are decidedly more rhythmic, making the work readily perceived as a kind of rondo form. McCabe has written that 'It was the rhetorical power of this very fine poem (whose original title was *Gone in the Wind*) and some aspects of its contemporary significance, that attracted me to it, and in its vivid, subtle and dramatic verbal power it seems to me to reflect the essential characteristics of Irish poetry throughout the ages.'

Siberia, composed a year later, is the bleakest portion of the triptych. The structure of a quasi-rondo form is given up in favour of a through-composed setting, and the text reveals Mangan's obsession with death, pain and the implacable forces of nature: 'Siberia doth reveal / Only blight and death. / No summer shines. / Night is interblent with Day.' The work is in a predominantly slow tempo with occasional rhythmic outbursts, but a doom-laden heaviness is sustained throughout. Stephen Wilkinson, to whom the work is dedicated, conducted the premiere with the William Byrd Singers of Manchester.

The last of the three movements, *Visions*, was composed for the BBC Northern Singers in 1983. The text is a conflation of two poems *And Then No More* and *Shapes and Signs*, which McCabe felt captured the poet's perception of a personal, emotional and dream-like world. Although not as 'formal' as the use of a ritornello in *Motet*, McCabe does shape *Visions* by periodic repetitions of the phrase 'I saw her once, one little while, and then no more', albeit with subtle alterations. Unlike the other movements of the triptych, here the chorus is divided into eight parts throughout the entire work. The florid lines, the rhythmic demands and harmonic densities all point to the fact that McCabe was aware of the abilities of his performers. In fact, this is a hallmark of his later choral works – writing to the special strengths of each particular ensemble. Although he states that is not obligatory, McCabe prefers that the order of performance be *Visions*, *Siberia* and finally *Motet*.

McCabe has confessed a fascination with the American desert, an area of the country he has visited often on his concert tours, so it comes as no surprise that when he was commissioned in 1986 by the King's Singers to compose a work, he chose his text from Reyner Banham's classic book *Scenes in America Deserta*. He selected the particular sections 'not so much to convey the picturesque aspects of the desert, but rather to touch on several points: the nature of the colouring, the silence and the heat, of course, but also the human element in the man-made structures, decorations and pastimes'.

McCabe claims that he used only a few pictorial effects in this composition and relied on colouristic textures produced by the syllables of the words themselves, but the overall impact on the listener is quite the opposite. Revelling in the fact that he was writing for a unique orchestra of voices, McCabe constructed a totally virtuosic showpiece for his performers. While never stretching them beyond the limits of vocal appropriateness, almost every pyrotechnic the ensemble is capable of can be found in the work. One can hear the wind blowing in the opening and closing moments, one can almost see the undulation of the waves of sand, feel the relentless heat and shudder at the sound of a rattlesnake just a few paces away. It is a brilliant piece of writing, but, like a watercolour, it does not reach deeply into the canvas.

To celebrate its twentieth anniversary in 1991, the William Ferris Chorale commissioned a series of works based on the text 'Amen, Alleluia'. Naturally John McCabe was the first composer on our list. John had worked with us on several occasions, so he was aware of the Chorale's particular gifts. He describes the work this way:

Opposite: Scenes in America Deserta, *extract.*

196

This little tribute to William Ferris and the William Ferris Chorale, dedicated to them with love, consists of two sections, the first slow and the second quick. The text is simply the two words of the title, the Amen being the first section and (with minimal overlap of the text) the Alleluia the second. In each part, the relevant word is cumulatively built up from its component syllables or sounds (in the Amen, at one point, all four letters are sung simultaneously), and the second section is a gradual progress from a quiet, light texture to a blazing final cadence.

Amen/Alleluia is written for an eight-part chorus with a quintet of soloists and is filled with ostinati, mini-canons, and an almost frighteningly wide range of dynamic expression. The four-minute work progresses logically and inevitably to its conclusion and is a delight for the performers as well as for the audience, who can revel in the robust and intriguing sounds swirling around the two familiar words.

A recurring theme in McCabe's music, both vocal and instrumental, has been the relationship of man to nature, and through it, perhaps, to God. This sensibility was one of the underlying inspirations for his 2004 work, *Songs of the Garden*, the other being a book entitled *Picture Book of Selected Insects* by the eighteenth-century Japanese artist Kitagawa Utamaro. Utamaro's charming drawings of insects, birds, plants and animals found in the garden are paired with short verses by his contemporary, the poet Tsulaya Juzaburo. McCabe selected his texts from a wide range of English (and one American) poets: John Clare, Robert Herrick, John Skelton, Thomas Hardy, William Blake and Walt Whitman. Using organ and brass quintet to accompany four soloists and SATB choir, McCabe has created an unabashedly lyrical portrait of the garden in spring, summer and autumn. The work was commissioned by The John Armitage Memorial Trust.

An area of vocal music that McCabe has yet to fully explore is that of songs for voice and piano. Counting the 1963 *Fünf Gedichte* written to German texts (perhaps as a tribute to his mother's heritage) there are just a dozen works, and many of those call for obbligato instruments, chamber ensembles or orchestras.

The Three Folksongs from 1963 are a delightful reworking of traditional melodies for high voice and piano (with optional clarinet), which he expanded into a five-song set for soprano and horn in 1976. He continued using folk material in the 1986 *Weaving Song*, an arrangement of a Scottish melody for soprano and piano duet.

When commissioned by Claire-Louise Lucas and Jonathan Darnborough

Opposite: Amen/Alleluia, *extract.*

in 1993, McCabe's original intention was to compose a cantata or a formal song cycle with a specific unifying theme. The more he searched for texts, however, the more he found himself drawn to Irish poetry, whose rich language always has been a source of inspiration for him. The result was *Irish Songbook, Part One*, settings of poems by William Laramie, Aubrey de Vere, W.B. Yeats, Padraic Pearse, John Boyle O'Reilly and J.M. Synge. 'What does perhaps unify this set for mezzo-soprano and piano is the theme of time and memory', McCabe wrote. 'In Irish poetry, the most inspiring aspect for me is not that the words lead one to want to *pictorialise* the images musically, but rather that in every poem there is an underlying atmosphere or feeling quite different to the superficial appearance of the words.' The vocal line is more diatonic than chromatic in these settings, with repetitive patterns and declamatory phrases the norm as opposed to long-lined melody. The piano is alternately in the forefront with aggressive filigree or providing bell-like chords underpinning the voice. McCabe feels a great affinity for these 'Irish' songs and has stated that he wants to continue his exploration of them with more settings in parts two and three.

The *Gladestry Quatrains*, a setting of twelve short poems by Jo Shapcott, is the end result of a commission for two songs to be premiered at the 2003 Presteigne Festival celebrating the Welsh countryside. McCabe was so charmed by Shapcott's pithy and epigrammatic sketches of landscape and human nature that once the two songs were finished he began writing ten more. Paul Conway, reviewing the premiere, remarked on the 'strongly characterised and fastidiously fashioned settings, matching the range and depth of the poems, from the intimacy of a shared joke to the touching acceptance of the transience of all things'.[2]

In 2005, to mark the end of her tenure as Creative Arts Fellow at Wolfson College, Oxford, Kathryn Whitney commissioned McCabe's *Heloise to Abelard*, a *scena* for mezzo-soprano and piano based on the correspondence between the famous medieval lovers. Rather than using their actual letters, McCabe chose to write his own text hoping to convey more concisely the changes in their relationship from passionate lovers to loving friends. The work, while continuous, is divided into four sections: Heloise depicting the first feelings of love; Abelard voicing his fear of their growing passion and the turbulence it will bring upon them both; Heloise raging against the hatred of outside forces; finally her resignation to the new nature of their love. By framing each section with tone-setting salutations and conclusions, McCabe has given himself a tailor-made book to support his imaginative music. The interplay between the piano and voice is especially telling – in fact, the piano seems almost a third protagonist in the story – and the

2 Paul Conway, 'Presteigne Festival 2005: Cecilia McDowall and John McCabe', *Tempo* 60(235) (January 2006), pp. 75–6.

farewells that close the sections (each one subtly varied from the previous) *John McCabe.*
sum up the transformation of their love with eloquence. Composers who
write their own libretti allow us an interesting look into the creative process. The musical invention that conventional wisdom decrees follows the
text, here, without doubt, is the force that actually generates and frames the
text; that is to say, the text foreshadows the music the composer has already
envisioned. Given the beauty and poignancy of *Heloise to Abelard*, one can
only hope that John McCabe will allow us many similar opportunities to
view the landscape of his brilliantly creative mind.

10
Music for theatre, film and television

Guy Rickards

As a composer, John McCabe built his reputation on his output of symphonies, concertos, chamber and instrumental works. In the 1990s, however, he achieved sustained success with three full-evening ballets: *Edward II* (1994–95) – written for the Stuttgart Ballet – and the diptych *Arthur* (1998–2001), for Birmingham Royal Ballet. However, McCabe's involvement with music for theatrical media is far more wide-ranging than this suggests, with over two dozen scores reaching back to much earlier in his career and featuring operas, entertainments, ballets, music for film and television – even a TV commercial for car tyres.

McCabe's first acknowledged venture onto the stage was with the children's opera *The Lion, the Witch and the Wardrobe* (1968). It was commissioned for the Manchester Cathedral Festival in 1969 and the desire seems to have been to create an alternative to Britten's then still very new *Noye's Fludde*, in its mix of adult and children performers. The first performance took place on 29 April that year at Chetham's Hospital School, Manchester, conducted by Gerald Littlewood and featuring Caroline Crawshaw and Patrick McGuigan as the White Witch and Aslan respectively, the remaining roles being taken by a troupe of nine children. Gerald Larner wrote the libretto, adapting C.S. Lewis's famous Christian allegory (actually the second, albeit first to be published, of his seven *Chronicles of Narnia*) of four children, evacuated away from London during the Second World War, who find the door to a magic kingdom through an old wardrobe and become embroiled in the life-and-death struggle to overcome the evil White Witch. The four acts (which play in total for around 80 minutes) chart the seduction of Edmund by the Witch, his eventual redemption by Aslan and the downfall of the Witch following Aslan's resurrection. The music is lyrical and almost romantic in places – as in Aslan's motif, played on the horn

Opposite: Edward II, *opening.*

203

Two scenes from the Bath College of Higher Education production of The Lion, the Witch and the Wardrobe.

– and the scoring luminous and rich. The climactic battle-scene, with its prominent percussion and in which the White Witch is at last overthrown, is highly effective in performance. George Odam, who conducted several performances at the then Bath College of Higher Education (now Bath Spa University), suggested that the instrumental writing was too difficult for the average school orchestra, requiring a specialist music-school ensemble to do the work justice. Musically, too, *The Lion, the Witch and the Wardrobe* is a subtler, more traditionally operatic work than *Noye's Fludde.*

The Bath production did not use children in the cast but proved equally successful; with its wintry theme the opera would prove a novel alternative to pantomime, especially if using a pared-down orchestration like that of the fine short concert suite McCabe arranged in 1971 to a commission from Stonyhurst College. Designed to be playable by amateur or youth ensembles, its luminous scoring with many solos is a delight and McCabe must have believed both opera and suite would have bright futures. However, as is described on p. 20, copyright restrictions have prevented all but a few isolated performances of the opera for a period of over 30 years. In the meantime, McCabe had produced another theatrical work: the 40-minute 'entertainment with texts by Liverpool poets' *This Town's a Corporation Full of Crooked Streets.* Composed in 1969, the work sets poems by Adrian Henri, Roger McGough and Brian Patten alongside children's rhymes (from a collection by Frank Shaw) in a five-part tapestry requiring solo speakers, a tenor singer, children's and mixed choruses, and a small instrumental ensemble including a string quintet, a percussion section of at least nine players and a Philicorda, a 1960s electric organ.

Commissioned by Madeley College of Education, *This Town's a Corporation Full of Crooked Streets* was designed specifically, unlike *The Lion, the Witch and the Wardrobe,* for young adults. Its themes – as can be

204

gleaned from the very title – derive from experience in real-life rather than make-believe, although as with the opera the expressive intention was to expand the awareness of its target audience. The opening movement, entitled *Liverpool 8* (from the old postal district and the subject of a study by John Cornelius), is a portrait of one of the key areas of the city, ethnically diverse, dominated by the massive Anglican Cathedral, a 'district of beautiful, fading, decaying Georgian terrace houses'.[1] It has been commented that this opening movement reveals the composer's affection for his native city, describing everything from its bustle and vigour to 'the smell of breweries and engine oil from the ferry boats'. By contrast, the succeeding *Domestic Life* is a scherzo, a 'fun-piece' according to the composer, where kitchen utensils come to life (and without a hint of Martinů). In 2000, McCabe composed a recorder and piano duet with the title *Domestic Life for Margaret Turner on her 60th birthday*, reusing some tunes from *This Town's a Corporation* in the process. The centrepiece is a nocturne describing the city around midnight, in the words of John Pattinson 'magically redolent of the ardour ... of young lovers, whose shadowy forms at times emerge from, or merge with, the close-knit but delicately scored texture'. The fourth movement is a *Dance of Death*, set here as a square-dance through which the medieval plainchant Dies Irae weaves in and out. Its subject is war – the city having been severely hit by bombing in the Second World War – and the folly of war, and it concludes with an unaccompanied choral setting of Brian Patten's *Sleep Now*. The finale, a panoply of diverse texts, is lighter in tone including nonsense songs such as 'Poor ould Billy Nitt' and 'One fine September Morning, October in July'. The work culminates in the Latin hymn 'Non nobis solum, sed toti mundo nati' ('Not only for us, but unto the whole world born'), the motto of Liverpool Institute for Boys, McCabe's old school, although at the last the children's chorus deflate any solemnity by counterpointing the tune of 'Poor ould Billy Nitt'. *This Town's a Corporation Full of Crooked Streets* was premiered at Madeley College in 1970.

Two years later, McCabe produced his one and only original film score, for the Hammer thriller *Fear in the Night* (also known by the titles *Dynasty of Fear* and *Honeymoon of Fear*). Produced, co-written and directed by Jimmy Sangster, *Fear in the Night* starred a young Judy Geeson as an 'emotionally unstable' young wife who had been attacked by a man with an artificial hand. She moves with her husband (played by Ralph Bates) to a creepy school run by Peter Cushing, who has an artificial hand, and his bitchy wife Joan Collins. Unremarkable as the film may have been, it proved a valuable experience for McCabe and was the first of a series of projects

1 John Cornelius, *Liverpool 8* (Liverpool: Liverpool University Press, 2001).

for film and television over the next sixteen years. The first of these were a couple of short pieces for instrumental ensemble commissioned in early 1973 by the independent Granada Television Company to be used as background pieces to accompany the station signal: *Madrigal* is a two-minute miniature and was succeeded by the much longer *Arabesque*. McCabe was then commissioned that same year by Granada to write what has remained his best-known work for TV or film, the theme to the hit drama series *Sam*. Scripted by John Finch, this ran to two series and a total of 39 episodes tracking the adventures of its eponymous hero, played by Mark McManus, who later became a household name for his portrayal of tough Scottish detective Taggart. *Sam*, however, was set in a South Yorkshire mining community and covered the period from 1936 to the then present-day, 1974 (by the end of series two). The series was an international hit and in 1975 McCabe made arrangements of the theme for small orchestra (premiered by Jack Parnell and the Royal Philharmonic Orchestra at the Royal Albert Hall) and for brass band. In 1989, McCabe re-used the theme as the basis of his piano quintet *Sam* Variations.

The first half of 1973 also saw the creation of McCabe's first ballet score, the single-act *The Teachings of Don Juan*, its subject not the rakish misadventures of Don Giovanni or Don Juan (as immortalised by Mozart and Strauss), but the Yaqui Indian shaman Don Juan Matus who featured in Carlos Castaneda's powerful and now controversial anthropological study of the same name. Scored for a small ensemble of flute, clarinet, horn, trumpet, percussion (requiring two players), violin and cello, McCabe's ballet was commissioned by the Northern Dance Theatre with choreography by Suzanne Hywel, and features, unusually, a solo baritone – placed onstage – who sings a text devised by the composer's future second wife, Monica Smith, from Castaneda's book. Don Juan Matus used hallucinogenic drugs to attain the status of a *naqual*, or 'man of knowledge', enabling him to move into and out of the 'Other World', and he acts as guide and interpreter for the Pupil (in the books, Castaneda himself) in his efforts to achieve a similar enlightenment. Only at one point does the singer, as the shaman, become directly involved in the action. One of McCabe's most experimental works, the ballet's idiom is markedly different to his other works of the time (although one critic thought it closer to *Notturni ed Alba* and the Second Symphony), its economical scoring pointing the way towards the later ballets of the 1990s. The extensive vocal part is a device that McCabe has not re-used in later dance pieces and acts as an alternative – and in the composer's words 'emotionally static' – point of focus to the visual element. The virtuosic vocal part is the most prominent element, despite some highly virtuosic solo writing for the winds especially, and its enormous range of declamatory styles from speech to falsetto make *The Teachings of Don Juan* a satisfying chamber cantata away from the stage. The first performance of this imaginative work took place in Manchester on 30 May 1973, conducted by Christopher Robbins. Since McCabe's ballet was produced, however, serious doubts as to the veracity of Castaneda's writings have been raised, primarily by Richard DeMille, dividing opinion between those who regard him as one of the great modern gurus and those who think him a fraud. This in no way undermines the effectiveness of McCabe's expressive vision, as the composer himself is well aware: 'I was fascinated by the Castaneda book, well the first two, actually. After that we both [composer and librettist] began to think it might be a fraud, but I still find the sheer imagination and conviction of it quite exciting – after all, it's a novel rather than reportage and can be assessed in that light. There wasn't any hint of the controversy when we wrote the ballet, so far as I remember, but we were suspicious.'

From the medium of vocal ballet, McCabe moved the next year to chamber opera in what is the most ambitious project of his early theatrical output, *The Play of Mother Courage*. Once again, Monica Smith provided the libretto, drawn from the Grimmelshausen book rather than Bertolt Brecht's better-known play, *Mother Courage and Her Children*. As the composer commented to the present writer, 'The choice of Grimmelshausen was deliberate – indeed, to this day (despite having a copy of it) I have neither seen nor read the Brecht (I loved *Galileo* when I saw it at the Mermaid Theatre many years ago, and bought it recently, but I'm very suspicious of a lot of Brecht).' Running to a little under two hours in length, this five-scene opera was McCabe's longest work to date and relied heavily on its mezzo-soprano lead; the 39 other parts can, thanks to doublings, be performed by a relatively small company of singers. The orchestral accompaniment is larger than for *The Teachings of Don Juan* but once again restrained, using single woodwinds and brass (no tuba), two percussionists, piano and string quintet. Commissioned by Opera Nova, *The Play of Mother Courage* was premiered in Middlesbrough on 3 October 1974, conducted by Iris Lemare.

The action takes place in flashback, as related by the aged Mother Courage, in a series of episodes during the Thirty Years' War (1618–48), a calamitous conflict in which the rival powers of Austria, Denmark, France, Spain and Sweden swept back and forth across the disparate states of Germany. The devastation was such that it is estimated that over a third of the population died. To survive, Mother Courage had in her youth become an army prostitute, prospering until defeat stripped her of all she had earned. After fortuitous friendships with an aging nurse and a colonel from another army helped her survive, she rebuilt her fortune by becoming a whore again and attained respectability until losing everything through an ill-advised attempt at marriage. In her final years, she espouses a 'pragmatic morality' of which her life is exemplar. McCabe's music is fast-paced for much of the time and the vocal writing shows greater skill and variety than in his previous stage works and is worlds away from *The Lion, the Witch and the Wardrobe*. *The Play of Mother Courage* has been called by Michael Kennedy 'a chamber opera in the Britten style', although this is perhaps misleading. As the composer has commented, 'the chamber opera concept really stems from him [Britten] ... I was very strongly influenced by a score of [Karl Amadeus Hartmann's] *Simplicius Simplicissimus*[2] ... and Hindemith's *Cardillac*, which I am still knocked out by. The mood and musical ethos of it was much affected by those two.'

2 Also derived from the work of Grimmelshausen.

Following the opera's completion, McCabe was asked to provide incidental music for the BAFTA-winning BBC TV drama *Leeds – United* (1974). Written by Colin Welland and directed by Roy Battersby, the story concerned a successful strike by textile workers that was mishandled by the union leadership into a humiliating defeat. The following year McCabe wrote the theme music (scored simply for solo piano) for Tony Parker's drama series *Couples*, produced for Thames TV by June Roberts and Verity Lambert. By the time of its first broadcast, on 14 October 1975, McCabe was putting the finishing touches to his first full-length ballet, *Mary, Queen of Scots*. The ballet was commissioned by Scottish Ballet in Glasgow with choreography by Peter Darrell to a scenario by Noel Goodwin charting Mary's turbulent and tragic life. She had been born in Linlithgow Castle on 8 December 1542, the daughter of Mary of Guise, and succeeded to the throne six days later on the death of her father, James V. Before the age of two she had been betrothed to the French King's heir Francis (later Francis II) and sent to France. At fourteen she was married to Francis and crowned queen three years later, in 1559. (Act I of McCabe's ballet opened with a tennis match at Fontainebleau at this tranquil time in her life.) Tragedy followed when Francis died the following year and by 1561 Mary had returned to Scotland, her homeland but culturally an alien country. At Holyrood Palace she set up a Francophile court (Scene iii), which did not endear her to the local nobility; nor did her favourite, Rizzio, who was assassinated in due course. Mary fared little better with her second husband, Lord Darnley. He, like her, had a claim to the English throne and their marriage in 1565 alarmed Elizabeth I; the rest of Mary's life was dominated by the relationship with her cousin to the south, encapsulated in the Prologue to the ballet in which the adult Mary and her cousin Elizabeth I dance a double *pas de trois*. Mary bore a son but in 1567 Darnley was murdered, at which point the first act concludes with the Earl of Bothwell's thwarting of the conspiracy to seize the infant prince. Before the year was out Mary had further offended Scottish opinion by marrying Bothwell, had been deposed, imprisoned in Lochleven Castle and seen her infant son crowned as James VI. Escaping to England the next year, aged still only 25, she spent the rest of her remaining twenty years as a captive of the English crown, the focal point for Catholic conspiracies against Elizabeth which led to her eventual execution, aged 44, in the Great Hall of Fotheringay Castle in 1587.

McCabe found his way into the project through the character of Mary herself, or what he imagined her musical character to be like. The end result was 'full of my mother', as he remarked to the present writer, which was not to suggest any biographical similarities or self-destructive tendencies, but rather a way of making the historical person flesh and blood within the score. *Mary, Queen of Scots* proved a notable success after its premiere on 3 March 1976, although working on the ballet for McCabe was not, as his wife Monica has recalled, ultimately, 'entirely satisfactory as a musical experience'. This was due largely to the score – which plays for two-and-a-quarter hours – being 'severely cut about, as a result of changes in the scenario'. Once again, the orchestral requirements were fairly modest with single woodwinds, pairs of horns and trumpets, percussion and strings. The music is vivid and dramatic, eminently danceable but, even more than with *The Teachings of Don Juan*, has a musical integrity that works away from the theatre. Accordingly, in 1976 the composer arranged two substantial suites that can be played by chamber or full orchestras. The First Suite comprises music mostly from Act I, opening with Introduction and Tennis Match and closing with the first act close of Mary and the Conspirators, which frame a succession of dances including the *pas de deux* of Mary and Bothwell from Act II, Scene ii and Mary's Mourning Dance for François. The Second Suite comprises episodes extracted in musical rather than chronological sequence, concluding with the Prologue to Act I. Both suites had to wait over ten years before being premiered, in each case by youth orchestras, respectively from the Purcell School conducted by Colin Durrant at the Queen Elizabeth Hall in March 1987 and the Harlow Youth Orchestra under George Caird in October 1988. In 1977, McCabe arranged two of the dances for harp and strings and music from the ballet formed the basis of the fifth of his Piano Studies in 1979.

A month after the premiere of *Mary*, his concert work *Notturni ed Alba* for soprano and orchestra was turned successfully into a ballet by Münster State Ballet in Westfallen, Germany, and in 1978 the music of the Second Symphony (1971), incorporating passages from the Variations on a Theme of Karl Amadeus Hartmann (1964), received a similar treatment under the title *Shadow-Reach*, by the Irish Ballet Company in Dublin. The scenario, with choreography by Domy Reiter-Soffer, was based on Henry James' famous ghost story, *The Turn of the Screw*, in which a governess struggles with the shades of her predecessor, Miss Jessel, and the menacing Peter Quint for control of her two wards, Miles and Flora. Less than two years later, Rosemary Helliwell created an acclaimed ballet using the music of *The Chagall Windows* for Stuttgart Ballet under the title *Die Fenster* ('The Windows'), premiered on 16 February 1980, at the Staatstheater, Stuttgart. Despite these successes, it was not until 1994 that McCabe would be commissioned to write another score for the theatre.

If the flow of commissions for the live stage now ran dry, there was a steady flow of those for television, the first being for *Come Back, Little Sheba* by the American playwright William Inge. This was one of six plays selected, co-produced by and starring Laurence Olivier for the series 'Great Plays of the Twentieth Century' broadcast by Granada TV in 1977; the cast included Joanne Woodward – playing Lola, the wife of Olivier's character, Doc Delany – and Carrie Fisher, fresh from creating the role of Princess Leia in the first *Star Wars* film, as Marie, whose renting of a room in the Delany house (and Doc's interest in her) is the catalyst for the drama. McCabe provided the incidental music but the title theme was an adaptation by Michael Lankester of a Purcell tune. In 1979, McCabe wrote the theme tune for Granada TV's long-running – and not infrequently controversial – docu-drama series *Hypotheticals*, featuring dramatisations of then current events. The following year, McCabe produced incidental music for two episodes of the *Hammer House of Horror* TV series. In *The Thirteenth Reunion*, directed by Peter Sasdy and aired originally on 20 September 1980, Julia Foster played a newspaper reporter who stumbled across a group of cannibals in leafy suburbia, who celebrated the anniversary of their rescue from a plane crash (they had survived by consuming the dead passengers) by feasting on one of the larger members of the local weight-watchers group. *Guardian of the Abyss* was broadcast two months later, on 15 November. Its preposterous plot, written by David Fisher, centred on the ownership of a magic mirror and featured various occult practices including human sacrifice and devil worship as well as hypnosis.

Drama of a more elevated nature was the subject of his next score, *The Good Soldier*, the first of three new commissions from Granada. An

210

adaptation of Ford Madox Ford's loosely autobiographical novel of adultery and marital disharmony in the period just before the outbreak of the Great War, the teleplay – adapted by Julian Mitchell – starred Jeremy Brett, Vickery Turner (herself a distinguished playwright and novelist), Robin Ellis and Susan Fleetwood and was directed by Kenneth Billington. McCabe composed and selected the incidental music, and the drama was first broadcast on 15 April 1981. The second and third Granada projects were written the following year, both for the series *All for Love* (not to be confused with a 60-minute TV film produced by Granada in 1983). In *Combat*, Thomas Ellice adapted an Edith Revley story concerning the machinations of one Mrs Prior (played by Joyce Redman) in trying to guide her son from one disastrous marriage into another. By contrast, *A Bit of Singing and Dancing* centred on 40-year-old Esme Fanshow (played by June Ritchie) starting over after the death of her mother and the arrival of a lodger (Benjamin Whitrow) with a mysterious occupation. Were this not enough, before the year was out, McCabe had composed the theme tune for that year's BBC *Young Musician of the Year*.

After producing the music for a television commercial for Michelin MX tyres in 1983, McCabe composed two further scores for Hammer productions, this time the *Hammer House of Mystery and Suspense*. *Czech Mate*, broadcast in 1984, is widely regarded as one of the best instalments in this series (in thirteen episodes, running until 1986), a tale of Eastern bloc paranoia whose principal character was played by Susan George. By contrast, *The Sweet Scent of Death* was a more straightforward crime thriller. The broadcasts of both were, unusually for projects McCabe was involved in, not immediate, but were delayed until 1986: 24 January for *Czech Mate* and 4 April for *The Sweet Scent of Death*. What has proved to date his final television score was written for BBC TV Scotland's production of Elizabeth Spender's *These Foolish Things* (1988), a love triangle involving Opera House designer Gutrune Day (played by Lindsay Duncan) and newspaper editor Nick Verney (James Fox). Charles Gormley directed and the play was broadcast in 1989.

For the next six years McCabe composed no incidental or theatre music, the longest gap in his production since before he had written *The Lion, the Witch and the Wardrobe* in 1968. But in 1994 he began work on a new full-length ballet to a scenario and choreography by David Bintley, whose *Hobson's Choice* a couple of years earlier for the Birmingham Royal Ballet, to a score by Paul Reade, had been widely acclaimed. Monica McCabe has written of the start of Bintley's and McCabe's association:

Wolfgang Stollwitzer as Edward II. Photo: Bill Cooper.

David was, I believe, looking for a composer to work on a very different project from *Hobson's Choice*. He knew John's music, thought he might be the right composer, and Paul (who sadly was to die, much too young, from a form of cancer) very generously brought them together. The outcome of this was … *Edward II*, based on the Marlowe play, which was commissioned by Stuttgart Ballet, and first performed there in 1995. It caused a tremendous stir, receiving a 15-minute standing ovation. Somehow it fitted in very well with the zeitgeist of the time, both with the 'coming out' of homosexuality, and also the highly publicised troubles of the British monarchy.

Edward II was born in Caernarfon in 1284, the last of over a dozen children born to Edward I, the 'Hammer of the Scots' and his queen Eleanor of Castile. He ruled medieval England from 1307 to 1327, the tenth king to have done so since the Norman Conquest in 1066. He was never intended as the heir, but the deaths of all his elder brothers cleared the way for this solitary, self-obsessed and pious child to ascend the throne. Even before his accession, his unrestrained favouritism for the courtier Piers Gaveston – many historians now allege a homosexual liaison though there is no clear evidence of this – outraged his father, leading to Gaveston's exile. The ballet opens with Edward I's funeral; as the cortège (the musical accompaniment of which, in the form of a long plainchant-like melody – of McCabe's own invention – is the thematic reservoir of the entire ballet) departs, Gaveston, now recalled from exile by the new king, is revealed onstage. His presence at Edward's coronation and the open affection the men display for each other incense the barons and clergy and upset Edward's young queen, Isabella. Edward's indifference to her and clear preference of Gaveston is developed through a pair of *pas de deux* in the second scene, the lyricism of which is offset by a riotous meeting of the barons – led by Mortimer, Warwick and Lancaster – who seal a petition against the king's lover to a vigorous stamping dance coloured by the baleful sonority of an electric guitar, marked *verzerrt* ('with fuzz'). While Edward frolics in the countryside with Gaveston and a troupe of minstrels, Mortimer begins his seduction of Isabella by winning her support for the petition. The barons then present their demands to Edward – interrupting his mock wrestling bout with his

212

lover – who flatly dismisses them. Incensed at this and Gaveston's mockery, the barons revolt, and the first act concludes in civil war, with the grinning cadaverous figure of the Grim Reaper stalking the battlefields of England harvesting the dead with his enormous scythe. Gaveston is finally cornered and decapitated, his severed head delivered to the King.

The second act opens many years later (after the disaster of Bannockburn), with a new favourite installed, Hugh Despenser. Edward and Isabella have made sufficient accommodation to have created a son, the future Edward III. He and his mother journey to France ostensibly to finalise a treaty ending a two-year war. However, at the French Court the still disaffected Isabella falls under the sway of Mortimer, now in exile. In return for the betrothal of the child prince to his daughter, Philippa, the Duke of Hainault provides mercenaries for an invasion of England. In the ballet, Isabella, arrayed in armour as the 'She-Wolf of France', is given a ferocious sword-dance of naked aggression as she leads her army into battle – victoriously as it turns out. Edward and Despenser flee but are captured, Despenser executed and Edward deposed in favour of his son, though with Mortimer and Isabella firmly in control. Led away to Berkeley Castle, Edward is finally murdered but Mortimer's and Isabella's celebrations are cut short: the boy king has his mother banished and her lover hauled away for execution.

For this gripping story, full of opportunities for character painting, action sequences, raucous ribaldry and searing tragedy, McCabe provided his richest theatrical score to date. Robert Simpson, when justifying his exclusion of Stravinsky from the symposium *The Symphony*, drew a sharp distinction between the symphonic and the balletic. In the former 'the internal activity is fluid, organic', the music growing 'by the interpenetrative activity of all its constituent elements', whereas music for the ballet is 'episodic, sectional. When rhythm and melody are dominant, tonality marks time; when tonality changes, rhythm and melody wait'.[3] One of the most compelling achievements of McCabe's powerful score for *Edward II* is that it succeeds in both of these seemingly irreconcilable spheres equally well: on the one hand, it is eminently danceable, very rhythmic, full of soaring melody; on the other, its course evolves entirely satisfactorily through purely musical as well as dramatic reasoning.

Notwithstanding the 'interpenetrative activity' of the 'constituent elements' in the music, there are still some tremendous set-pieces: the burlesque entertainment in Act I, Scene iii devised by the minstrel Fauvel for the king and Gaveston; the terrifying dance of the scythe-wielding Reaper in Act I, Scene iv; the surreally colourful French court in Act II, Scene i with its very un-Britten-like courtly dances; and Edward's murder in the

3 Robert Simpson, ed., *The Symphony* (Harmondsworth: Pelican, 1967), pp. 11–13.

penultimate scene, portrayed graphically both on stage and in the orchestra. Yet much of the impact of these moments is cumulative, deriving from the place of each one, either as a climax or point of contrast, in the overall scheme of the whole work. It is because the score works as absolute music as well as accompanying the dramatic action that the climactic point of the entire ballet – Edward's death – is so cathartic, in turn preparing the swift downfall of Isabella and Mortimer and the new king's deadly retribution. Yet the heart of the ballet lies in its solos – especially those for the king – and particularly duos, which encapsulate the central relationships: Edward and Gaveston, with perhaps the most sheerly beautiful music in the ballet; Edward and Isabella, who dance with exquisite frigidity; Isabella and Mortimer in three *pas de deux* of accelerating passion and evil (Act I, Scene iii; Act II, Scenes ii and iv); Edward and Despenser; and Edward and Fauvel, the clown who transforms into Edward's gaoler and executioner, Lightborn. This last pairing underlines the symphonic unity of the score with a veiled recapitulation – almost a torment – of the love duet with Gaveston in Act I. And as with *Mary, Queen of Scots*, Edward's musical character owed much to McCabe's own mother, though self-evidently a rather different side to her personality than had been echoed in the Scottish Queen.

Following its successful initial run of nearly 30 performances, Bintley revived the ballet on being appointed Artistic Director of Birmingham Royal Ballet in 1997, winning several awards in the process. The company then toured the ballet around Britain – during which time the orchestra made a critically acclaimed commercial recording of the full score (for Hyperion Records) – and took it to Hong Kong for the 2000 Festival, where it was a smash hit, and in autumn of the following year to New York. A further revival is set for 2007. In the meantime, some of the music made its way to the concert platform in its own right, most notably the six key episodes that comprise his fifth – and longest – symphony (1998, receiving its first performance three years later), but also the trio for clarinet, violin and piano *Fauvel's Rondeaux* (1995–96) and, its material rather more distantly derived, the Cello Sonata (1999).

By this time, McCabe was already planning his most ambitious theatrical project, again with David Bintley, the diptych of full-evening ballets *Arthur*. The ballets were a special commission for the Birmingham Royal Ballet to mark the millennium, the first section – rather prosaically billed as simply Part I – completed in 1999 and premiered at the Birmingham Hippodrome on 25 January 2000 and Part II completed in 2000 and premiered at Sadler's Wells in London on 9 May 2001. McCabe gave alternative titles to his musical scores, Part I being *Arthur Pendragon* and dealing with the boy

Opposite: Arthur *Part I:* Arthur Pendragon, *opening bars.*

214

David Justin as Uther and Joseph Cipolla as Merlin in Arthur Pendragon. *Photo: Bill Cooper.*

king's rise to power and Part II, dealing with the tragedy of his fall, entitled *Morte d'Arthur*. The resonances this title gives of Sir Thomas Malory's famous fifteenth-century treatment of the legends is misleading as Bintley, who devised the scenario with the help of David Day, followed rather Fay Sampson's novel sequence, in which Arthur's half-sister Morgan is a much larger character. Indeed, McCabe's original focus for the ballet was Morgan rather than Arthur. He was much moved by the image from the close of the first book where Morgan, still a child, stands on the bridge between Tintagel and the mainland being pulled in two conflicting directions, almost torn apart in the process. However, Bintley's idea was to focus on the key relationships: Arthur and Morgan certainly, but also Lancelot, Guinevere and Arthur's son by Morgan, Mordred. Indeed, most of the principal characters interact in triangles: in the opening scenes Uther Pendragon, Gorlois of Cornwall and his wife Igraine; and two later centred on Arthur and his wife Guinevere, the first with Morgan, the second with Arthur's champion, Lancelot du Lac. Once again it was the characters that drew the composer into the music and together he and the choreographer evolved the scenario in a true collaboration, albeit that Bintley controlled the plot lines and McCabe the music.

Arthur Pendragon is a very different proposition from *Edward II*. The music again blends the seemingly irreconcilable disciplines of the balletic and the symphonic but, befitting the subject, there is more light and variety of mood in both the music and choreography with moments of high comedy unthinkable in its predecessor. The ballet opens in the lawless Britain of post-Roman decay with a rape and murder; lust is the prime motivating force in the ballet. The first three scenes of Act I deal with the circumstances of Arthur's conception and birth: how Uther Pendragon brings order to the kingdom but risks everything to steal a night with the wife of his crucial ally, Gorlois of Cornwall. It is Merlin who disguises Uther in order that he can invade Igraine's bed and he remains a character apart for most of the ballet except in Scene iii, where he steps forward to wrest the sword of power, here called Caliburn (rather than the more familiar Excalibur), as well as the infant Arthur from Uther. The pivot of the first ballet is the long fourth scene, which features the tournament where knights joust to

216

win the right to draw Caliburn from the stone (only in later versions were the Sword in the Stone and Excalibur, the latter gifted by the Lady of the Lake, different weapons). Arthur it is who finally succeeds and assumes royal power at the apex of the ballet. The second act then follows episodes in the early years of Arthur's reign, including the wooing of Guinevere by Lancelot's proxy – leading to their fateful romance – and the king's seduction by Morgan as an instalment of her revenge of her father Gorlois' betrayal and death. The conclusion is compelling and graphic: as Arthur and Guinevere marry, a Herod-like massacre of infant boys is ordered in a vain attempt to seek out and destroy Mordred, the fruit of Arthur's incestuous union with Morgan. In the second ballet, *Morte d'Arthur*, the seeds of Arthur's downfall sown at the end of Part I ripen to full fruit. Mordred and Morgan form an alternative triangle of hate with Arthur to offset that of Arthur, Lancelot and Guinevere, and bring about the destruction of his kingdom, and the Fellowship of the Round Table, at the battle of Camlann. As this second panel of the diptych progresses, Morgan assumes an ever more central role, her actions determining the destinies of all. No sacrifice is too great for her to achieve her ends: incest with her half-brother, and the destruction of Merlin, the kingdom and even her son Mordred, her ultimate instrument of revenge, whom she kills after he finally rejects her. At the end, as Morgan finally abdicates the world to accompany Arthur's body to Lyonesse, only the exhausted Lancelot and the dying Guinevere remain to contemplate the ruin of Arthur's domain.

The finale of Act I of *Arthur Pendragon*, one of a series of hugely impressive set-pieces in both ballets, is far removed from the divertissement-like scenes typical in classical ballets such as *Raymonda*, where the dance company has a chance to display its collective virtuosity while the story marks time. Even *Edward II* had had one such scene, early in the second act when the plot drove the action to the French court, but any attempt to write a section of this type would have been dangerously anti-climactic. Here and in *Morte d'Arthur*, McCabe also avoided trying to write either pastiche or pseudo-Dark-Age music in an attempt to create a fifth-century sound-world (a highly speculative enterprise at best, given the paucity of material to have survived from that time). However, there is at the heart of both ballets a connection with William Byrd's Mass for Three Voices, the Kyrie of which seems to have 'imbued so many of the thematic ideas of both ballets', though it was not until working on the satellite piece *The Golden Valley* (2000), the musical material of which is drawn from both ballets, that the composer fully appreciated this.

A feature of the scoring for *Arthur Pendragon* is the relative economy of the orchestra, unlike the large ensemble required for *Edward II* (for which a scaled-down version was prepared for performances in smaller theatres). Only double woodwind is needed, but with an alto saxophone often used to portray Morgan; Arthur is represented usually by a solo horn. However, the percussion section is greatly, indeed exuberantly, expanded even though only two players (aside from the timpanist) are required. Alongside the conventional battery of cymbals, gong, side and bass drums, tambourine, triangle, bells, glockenspiel and xylophone, McCabe includes instruments that are decided strangers to the ballet orchestra pit: crotales, flexatone, roto-toms, whip, anvil and some real exotica – rainstick (an Aboriginal instrument), Agogo bells and a waterphone. This last has been described by the composer as 'a kind of metal bowl with protruding rods which are played with a cello bow'. McCabe spent a most entertaining day with the Birmingham Royal Ballet's principal percussionist experimenting and exploring sonorities. For *Morte d'Arthur*, many of the more unusual instruments were dropped but with no loss in the richness of texture.

The reception of this ambitious project was more muted than that accorded to *Edward II*. The division of the action across two evenings attracted much attention but Bintley's choreography found less favour. McCabe's powerful music was praised but, as with *Mary, Queen of Scots*, the Arthur ballets have yet to find their place as repertoire items. Unlike *Edward II*, the music of *Arthur* remains unrecorded, although a suite of four movements extracted from *Arthur Pendragon* with the assistance of conductor Christopher Austin has been issued on CD by Dutton Epoch. The music is drawn mostly from the first act, the opening *Allegro deciso* describing Uther and the Tribes while the second movement is the first of the ballet's great *pas de deux*, Igraine and Uther. The third movement is entitled *The Tourney* and is drawn from the pivotal fourth scene, though does not feature the episode where Arthur draws Caliburn from the stone. The complex, compound finale is entitled *The Lovers*, a conflation of two *pas de deux* for Lancelot and Guinevere and *Arthur Pendragon*'s climax, featuring Arthur's misguided massacre of the innocents.

After composing around a dozen emotionally charged duos in *Edward II* and the *Arthur* diptych, McCabe has commented at being 'all *pas de deux*ed out'. He has hinted at having ideas for a full-scale opera but without a commission this is unlikely to see the light of day. For the moment he has turned his main attention back to concert works. A second suite from the *Arthur* ballets is on the cards but this aside he has no further plans at present for additional stage works. However, McCabe remains in full vigour as a composer so nothing is impossible. Even should *Arthur* prove to be his theatrical swansong, his contribution to European music drama, in all its forms, will prove to be of lasting importance, as strong and varied a body of work as any composer has produced in the past hundred years.

Discography

McCabe compositions

Orchestral (see also Theatrical)

The Chagall Windows
Hallé Orchestra / Loughran

(LP) HMV ASD 3096
(LP) HMV ED 29 12191
(Cassette) HMV ED 29 12194
(CD) EMI CDM 7 63176 2
(CD) EMI CDM 5 67120 2

London Philharmonic Orchestra / Bernard Haitink

(CD) LPO–0023

Clarinet Concerto
Hilton / BBC Scottish Symphony Orchestra / Gamba

(CD) Clarinet Classics CC0034

Concertante Variations on a Theme of Nicholas Maw
St Christopher Chamber Orchestra / Donatas Katkus

(CD) Dutton Epoch CDLX 7133

Concertino for Piano Duet
Wibaut / Rutherford / Frensham Heights School / Latham

(LP) Erase EO 253 S
Limited private edition

***Concerto funebre* for Viola and Chamber Orchestra**
Bradley / Orchestra Nova / Vass

(CD) Dutton Epoch CDLX 7186
[Album: *British Viola Music*]

Concerto for Orchestra
RLPO / Bostock [+ Gregson/Hoddinott]

(CD) Classico CLASSCD 384

London Philharmonic Orchestra / Sir Georg Solti
(world premiere performance)

(CD) LPO–0023

Domestic Life
Turner / Royal Ballet Sinfonia / Gavin Sutherland

(CD) ASV CD WHL 2143

Flute Concerto
Beynon / BBC Symphony Orchestra / Vernon Handley

(CD) Hyperion CDA 67089

Hartmann Variations
Hallé Orchestra / Loughran

(LP) HMV ASD 3096
(LP) HMV ED 29 12191
(Cassette) HMV ED 29 12194
(CD) EMI CDM 7 63176 2

Notturni ed Alba
Gomez / CBSO / Frémaux

(LP) HMV ASD 2904
(LP) HMV ED 29 12191
(Cassette) HMV ED 29 12194
(CD) EMI CDM 7 63176 2
(CD) EMI CDM 5 67120 2 Quaife/State Orchestra of
Victoria/Mills(CD) Recorded in Melbourne, 1995
[not issued]

Piano Concerto No. 1
McCabe / BBC Scottish Symphony Orchestra / Christopher Austin

(CD) Dutton Epoch CDLX 7179

Piano Concerto No. 2 (Sinfonia Concertante)
Tamami Honma / St Christopher Chamber Orchestra / Donatas Katkus   (CD) Dutton Epoch CDLX 7133

***Pilgrim* for Double String Orchestra**
BBC Scottish Symphony Orchestra / Christopher Austin   (CD) Dutton Epoch CDLX 7179

Red Leaves
Brunel Ensemble / Austin   (CD) Cala The Edge CACD77005
(CD) Signum SIGCD053 [reissue 2005]
[Album: *Red Leaves*]

Six-minute Symphony
St Christopher Chamber Orchestra / Donatas Katkus   (CD) Dutton Epoch CDLX 7133

Sonata on a Motet
St Christopher Chamber Orchestra / Donatas Katkus   (CD) Dutton Epoch CDLX 7133

Symphony No. 1 (*Elegy*)
LPO / Snashall   (LP) Pye TPLS 13005

Symphony No. 2
CBSO / Frémaux   (LP) HMV ASD 2904
(CD) EMI CDM 5 67120 2

Symphony 'Of Time and the River' (Symphony No. 4)
BBC Symphony Orchestra / Vernon Handley   (CD) Hyperion CDA 67089

Tuning
NYOS / McCabe   (Cass.) Alpha CAPS 367
[limited edition]

Chamber and instrumental
***Canto* for Guitar**
Behrend   (LP) DG 2530079

The Castle of Arianrhod
James / McCabe   (LP) Cornucopia [Not issued]

Concerto for Piano and Wind Quintet
Fibonacci Sequence   (CD) Dutton Epoch CDLX 7125

Dance-Prelude for Oboe d'amore and Piano
Paull / Gainsford   (CD) AmorisEdition AR 1003

Dances for Trumpet and Piano
3 movements
Paulin / Vorster   (CD) Move MCD 060

Desert III: Landscape
Australian Piano Trio   (LP) Pagecoll S-1 (Australia)

Fauvel's Rondeaux
Fibonacci Sequence   (CD) Dutton Epoch CDLX 7125

***Goddess* Trilogy for Horn and Piano**
Williams / Covert   *(CD) Music from Northwestern Vol. 5

***Maze Dances* for Solo Violin**
Sheppard Skærved   (CD) Metier MSV CD92029

Musica Notturna
Fibonacci Sequence   (CD) Dutton Epoch CDLX 7125
[cello edition]
Australian Piano Trio   (LP) Pagecoll S-1 (Australia)

Partita for Solo Cello
J.L. Webber   (LP) L'Oiseau Lyre DSLO 18

Laurs   (LP) Pagecoll S-1 (Australia)

Three Pieces for Clarinet and Piano
Schweickhardt / Cobb   (LP) Coronet 3116 (USA)

Carpenter / McArthur   (CD) Herald HAVPCD 152

Puddy / Martineau   (CD) Veloce Classics VELCD9503

Portraits for Flute and Piano
Threes and Twos
Adrian Ashton (piano) [Album: *Pocket Pianist for Flute*]   (LP/Cassette) Oakland Music OMPP 4 FA

Postcards for Wind Quintet
Fibonacci Sequence   (CD) Dutton Epoch CDLX 7125

Pueblo for Solo Double Bass
Leon Bosch   (CD) Meridian [recorded 2006]

Rounds for Brass Quintet
Hallé Brass Consort   (LP) Pye GSGC 14114

Beaux Arts Quintet, Belgium   (CD) BBQ-003 [Belgium]

Star-Preludes for Violin and Piano
Sheppard Skærved / Honma   (CD) Metier MSV CD92029

String Quartet No. 2
Camerata Ensemble   (CD) Campion CAMEO 2027

String Quartet No. 3
Vanbrugh Quartet   (CD) Hyperion CDA67078

String Quartet No. 4
Vanbrugh Quartet   (CD) Hyperion CDA67078

String Quartet No. 5
Vanbrugh Quartet   (CD) Hyperion CDA67078

String Trio
Cardiff University Ensemble   (LP) Argo ZRG 761

Camerata Ensemble   (CD) Campion CAMEO 2027

Keyboard

Afternoons and Afterwards **for Piano**
Catherine Nardiello   (CD) CN-127

The Artful Dodger / Harvey   (Cassette) Associated Board 1994 Grades 6/7

Aubade **(Study No. 4)**
McCabe   (LP) RCA RL 25076

McCabe   (CD) British Music Society BMS424CD

Honma   (CD) Metier MSV CD 92071

Five Bagatelles for Piano

McCabe   (LP) Pye GSGC 14116
                                                       (LP) PRT GSGC 2069 reissue

McCabe   (CD) British Music Society BMS424CD

Basse Danse for Two Pianos
McCabe / Vorster   (CD) Recorded Melbourne, 1995

McCabe / Honma   (CD) Dutton Digital CDSA6881

Capriccio **(Study No. 1)**
McCabe   (LP) RCA RL 25076

Honma   (CD) Metier Metier MSV CD 92071

Dies Resurrectionis **for Organ**
Cook   (LP) RCA LVL1 5019

Bowers-Broadbent   (LP) Abbey LPB 665 [MONO]

Elegy for Organ

Higginbottom   (LP) Decca Eclipse ECS 626

Evening Harmonies **(Study No. 7 –** ***Hommage à Dukas*****)**

Nadiradze   (CD) Classical Rec. Co. CRC1115-2
                                                       [*Prelude to Dreams* – Scottish International Piano
                                                       Competition 2001]

Honma   (CD) Metier MSV CD 92071

Fantasy on a Theme of Liszt

McCabe   (LP) RCA RL 25076

Caskie   (CD) Metier MSV CD92004

Gaudí **(Study No. 3)**
McCabe   (LP) RCA RL 25076

McCabe   (CD) British Music Society BMS424CD

Haydn Variations (1982)

McCabe   (CD) British Music Society BMS424CD

Miniconcerto for Organ and Penny Whistles
Weir / Blades / Willcocks   (LP) Abbey APR 606 [MONO]

Mosaic **(Study No. 6)**
McCabe   (CD) British Music Society BMS424CD

Le Poisson magique **for Organ**
Barber   (LP) Vista VPS 1025

Two Scenes from *Edward II* **for Two Pianos**
McCabe / Vorster   (CD) Recorded Melbourne 1995

Scrunch **(Study No. 8 –** *Omaggio a Domenico Scarlatti***)**
Honma   (CD) Metier MSV CD 92071

Sostenuto **(Study No. 2)**
McCabe   (LP) RCA RL 25076

Honma   (CD) Metier MSV CD 92071

Tenebrae **for Piano**
Honma   (CD) Metier MSV CD 92071

Tunstall Chimes **(Study No. 10 –** *Hommage à Ravel***)**
Browell [British Music Society Piano Awards]   (CD) BMS ENV040CD

John [British Music Society Piano Awards]   (CD) BMS ENV039CD

Powell [British Music Society Piano Awards]   (CD) BMS ENV038CD

Tau Wey [British Music Society Piano Awards]   (CD) BMS ENV037CD

Variations **(1963) for Piano**
McCabe   (LP) RCA RL 25076

McCabe   (CD) British Music Society BMS424CD

Honma   (CD) Metier MSV CD 92071

Brass and wind band
Canyons
Guildhall School of Music & Drama Symphonic Wind Ensemble / Gane   (CD) Polyphonic QPRM 127 D

Royal Northern College of Music Wind Band / Rundell   (CD) Chandos CHAN 10409

Cloudcatcher Fells
Black Dyke Mills Band / Parkes   (LP) Chandos BBRD 1032
                                                           (CD) Chandos CHAN 8483
                                                           (Cassette) Chandos BBRD 1032
                                                           (CD) Chandos CHAN 4509 reissue

Brass Band de Waldsang / Weide	(CD) Heavyweight HR005/D
	(Cassette) Heavyweight HR005
Leyland DAF Band / Evans	(CD) Doyen DOY CD 008
	(Cassette) Doyen DOY MC 008
Brass Band Bienne /Eicher	(CD) GMS 8905
Britannia Building Society Band / Snell	(CD) Doyen DOY CD 030
	(Cassette) Doyen DOY MC 040

Desert II: Horizon

Massed Bands / Snell	(CD) Polyphonic QPRL039D
	(Cassette) Polyphonic CPRL039D
Britannia Building Society Band / Snell	(CD) Doyen DOY CD 030
	(Cassette) Doyen DOY MC 040

***Images* for Brass Band**

Sun Life Band / Hurdley	(CD) Stanshawe STA 004CD
	(Cassette) Stanshawe STA 004T
Britannia Building Society Band / Snell	DOY CD 030
	(Cassette) Doyen DOY MC 040

Overture: *Northern Lights*

Britannia Building Society Band / Snell	DOY CD 030
	(Cassette) Doyen DOY MC 040
US Air Force Band	(CD) Altissimo 5556

***Salamander* for Brass Band**

Britannia Building Society Band / Snell	DOY CD 030
	(Cassette) Doyen DOY MC 040
European Brass Band Championships, 1997	DOYCD062
Grimethorpe Colliery Band / Parkes	(CD) Chandos 4549

Choral and vocal
Amen/Alleluia

Ferris Chorale / Ferris	(CD) WFC LIVE! 869914

Coventry Carol

Elizabethan Singers / Halsey	(LP) Argo ZRG 5499
	(CD) Decca 425 515-2 reissue
Leeds Parish Church / Hunt	(LP) Abbey XMS 697
	(LP) Abbey MVP 756 reissue

Three Folksongs

Eaves / King / Kenny	(LP) Cameo Classics GOCLP 9020
Alexandra Ensemble	(Cassette) Whitetower ENS 153
Catrin Hughes Ensemble	(Cassette) Gareth Hughes CATN 1

Blase / Berk / Berk-Seiz	(CD) cordAria CACD 561
Wells / Turner / Swallow	(CD) Campion CAMEO 2021

Gladestry Quatrains
Gwaithla Brook; Cefn hir

Keith / Lepper	(CD) Metronome CD 1065

Great Lord of Lords

Thomas Weisflog / William Ferris Chorale / William Ferris	(CD) WFC Live! 57506 [Album title: *Toward the Unknown Region*]

Mangan Triptych
Siberia; Visions

William Byrd Singers / Wilkinson	(CD) ASC CS CD 58

Mary Laid her Child

Norwich Cathedral Choir / Nicholas	(LP) Abbey LPB 748

Proud Songsters

Sine Nomine / Hollingworth	(CD) Cloister CLOCD0205

Scenes in America Deserta

The King's Singers	(CD) Signum SIGCD090 [Album: *Landscape & Time*]

To Us in Bethlem City

King's Singers	(CD) Signum SIGCD502

Upon the High Midnight

Worcester Cathedral Choir / Hunt	(LP) Abbey LPB 787

Dormi Jesu

William Ferris Chorale / Ferris	(CD) WFC 128689

Theatrical
Arthur, Part I: Arthur Pendragon (ballet)
Ballet Suite No. 1

BBC Scottish Symphony Orchestra / Christopher Austin	(CD) Dutton Epoch CDLX 7179

Edward II (ballet)
Complete Recording

Royal Ballet Sinfonia / Wordsworth	(2CD) Hyperion CDA 67135/6 *(2CD) Hyperion SACDA 67135/6 * Super Audio CDs

Mary, Queen of Scots (ballet)
Two Dances for Strings and Harp

Northern Chamber Orchestra / Ward	(CD) ASC CS CD45

TV and film
Fear in the Night (film)

Orchestra / Martell	DVD

226

Fear in the Night – film extract
Orchestra / Martell

(LP) EMI Studio Two TWOA 5001

Orchestra / Martell [Hammer Film Music Collection Vol. 2]

(CD) GDI GDICD005

Hammer House of Horror (TV series)
Growing Pains; Guardian of the Abyss; The Thirteenth Reunion
In: *Hammer House of Horror* (4-DVD set)

(4 DVD) Carlton 37115 04093

Sam – TV theme tune
Jack Parnell Orchestra

(LP) Music for Pleasure SPR 90035

Arrangements
Rawsthorne: Suite for Recorder
Turner / NCO / Lloyd-Jones [Rawsthorne Orchestral Music]

(CD) Naxos 8.553567

* Music from Northwestern is the record label of Northwestern University, Chicago, Illinois, USA

Recordings as performer

Solo piano recordings
ADAMS
Phrygian Gates
[+Bennett, Carter, Copland, Previn, Rochberg]

Continuum (2CD)
CCD 1028/9
Published 1991
Album: *Transatlantic Piano*

BAX
Sonata in E flat (original version of Symphony No. 1); Sonata No. 2 in G; *Legend*

Continuum (CD)
CCD 1045
Published 1992

Sonata No. 4 in G: Allegretto quasi andante
[+ Holst, Ireland, Moeran, Vaughan Williams, Warlock]

Decca (LP)
SDD 444
Published 1974
Album: *Pastorale*

BEARDSLEY, C.
Stars in a Dark Night (Diptych No. 1)
[+ Ellis, Forshaw, Golightly, Pitfield, Rawsthorne, J.R. Williamson]

ASC Classical Series (CD) CS CD3
Album: *Contemporary British Piano Music* [NWCA disc]
Published 1998

BENNETT
Noctuary
[+ Adams, Carter, Copland, Previn, Rochberg]

Continuum (2CD)
CCD 1028/9
Published 1991
Album: *Transatlantic Piano*

BRAHMS
Variations and Fugue on a Theme of Handel, Op. 24; Three Pieces, Op. 117; Four Pieces, Op. 119

Oryx (LP) BRL 78 / (Cassette) BRL 78

Recorded 1972

BRITTEN
Notturno **(Night Piece) (1963)**
[McCabe, Nielsen, Rawsthorne, Schönberg, Webern]

Pye (LP)

GSGC 14116

Published 1969

Reissued: PRT (LP)GSGC 2069 / (Cassette) ZCGC 2069

Reissued 1983

Album: *Twentieth-Century Piano Music*

CARTER
Sonata (1945–46)
[+ Adams, Bennett, Copland, Previn, Rochberg]

Continuum (2CD)

CCD 1028/9

Published 1991

Album: *Transatlantic Piano*

CLEMENTI
Sonata in D, Op. 40, No. 3; Sonata in F, Op. 33, No. 2; Sonata in G minor,
Op. 50, No. 3 (*Didone Abbandonata*); Three Monferrine, Op. 49, Nos. 3, 4, 12

Hyperion (LP)

A66057

Published 1982

COPLAND
Sonata (1939–41)
[+ Adams, Bennett, Carter, Previn, Rochberg]

Continuum (2CD)

CCD 1028/9

Published 1991

Album: *Transatlantic Piano*

Variations (1930)
[McCabe, Nielsen, Rawsthorne, Schönberg, Webern]

Pye (LP)

GSGC 14116

Published 1969

Reissued: PRT (LP)GSGC 2069 / (Cassette) ZCGC 2069

Reissued 1983

Album: *Twentieth-Century Piano Music*

ELGAR
Adieu; Chantant; **Concert Allegro;** *Griffinesque; In Smyrna; May Song;* **Minuet; Serenade; Skizze; Sonatina**

Prelude (LP)

PRS 2503

Published 1976

ELLIS, DAVID
Piano Sonata No. 1
[+ Beardsley, Forshaw, Golightly, Pitfield, Rawsthorne, J.R. Williamson]

ASC Classical Series (CD) CS CD3

Published 1998

Album: *Contemporary British Piano* Music [NWCA disc]

228

FORSHAW, D.
Four Pieces after Charles Messier
[+ Beardsley, Ellis, Golightly, Pitfield, Rawsthorne, J.R. Williamson] ASC Classical Series (CD) CS CD3
Published 1998
Album: *Contemporary British Piano Music* [NWCA disc]

GOLIGHTLY, D.
Piano Sonata
[+ Beardsley, Ellis, Forshaw, Pitfield, Rawsthorne, J.R. Williamson] ASC Classical Series (CD) CS CD3
Published 1998
Album: *Contemporary British Piano Music* [NWCA disc]

GRIEG
Slåtter, Op. 72; Stimmungen, Op. 73 RCA (LP) GL 25329 / (Cassette) GK 25329
Published 1980

Lyric Pieces, Op. 43 (Complete); Lyric Pieces, Op. 54, Nos. 3, 4; Lyric Pieces, Op. 65 (Complete); Lyric Pieces, Op. 71, Nos. 2, 3;
Four Humoresques, Op. 6 Oryx (LP)
BRL 97 / (Cassette) BRL 97
Recorded 1972

HAYDN
Sonata in E flat, L62 (Hob. 52); Sonata in G, L13 (Hob. 6); Sonata in E, L15 (Hob. 13)
HMV (LP)
HQS 1301
Published 1973

Complete Sonatas; plus
Adagio in F; Capriccio in G; Fantasia in C; *Seven Last Words of the Redeemer on the Cross*; Seven Minuets from *Kleine Tänze*
***für die Jugend*; Twenty Variations in A; Six Variations in C; Five Variations in D; Twelve Variations in E flat; Andante con**
Variazioni in F minor Decca/London (12 CDs) 443 785-2
Reissued 1995

Complete Sonatas (Landon numberings): Volume 1:
Sonata in C, L6; Sonata in C, L10; Sonata in E flat, L18; Sonata in B minor, L47; Sonata in D, L50; Sonata in G, L52; Sonata in
C, L60 (English); Fantasia in C; Andante con Variazioni in F minor Decca (3LP)
1HDN 100/2
Published 1975

Complete Sonatas (Landon numberings): Volume 2:
Sonata in D, L9; Sonata in E flat, L17; Sonata in A flat, L31; Sonata in C, L36; Sonata in E flat, L43; Sonata in A, L45; Sonata
in E, L46; Sonata in C, L48; Sonata in G, L54; Sonata in B flat, L55; Sonata in D, L56; Variations in A
Decca (3LP) 2HDN 103/5
Published 1975

Complete Sonatas (Landon numberings): Volume 3:
Sonata in G, L1; Sonata in G, L4; Sonata in B flat, L20; Sonata in D, L30; Sonata in G minor, L32; Sonata in A flat, L35;
Sonata in A, L41; Sonata in G, L42; Sonata in E minor, L53; Sonata in F, L57; Sonata in E flat, L59; Adagio in F; Variations in C
Decca (3LP)
3HDN 106/8
Published 1976

Complete Sonatas (Landon numberings): Volume 4:
Sonata in C, L2; Sonata in F, L3; Sonata in G, L5; Sonata in D, L7; Sonata in B flat, L11; Sonata in G, L13; Sonata in D, L16; Sonata in E minor/major, L19; Sonata in D, L34; Sonata in E flat, L40; Sonata in F, L44; Sonata in C sharp minor, L49; Sonata in E flat, L51; Sonata in C, L58; Capriccio in G

Decca (3LP)
4HDN 109/11
Published 1977

Complete Sonatas (Landon numberings): Volume 5:
Sonata in A, L8; Sonata in A, L12; Sonata in C, L14; Sonata in E, L15; Sonata in E flat, L29; Sonata in E, L37; Sonata in D, L61; Sonata in E flat, L62; Sonata in D, L28 (completed McCabe); Sonata in B flat (Hob. 17 – now attributed to Schwanenberg); Sonata in E flat (Hob. 16 – now attribution unknown); Variations in E flat; Variations in D (attributed to Haydn); *Seven Last Words of the Redeemer on the Cross*; Seven Minuets from *Kleine Tänze für die Jugend* (Hob. IX/8, Nos.1, 2, 5, 7, 8, 10, 11)

Decca (4LP)
5HDN 112/15
Published 1977

Variations in D; Variations in A; Variations in C; Adagio in F; Fantasia in C; Capriccio in G; Seven Minuets

Decca (LP)
6.42455AS [German compilation disc]
Published 1977

Sonatas: in F, L3; in G minor, L32; in G, L42; L47; in E flat, L59

Pye (LP) Not issued
Recorded 1968

HINDEMITH
Ludus Tonalis; 1922 Suite

Hyperion (CD)
CDA66824
Published 1996

HOLST
Nocturne; Jig; Two Folksong Fragments, Op. 46 Nos. 2, 3
[+ Bax, Ireland, Moeran, Vaughan Williams, Warlock]

Decca (LP)
SDD 444
Published 1974
Album: *Pastorale*

HOWELLS
Lambert's Clavichord; Howells' Clavichord

Hyperion (CD)
CDA66689
Published 1994
Hyperion Helios (CD)
CDH55152
Reissued 2005

IRELAND
Sonatina
[+ Bax, Holst, Moeran, Vaughan Williams, Warlock]

Decca (LP)
SDD 444
Published 1974
Album: *Pastorale*

JOUBERT
Sonata No. 1, Op. 24; Sonata No. 2, Op. 71; Dance Suite, Op. 21

Pearl (LP)
SHE 520
Published 1975
Reissued: Maxsound (Cassette)
MSCB 33
Reissued 1986

LAMBERT
Piano Sonata
[+ other pianists: Bridge, Reizenstein]

Continuum (CD)CCD 1040
Published 1992
Album: *Best of British Piano*

Trois Pièces Nègres for piano duet (see also Rawsthorne)
with Tamami Honma (piano)

Dutton (CD)
For release 2006

McCABE
Five Bagatelles (1964)
[+ Britten, Copland, Nielsen, Rawsthorne, Schönberg, Webern]

Pye (LP)
GSGC 14116
Published 1969
Reissued: PRT (LP)GSGC 2069 / (Cassette) ZCGC 2069
Reissued 1983
Album: *Twentieth-Century Piano Music*

Variations (1963); Fantasy on a Theme of Liszt (1967); *Capriccio* **(Study No. 1) (1969);** *Sostenuto* **(Study No. 2) (1969);** *Gaudí*
(Study No. 3) (1970); *Aubade* **(Study No. 4) (1970)**

RL 25076
Published 1977

Haydn Variations; Variations (1963); *Gaudí* **(Study No. 3);** *Aubade* **(Study No. 4);** *Mosaic* **(Study No. 6); Five Bagatelles**

British Music Society (CD) BMS424CD
Published 1999

MENDELSSOHN
Capriccio Brillant (arr. Brockway)
[with Besses o' th' Barn Band / Ifor James]
[+ Brass Band works]

Pye (LP) GSGL 10510
Published 1974
Album: *Capriccio Brillante*

MOERAN
Bank Holiday
[+ Bax, Holst, Ireland, Vaughan Williams, Warlock]

Decca (LP
SDD 444
Published 1974
Album: *Pastorale*

Rhapsody in F sharp for Piano and Orchestra
[with NPO / Nicholas Braithwaite]
[+ Bridge (Wallfisch)]

Lyrita (LP) SRCS 91
Published 1977

MOZART
Sonata in A minor, K310; Sonata in F, K533/494; Sonata in C, K545   Oryx (LP)
BRL 27 / (Cassette) BRL 27
Recorded 1972

**Fantasia in C, K395; Fantasia in C minor, K 396; Fantasia in D minor, K 397; Rondo in D, K485; Rondo in A minor, K511;
Andante in F, K616; Allegro (Sonata movement) in G minor, K312; March in C, K408; Marche funèbre in C minor, K 453a;
Gigue in G, K574; Minuet in D, K355; Adagio in B minor, K540**   Oryx (LP)
BRL 28 / (Cassette) BRL 28
Recorded 1972

NIELSEN
Chaconne, Op. 32
[+ Britten, Copland, McCabe, Rawsthorne, Schönberg, Webern]   Pye (LP)
GSGC 14116
Published 1969
Reissued: PRT (LP)
GSGC 2069 / (Cassette) ZCGC 2069
Reissued 1983
Album: *Twentieth-Century Piano Music*

**Festival Prelude; Piano Music for Young and Old, Books 1 and 2; Symphonic Suite, Op. 8; Five Pieces, Op. 3; Three Pieces,
Op. 59**   Decca (LP)
SDD 475
Published 1975
Album: *Nielsen Piano Music, Vol. 1*

Humoresque-Bagatelles, Op. 11; Suite, Op. 45; Chaconne, Op. 32; *Dance of the Lady's Maids*; Theme with Variations, Op. 40
Decca (LP)
SDD 476
Published 1975
Album: Nielsen Piano Music, Vol. 2

PITFIELD
Prelude, Minuet and Reel; Studies on an English Dance-Tune; Novelette in F
[+ other Pitfield works] [see also Chamber Music discography]   RNCM (CD) RNCMTP3
Published 1994

Prelude, Minuet and Reel
[+ Beardsley, Ellis, Forshaw, Golightly, Rawsthorne, J.R. Williamson]   ASC Classical Series (CD) CS CD3
Published 1998
Album: *Contemporary British Piano Music* [NWCA disc]

PREVIN
The Invisible Drummer
[+ Adams, Bennett, Carter, Copland, Rochberg]   Continuum (2CD)
CCD 1028/9
Published 1991
Album: *Transatlantic Piano*

RAWSTHORNE
**Four Bagatelles (1938); Sonatina (1949); Theme and Four Studies; Four Romantic Pieces (1954); Ballade (1938); Valse
(1927); Ballade in G sharp minor (1929); *The Creel** (see also Lambert)
with Tamami Honma (piano)   Dutton (CD)
For release 2006

Four Bagatelles (1938)
[+ Britten, Copland, McCabe, Nielsen, Schönberg, Webern]

Pye (LP)
GSGC 14116
Published 1969
Reissued: PRT (LP)GSGC 2069 / (Cassette) ZCGC 2069
Reissued 1983
Album: *Twentieth-Century Piano Music*

Theme and Four Studies
[+ Beardsley, Ellis, Forshaw, Golightly, Pitfield, J.R. Williamson]

ASC Classical Series (CD) CS CD3
Published 1998
Album: *Contemporary British Piano Music* [NWCA disc]

ROCHBERG
Carnival Music
[+ Adams, Bennett, Carter, Copland, Previn]

Continuum (2CD)
CCD 1028/9
Published 1991
Album: *Transatlantic Piano*

SATIE
Trois gymnopédies; Sonatine bureaucratique; *Véritable préludes flasques; Sports et divertissements; Vieux sequins et vieilles cuirasses*; Gnossiennes Nos. 1, 4, 5; Sarabandes Nos. 1, 3; Nocturne No. 1; Passacaille; Six Posthumous Pieces; *Rag-time Parade* (trans. Ourdine)

Saga (LP)
SAGA 5387 / (also Cassette)
Published 1974
Album: *Satie Piano Music*
Reissued: Saga (CD) EC 3369-2

Chapitres tournés en tous sens*; Gnossiennes Nos. 2, 3; *Les Trois Valses distinguées du précieux dégoûtée; Avant-dernières pensées; Première pensée rose + Croix; Deux rêveries nocturnes; Je te veux* (Valse); *Pièces froides; Prélude de la porte héroïque du ciel; Le Piège de Méduse*; Nocturnes Nos. 3, 5; *Le Fils des étoiles; Valse-Ballet; Rêverie du pauvre; Les Pantins dansent; Cinq Grimaces

Saga (LP)
SAGA 5472 / (Also Cassette)Published 1980
Album: *More Satie Piano Music*
Reissued: Saga (CD) EC 3393-2
Reissued 1994

***Avant-dernières pensées; Chapitres tournés en tous sens; Cinq grimaces*; Gnossiennes 1–5; Gymnopédies 1–3; *Je te veux* (Valse); Nocturnes 1, 3, 5; Passacaille; *Pièces froides; Le Piége de Méduse; Ragtime Parade; Rêverie du pauvre; Sonatine Bureaucratique; Sports et divertissements*; Valse-Ballet**

Regis (CD) RRC 1227
Album : *Satie Piano Masterpieces*
Reissued 2005

Le Fils des étoiles*; Trois Gymnopédies; *Sports et divertissements; Les Trois Valses distinguées du précieux dégoûtée; Vieux sequins et vieilles cuirasses

Continuum (CD) not issued
(Recorded 1992)

SAXTON
Chacony for Left Hand

NMC (CD)
D065
Published 2000
Album: *Saxton Piano and Chamber Music*

SCARLATTI
Sonatas: in G, K105; G minor, K426; D minor, K517; D, K490; F minor, K69; F, K518; E, L28; E, K215; C, K133; G, K259; G minor, K43; C, K460
Hyperion (LP)
A66025
Published 1981

SCHOENBERG
Six Little Pieces, Op. 19
[+ Britten, Copland, McCabe, Nielsen, Rawsthorne, Webern]
Pye (LP)
GSGC 14116
Published 1969
Reissued: PRT (LP)
GSGC 2069 / (Cassette) ZCGC 2069
Reissued 1983
Album: *Twentieth-Century Piano Music*

SCHUBERT
Sonata in C, D840 (Relique); Three Piano Pieces (Impromptus), D846
Davjohn – not issued
Recorded 1968

SCHUMAN, WILLIAM
Piano Concerto
[with Albany SO / David Alan Miller][+ Credendum; Symphony No 4]
Albany (CD)
TROY566
Published 2003

SCHUMANN
Fantasiestücke, Op. 12, Nos. 2, 3, 4; *Waldszenen*, Op. 82, Nos. 1, 3, 4, 5, 6, 7; *Kinderszenen*, Op. 15; *Romances*, Op. 28, Nos. 2, 3
Oryx (LP)
BRL 59 / (Cassette) BRL 59
Recorded 1972

VAUGHAN WILLIAMS
The Lake in the Mountains; **Hymn-Tune Prelude on** *Song 13* **(Gibbons); Suite of Six Short Pieces**
[+ Bax, Holst, Ireland, Moeran, Warlock]
Decca (LP)
SDD 444
Published 1974
Album: *Pastorale*

WARLOCK
Five Folk-song Preludes
[+ Bax, Holst, Ireland, Moeran, Vaughan Williams]
Decca (LP)
SDD 444
Published 1974
Album: *Pastorale*

WEBERN
Variations, Op. 27
[+ Britten, Copland, McCabe, Nielsen, Rawsthorne, Schönberg]
Pye (LP)
GSGC 14116
Published 1969
Reissued: PRT (LP)GSGC 2069 / (Cassette) ZCGC 2069
Reissued 1983
Album: *Twentieth-Century Piano Music*

WILLIAMSON, J.R.
Three Palindromic Preludes
[+ Beardsley, Ellis, Forshaw, Golightly, Pitfield, Rawsthorne]

ASC Classical Series (CD) CS CD3
Published 1998
Album: *Contemporary British Piano Music* [NWCA disc]

Piano performance with other artists
ABBOTT
Alla Caccia
[with Ifor James, horn]
[+ Hindemith, Fricker, Nielsen]

Pye (LP) GSGC 14087
Published 1968

ATHANASIADIS, BASIL
Terpsichore bemused
[with Tamami Honma, piano]

Dutton Digital (CD) CDSA6881
Published 02/2005

BAX
Piano Quartet
[with members, English String Quartet]
[+ Bax: Harp Quartet; String Quartet No. 1]

Chandos (LP) ABRD 1113 / (CD) CHAN 8391 / (Cassette)
ABTD 1113
Published 1984

Violin Sonata No. 1 in E
Violin Sonata No. 2 in D
[with Erich Gruenberg, violin]

Chandos (CD) CHAN 8845 / (Cassette) ABTD 1462
Published 1990

BERKELEY, L.
Duo for Cello and Piano
[with Julian Lloyd Webber, cello]
[+ Dalby, Fricker, (McCabe)]

L'Oiseau Lyre (LP) DSLO 18
Published 1977
Album: *Julian Lloyd Webber plays British Cello Music*

BRAHMS
Clarinet Sonata in F minor, Op. 120, No. 1
Clarinet Sonata in E flat, Op. 120, No. 2
[with Murray Khouri, clarinet]
[+ Gal]

Continuum (CD) CCD 1027
Published 1991

BRIDGE
Elegy for Cello and Piano
[with Julian Lloyd Webber, cello]
[+ Ireland, (Britten)]

ASV (LP) ACA 1001 / (Cassette) ZCACA 1001
Published 1980
Album: *Julian Lloyd Webber plays Britten, Ireland and Bridge*

Elegy for Cello and Piano
[with Julian Lloyd Webber, cello]

Album: *The Four Seasons Vol. 3: Autumn*

Elegy for Cello and Piano
Scherzetto for Cello and Piano
[with Julian Lloyd Webber, cello]
[+ Ireland, Stanford]

ASV (CD) DCA 807
Published 1992
Album: *British Cello Music Vol. 2*
Reissued 1996

BRITTEN
Cello Sonata in C, Op. 65
[with Julian Lloyd Webber, cello]
[+ Prokofiev, Shostakovitch]

Philips (CD) 422 345-2
Published 1989

***Mazurka elegiaca*, Op. 23 No. 2**
[with Tamami Honma, piano]

Dutton Digital (CD) CDSA6881
Published 02/2005

CASKEN
Ia orana, Gauguin
[with Jane Manning, soprano]
[+ other Casken works]

Wergo (LP) WER 60104
Published 1984
Album: *The Moving Fires of Evening*

COOKE
Rondo in B flat for Horn and Piano
[+ Eccles, Gwilt etc]

Cornucopia (LP) IJ 100
Published 1979
Album: *Pot-pourri*

COPLAND
Danzón Cubano
[with Tamami Honma, piano]

Dutton Digital (CD) CDSA6881
Published 02/2005

DALBY
Variations for Cello and Piano
[with Julian Lloyd Webber, cello]
[+ Berkeley, Fricker, (McCabe)]

L'Oiseau Lyre (LP) DSLO 18
Published 1977
Album: *Julian Lloyd Webber plays British Cello Music*

ECCLES
Horn Sonata in G minor (arr. Eger)
[with Ifor James, horn]
[+ Cooke, Gwilt etc]

Cornucopia (LP) IJ 100
Published 1979
Album: *Pot-pourri*

ELGAR
From the Bavarian Highlands
[with William Ferris Chorale / Ferris]
[+ choral items]

WFC (Cassette) WFC
Published 1992
WFC (CD) 90246
Published 1997
Album: *A Gift of Love*

FRICKER
Horn Sonata, Op. 24
[with Ifor James, horn]
[+Abbott, Hindemith, Nielsen]

Pye (LP) GSGC 14087
Published 1968

Cello Sonata, Op. 28
[with Julian Lloyd Webber, cello]
[+ Berkeley, Dalby, (McCabe)]

L'Oiseau Lyre (LP) DSLO 18
Published 1977
Album: *Julian Lloyd Webber plays British Cello Music*

GÁL
Clarinet Sonata, Op. 84
[with Murray Khouri, clarinet]
[+ Brahms]

Continuum (CD) CCD 1027
Published 1991

GOEHR
Four Songs from the Japanese
[with Marni Nixon, soprano]
[+ Ives, Schurmann]

Pye (LP) GSGC 14105
Published 1967
Nonesuch (LP) H 71209

GWILT
Horn Sonatina
[with Ifor James, horn]
[+ Cooke, Eccles, etc]

Cornucopia (LP) IJ 100
Published 1979
Album: *Pot-pourri*

HINDEMITH
Horn Sonata in F (1939)
[with Ifor James, horn]
[+ Abbott, Fricker, Nielsen]

Pye (LP) GSGC 14087
Published 1968

Horn Sonata in F (1939)
Waldhorn Sonata in E flat
[with Ifor James, horn]
[+ R. Strauss]

Phoenix (LP) Not issued
Not issued

IRELAND
Cello Sonata in G minor
[with Julian Lloyd Webber, cello]
[+ Bridge, (Britten)]

ASV (LP) ACA 1001 / (Cassette) ZCACA 1001
Published 1980
Album: *Julian Lloyd Webber plays Britten, Ireland and Bridge*

[+ Bridge, Stanford]

ASV (CD) DCA 807
Published 1992
Album: *British Cello Music Vol. 2*
Reissued 1996
Album: *Ireland Chamber Music*
ASV (CD) GLD 4009
Reissued 2004

The Holy Boy
[with Julian Lloyd Webber, cello]
[+ Rawsthorne and cello solos]

ASV (LP) DCA 592 / (LP) DCA 592 / (Cassette) ZCDCA 592
Published 1987
ASV (CD) DCA 592
Reissued 1996
ASV (CD) Quicksilva CDQS 6116
Album: *The Four Seasons Vol. 4: Winter*
Album: *Ireland Chamber Music*
ASV (CD) GLD 4009
Reissued 2004

Piano Trio No. 2 in E
[with Daniel Hope/Julian Lloyd Webber]

Album: *Ireland Chamber Music*
ASV (CD) GLD 4009
Published 2004

Violin Sonata No. 1 in D minor
[with Daniel Hope, violin]

Album: *Ireland Chamber Music*
ASV (CD) GLD 4009
Published 2004

IVES
Thirteen Songs
[with Marni Nixon, soprano]
[+ Goehr, Schurmann]

Pye (LP) GSGC 14105
Published 1967
Nonesuch (LP) H 71209

JOUBERT
Six Poems of Emily Brontë
Shropshire Hills
[with Lesley-Jane Rogers, soprano]

Kontakion for Cello and Piano
[with Richard Tunnicliffe, cello]

Improvisation for Recorder and Piano
[with John Turner, recorder]
[+ songs for soprano and recorder]

Toccata Classics
Recorded 2006

McCABE
Basse Danse
[with Tamami Honma, piano]

Dutton Digital (CD) CDSA6881
Published 02/2005

McPHEE
Balinese Ceremonial Music
[with Tamami Honma, piano]

Dutton Epoch (CD) CDSA6881
Published 02/2005

NIELSEN
Canto Serioso
[with Ifor James, horn]
[+ Abbott, Hindemith, Fricker]

Pye (LP) GSGC 14087
Published 1968

PITFIELD
Three Nautical Sketches for Recorder and Piano
Rondo alla Tarantella for Recorder and Piano
[with John Turner, recorder]
[+ Pitfield piano solos and other works]

RNCM (CD) RNCMTP3
Published 1994

PROKOFIEV
Ballade for Cello and Piano, Op. 15
[with Julian Lloyd Webber, cello]
[+ Britten, Shostakovitch]

Philips (CD) 422 345-2
Published 1989

RAWSTHORNE
Cello Sonata (1949)
[with Julian Lloyd Webber, cello]
[+ Ireland and cello solos]

ASV (LP) DCA 592 / (LP) DCA 592 /
(Cassette) ZCDCA 592
Published 1987
ASV (CD) DCA 592
Reissued 1996

Piano Quintet (1968)
[Rawsthorne Chamber Music]

Naxos (CD) 8.554352
Published 1999

SAXTON
Arias for Oboe and Piano
[with Alun Darbyshire]

Eloge for Voice and Ensemble
[with Cahill/Brunel Ensemble/Austin]
[Saxton Piano and Chamber Music]

NMC (CD) D065
Published 2000

SCHURMANN
Chuench'i
[with Marni Nixon, soprano]
[+ Goehr, Ives]

Pye (LP) GSGC 14105
Published 1967
Nonesuch (LP) H 71209

SHOSTAKOVICH
Cello Sonata in D minor, Op. 40
[with Julian Lloyd Webber, cello]
[+ Britten, Prokofiev]

Philips (CD) 422 345-2
Published 1989

STANFORD
Cello Sonata No. 2, Op. 39
[with Julian Lloyd Webber, cello]
[+ Bridge, Ireland]

ASV (CD) DCA 807
Published 1992
Album: *British Cello Music Vol. 2*
Reissued 1996

Clarinet Sonata in F, Op. 129
[with Murray Khouri, clarinet]
[+ other clarinet works]

Continuum (CD) CCD 1074
Published 1995
Album: *Best of British Clarinet Vol. 2*

STRAUSS, R.
Andante for Horn and Piano
[with Ifor James, horn]
[+ Hindemith]

Phoenix (LP) Not issued
Not issued

STRAVINSKY
Agon
[with Tamami Honma, piano]

Dutton Digital (CD) CDSA6881
Published 02/2005

WALTON
Piano Quartet
[with members, English Piano Quartet]
[+ String Quartet in A minor]

Meridian (CD) CDE 84139 / (Cassette) KE 77139
Published 1987

Index

John McCabe's works are indexed separately on pp. **254-7** below. Pages containing illustrations are in *italic* type.

242

244

248